T0360717

Relocating Development Economics

Originating in the nineteenth century, the European idea of development was shaped around the premise that the West possessed progressive characteristics that the East lacked. As a result of this perspective, many alternative development discourses originating in the East were often overlooked and forgotten. Indian Economics is but one example. By recovering thought from the margins, *Relocating Development Economics* exposes useful new ways of viewing development. It looks at how an Indian tradition in economic thought emerged from a group of Indian economists in the late nineteenth century who questioned dominant European economic ideas on development and agricultural economics. This book shows how the first generation of modern Indian economists pushed at the boundaries of existing theories to produce reformulations that better fit their subcontinent and opens up discursive space to find new ways of thinking about regress, progress and development.

MARIA BACH is Junior Lecturer and Postdoctoral Researcher at the University of Lausanne. As an historian of economics, she is interested in how economists from what we call the Global South today produced economic ideas. She wrote her thesis at King's College London in International Political Economy, which won the Joseph Dorfman Award for the Best Dissertation in the History of Economic Thought, 2020.

Series Editor: Professor Harro Maas, Walras-Pareto Centre for the History of Economic and Political Thought, University of Lausanne

This series contains original works that challenge and enlighten historians of economics. For the profession as a whole, it promotes better understanding of the origin and content of modern economics

Other books in the series:

Till Düppe, *The Closed World of East German Economists: Hopes and Defeats of a Generation* (2023)

Erwin Dekker, *Jan Tinbergen (1903–1994) and the Rise of Economic Expertise* (2021)

Jeff E. Biddle, *Progression through Regression* (2020)

Erwin Dekker, *The Viennese Students of Civilization* (2016)

Steven G. Medema, Anthony M.C. Waterman (eds.), *Paul Samuelson on the History of Economic Analysis: Selected Essays* (2014)

Floris Heukelom, *Behavioral Economics: A History* (2014)

Roger E. Backhouse, Mauro Boianovsky, *Transforming Modern Macroeconomics: Exploring Disequilibrium Microfoundations, 1956–2003* (2013)

Susan Howson, Lionel Robbins (2012)

Robert Van Horn, Philip Mirowski, Thomas A. Stapleford (eds.), *Building Chicago Economics: New Perspectives on the History of America's Most Powerful Economics Program* (2012)

Arie Arnon, *Monetary Theory and Policy from Hume and Smith to Wicksell: Money, Credit, and the Economy* (2011)

Malcolm Rutherford, *The Institutionalist Movement in American Economics, 1918–1947: Science and Social Control* (2011)

Samuel Hollander, *Friedrich Engels and Marxian Political Economy* (2011)

Robert Leonard, *Von Neumann, Morgenstern, and the Creation of Game Theory: From Chess to Social Science, 1900–1960* (2010)

Simon J. Cook, *The Intellectual Foundations of Alfred Marshall's Economic Science: A Rounded Globe of Knowledge* (2009)

Samuel Hollander, *The Economics of Karl Marx: Analysis and Applications* (2008)

Donald Moggridge, *Harry Johnson: A Life in Economics* (2008)

Filippo Cesarano, *Monetary Theory and Bretton Woods: The Construction of an International Monetary Order* (2006)

Timothy Davis, *Ricardo's Macroeconomics: Money, Trade Cycles, and Growth* (2005)

(Continued after the index)

Relocating Development Economics

The First Generation of Modern Indian Economists

MARIA BACH
The University of Lausanne

CAMBRIDGE
UNIVERSITY PRESS

CAMBRIDGE
UNIVERSITY PRESS

Shaftesbury Road, Cambridge CB2 8EA, United Kingdom

One Liberty Plaza, 20th Floor, New York, NY 10006, USA

477 Williamstown Road, Port Melbourne, VIC 3207, Australia

314–321, 3rd Floor, Plot 3, Splendor Forum, Jasola District Centre, New Delhi – 110025, India

103 Penang Road, #05–06/07, Visioncrest Commercial, Singapore 238467

Cambridge University Press is part of Cambridge University Press & Assessment, a department of the University of Cambridge.

We share the University's mission to contribute to society through the pursuit of education, learning and research at the highest international levels of excellence.

www.cambridge.org
Information on this title: www.cambridge.org/9781009438193

DOI: 10.1017/9781009438209

First published 2024

A catalogue record for this publication is available from the British Library.

Library of Congress Cataloging-in-Publication Data
Names: Bach, Maria, author.
Title: Relocating development economics : the first generation of modern Indian economists / Maria Bach, The American University of Paris, France.
Description: Cambridge, United Kingdom ; New York, NY, USA : Cambridge University Press, 2024. | Series: Historical perspectives on modern economics | Includes bibliographical references and index.
Identifiers: LCCN 2024015906 | ISBN 9781009438193 (hardback) | ISBN 9781009438216 (paperback) | ISBN 9781009438209 (ebook)
Subjects: LCSH: Economists – India.
Classification: LCC HB126.I43 B33 2024 | DDC 338.9–dc23/eng/20240514
LC record available at https://lccn.loc.gov/2024015906

ISBN 978-1-009-43819-3 Hardback

To my rock, Pierre

Contents

Figures

Tables

Acknowledgements

Fearlessness is a funny thing. My fearlessness has proved to be productive, rewarding and exhilarating, but also a lot of stress and hard work. Fearlessness got me to start my PhD with little understanding of what it would actually entail to write a thesis. Would I have started the PhD if I had known what it entailed? I am not sure. I will never be sure. But I do know that I changed. The PhD pushed me to grow and learn in ways I could not have imagined.

I want to thank Harro Maas for seeing the potential of my thesis and for proposing it to Cambridge University Press. As a PhD student, I believed that the contribution of this first major generation of modern Indian economists needed to be told louder and bolder. I hope with this book that the contributions of those Indian economists reach a bigger audience, in that clearer way that books do, compared to PhD theses.

I would like to thank my supervisors, Valbona Muzaka, Jon Wilson and Alex Callinicos. I am especially grateful to my first supervisor, Valbona Muzaka. I could not have completed my thesis, and thus this book, without her. Her constant support – emotional, academic and practical – was extraordinary throughout.

I owe a debt of gratitude to the London Arts and Humanities Partnership supported by the Arts and Humanities Research Council, INET's Young Scholar's Initiative and the Faculty of Social Science and Public Policy Research Fund from King's College London. In the final stages of the book writing, I was also gracefully helped by the University of Lausanne to pay for copyediting and the images in this book. The financial support has been invaluable.

I would like to thank the following people for consoling me when I was down and for being my very own cheerleaders: Oscar Dahl, Emilie Mendes de Leon, Susanne Spahn, Michael Karner, Mathilde Toulemonde, Rosie Brand, Ashley Acker, Elena Bordarier, Meg Gagnard, Lacy Audry, Alice Hertz and so many more. A brief but noteworthy mention must be made of Anne and Manuel Bénétreau for hosting and feeding me in the last months of my PhD.

Thank you to the PhD students in my department at King's College London and in the LSE Economic History department, as well as the brilliant group of scholars in the INET YSI Working Group on the History of Economic Thought. Thank you also to the members of Walras-Pareto Centre at the University of Lausanne, the regulars who joined my online writing group and the wider History of Economics community. Thank you especially to Cléo Chassonnery-Zaïgouche, François Allisson, Reinhard Schumacher, Camila Orozco Espinel, Christina Laskaridis, Mary Morgan, Béatrice Cherrier, Catherine Herfeld, Verena Halsmayer, Alex Thomas, David Philippy, Poornima Paidipaty and Cecilia Lanata-Briones. My thesis sister, as one could put it, Sharmin Khodaiji, needs a special thanks. It was such a pleasure sharing this journey with you. I hope that you gained the same amount of support and help that I received from you. I look forward to many close collaborations!

To everyone who saw me present, discuss and read my work, thank you! Researching and writing is a lonely work, but it is never completed alone. This book would not exist if it were not for a large community of brilliant researchers. And this book would not be as clear or enjoyable to read if it were not for my copy editor, Jon Bentley-Smith.

In the process of writing this book, my responsibilities have increased, namely to two small humans. I am thus impelled to thank the various professionals, friends and family (especially mormor, mamie and papi) who have taken care of my children when I was working or needed time off. You are modern-day heroes to me!

Last, but by far not the least, thank you to my family. To Anton, who came into this world just before I signed my book contract, and to Lucas, who came when I was in the middle of writing the manuscript, you may have forced me to leave work during a few (perhaps several) productive bursts of writing, but your laughs and love make the everyday magical. Finally, I want to thank my greatest support of all, my husband Pierre. His gracious encouragement and constant help is nothing short of a wonder. Jag älskar er!

Introduction: Relocating Development Economics

In the late 1860s, an economist stepped into a 'small room in a smoky lane' of London, 'crowded with members of a large family'.[1] The economist remarked that the mother, her teenage daughter and small baby were crammed into the space. He could not help but notice the coal absent from the furnace, the broken windowpanes and the light clothing on their starved bodies. It 'presents', wrote Romesh Chunder Dutt, 'a sight of misery compared to which the poorest classes of people in our own country are well off'.[2] Dutt, born and raised in Calcutta, Bengal, thousands of miles away, had sailed to London in 1868. He had come to take the Civil Service examination, which until recently had been open to only British candidates; Dutt himself would soon become the second Indian ever to serve as a civil servant in the British government in India. But he had also travelled to see with his own eyes the progressive and modern Britain and Europe that he had been taught and read about at home.

Dutt had graduated from Calcutta University in 1866. From 1856 to 1857, the British East India Company had established three universities in the main centres of imperialism in India: Calcutta, Bombay and Madras. These institutions were to diffuse 'the improved arts, science, philosophy and literature of Europe; in short, European knowledge'.[3] At the same time, in early 1857, a rumour had spread among the sepoys, Indian soldiers, in the service of the British East India Company that the grease to lubricate the cartridges in their guns was a mixture of pigs' and cows' lard. To load the guns, they had to bite off the ends of the lubricated cartridges. Oral contact with the cartridges, then, was an insult to both Muslims and Hindus. A revolt, referred to as the Indian Mutiny, broke out on 10 May 1857 in northern India, not far from Delhi, and eventually spread to Delhi, Kanpur and Lucknow.

---

[1] Dutt, *Three Years in Europe*, 27–8. [2] Ibid., 27–8.
[3] Wood's 1854 despatch, quoted in Seth, *Subject Lessons*, 2.

Prior to this, Indians had not mounted such an overt, organised attack against their foreign rulers. The British saw no other solution than to reorganise the Indian administration. Control over the Empire of India was passed from the British East India Company to the British Crown. To further secure and legitimise their rule, the British were now said to have a 'civilising mission': while India was regressive and poor, its foreign rulers preached that they would bring progress and modernity, qualities they themselves possessed.

Yet when Dutt saw that mother and her children freezing and hungry in a rundown room in London, the civilising mission did not hold up. How could a country civilise and enrich another if it had so much poverty of its own? 'The London Labourer', wrote Dutt, 'is one of the most harrowing sights that civilisation can hold up to your view'.[4] Dutt was reversing the gaze after centuries of Europeans, including British, travelling to India to observe a population perceived as drastically different from their own. Along with others, he used the scientific method of comparison to study the Indian economy. In such a way, he and his contemporaries gained authority, objectivity and credibility.

Dutt was a part of the first generation of modern Indian economists who had graduated from the imperial universities. Born predominantly between the 1840s and 1850s,[5] they spent their lives studying India's economy. They were a group of middle-class men from Bombay, Calcutta and Madras. Some were professors of economics, some judges, other merchants or bankers working for imperial companies and institutions. Some had seen their families lose their riches as foreigners took over such lucrative economic activities as tea plantations and jute production. Some sought to better understand the worrying poverty they witnessed in the course of interviewing the poor. All of them were convinced that India was not doing well, and that the British, as their rulers, were not doing enough to better the condition of the average citizen. The civilising mission was failing.

This group of economists became known as the Early Nationalists, as they began India's fight for independence. When historians and political theorists analyse them, they often portray them as political scientists and nation-builders who mostly regurgitated existing

---

[4] Dutt, *Three Years in Europe*, 27.
[5] Except Dadabhai Naoroji, who was born in 1825, but as he outlived most of the others he remains a key member of this group.

European economic thinking. Much less has been written on their contribution to economics, despite them being the first generation of modern economists in India. My intention here is to show how they produced original, forward-thinking knowledge on economic development. In the chapters that follow, I explore their understanding of how India's economy evolved (Chapters 3 and 4), their prescriptions for bringing progress back to India (Chapter 5), the economic consequences of imperialism, and a global plan for development (Chapter 6).

The First Generation of Modern Indian Economists

Speaking in his home state, Mahadev Govind Ranade coined the term 'Indian Economics' in a speech at the intellectual centre of western India, Deccan College, in 1892.[6] The lecture hall was filled with Indian students and probably some officials given that the college was in Poona, where the British administration moved during the warm summer months. As India's third oldest educational institute, it had been established on the initiative of the governor of the Bombay Presidency administration in 1821, Mountstuart Elphinstone.[7] The college was part of the imperial university system where the Indian middle and elite classes could get a higher education. It was through such an education that Ranade learned the skills that enabled him to understand this imperial system. Now he criticised it from within.

Ranade's lecture in 1892 is considered the main founding text of Indian Economics. Some ten years later, another Indian economist of the same generation, Ganapathy Dikshitar Subramania Iyer, published the other founding text.[8] Iyer was a leading journalist and founder of *The Hindu*, now the country's national newspaper. Ranade and Iyer argued that India needed its own economic thinking that considered India's past and present, different from that of western Europe where the thinkers they had been taught came from. Ranade and Iyer's initial idea proved popular with their contemporaries, enabling Indian Economics to emerge.

This book tells the story of the first generation of modern Indian economists. Thinkers focused on political economy had existed before,

---

[6] Ranade, *Essays on Indian Economics*, 1.
[7] First named Hindoo College, it was eventually renamed Deccan College in 1864.
[8] Iyer, *Some Economic Aspects of British Rule in India*, app. 1.

like in most other places, but they were found in the vernacular tradition, often isolated within their communities as they worked in their
regional languages.[9] The economists in the first generation wrote primarily in English because that was the dominant language at higher
educational institutions in India in the nineteenth century. But another
reason they used English was to inform their British rulers about their
conclusions regarding the problems facing the Indian economy and the
appropriate solutions they identified.

There were nine economists in this first generation: Dutt, Ranade,
Iyer, Dadabhai Naoroji, Dinshaw Edulji Wacha, Ganesh Vyankatesh
Joshi, Surendranath Banerjea, Kashinath Trimbak Telang and Gopal
Krishna Gokhale. They were a group of middle-class men from
Bombay, Calcutta and Madras. Some were professors of economics,
some judges, other merchants or bankers working for imperial com-
panies and institutions. Most were Hindus from the upper castes with
families that had the means to send them to school. Some of them, like
Ranade, Iyer and Telang, openly self-identified as Indian economists.
Others, like Naoroji and Dutt, were labelled as Indian economists later

---

[9] There is some literature on the history of vernacular political economy in India:
see, for example, Dasgupta, *A History of Indian Economic Thought*. The ancient
text, often thought of as the first ever manual on statecraft, *The Arthasastra*
(Treatise on Success) appeared in India in the second and third centuries. At the
time of writing, the most recent histories were published in 2019: McClish, *The
History of the Arthasastra*; Kamal, *Kautilya's Arthashastra*.

For a regional study of how political economy was brought into the vernacular
tradition in Bengal in the nineteenth century, to a large extent by translating
British and some European political economy treaties into Indian vernacular
languages, see Mitra, 'Exchanging Words and Things'.

There is one notable exception in this earlier period, Rammohun Roy, who
worked for the British imperial officials in Bengal between 1803 and 1815, later
becoming a private financier and public intellectual. His writings circulated in
Bengal, Europe and North America, and he was active in British political debates,
like Naoroji was later, and supported local free traders who criticised the British
East India Company's monopoly. Being from an era earlier than the Indian
economists, this book focuses on those who were later labelled the Early
Nationalists. Roy was for imperialism, arguing that the advanced nation of
Britain would bring progressive forces to India in the form of British capital and
labour. This book focuses on the second half of the nineteenth century when there
was a large group of economists, all eventually anti-imperialist, who engaged
in dialogue between themselves to build a larger thinking around Indian
economic development. For further discussion on Roy, see Ganguli, *Indian
Economic Thought*, 41, 56; Bayly, *Recovering Liberties*, 49, 83; Helleiner, *The
Contested World Economy*, 43.

because their research actively sought to understand and represent the Indian experience of economic development. Studies by this generation came first in the 1870s and continued into the early twentieth century, and led to the development of theories, concepts, ideas and solutions for India's idiosyncratic problems. Ranade's inauguration of an Indian Economics placed their growing number of studies under a new intellectual umbrella (see Chapter 2).

Members of the group were not all from the same place, although most were from northern India, where the British had the most control. Nor did they all take the same professional path, thus participating in and establishing diverse groups to build the then nascent nationalist movement. These Indian economists all fought for independence, but they were not always in agreement on how to bring about independence or how to, for example, alleviate poverty. Finding evidence of dialogue between them, however, is hard due to a lack of archival sources, making it difficult to flesh out their disagreements. Throughout this book, I show both the points of convergence and, where sources allow, the points of divergence among them.

Economics and Economic Change in the Nineteenth and Twentieth Centuries

The last three decades of the nineteenth century are pivotal in the history of economics. There were more and more economists worldwide working on ever more specialised topics. As economic societies and journals flourished and multiplied, debates on economic issues became more technical and addressed increasingly specific questions within the discipline. Economists could soon become professors of economics, as universities started to establish departments dedicated to the field by the early twentieth century. At the same time, they shifted their perspective on how they saw the dynamics of an economy. In what is often labelled the marginalist revolution, economists broke from classical economists who had conceived the labour theory of value, seeing the value of commodities as prescribed by the costs of production. The marginalist economists instead defined the value of commodities according to the utility that consumers gained from them.[10]

---

[10] For more discussion, see Backhouse, 'Marginal Revolution'.

Moreover, significant economic progress in Europe and North America in the second half of the nineteenth century meant that things were changing fast, and not always for the better. Germany and the United States had now become firmly established industrial powers. Material output was rising dramatically, but prices were falling. Business losses were common, and workers were constantly at risk of losing their jobs. Rapid progress was thus accompanied by instability, inequality and poverty. Nevertheless, the average living standard was rising, inciting a novel sense of power that saw workers revolt against increasing job insecurity as unemployment rose. Social reform and industrial organisation were reactions to such upheavals. Germany, the United States and Japan now saw growing support for state-led development, which challenged British imperialism and laissez-faire politics such as free trade.

Britain's industrialisation had put Indian manufacturers out of business, especially in the textile industry. Cheap North American wheat flooded Europe thanks to improved land and sea transportation, and European agriculturalists suffered a depression that spread to other sectors. The so-called Long Depression in Europe lasted from the early 1870s to the mid-1890s, hurting global aggregate demand and causing ripple effects the world over. With less demand for their goods, the Indian population grew poorer. The great famines in India of the late 1870s, 1890s and early 1900s claimed tens of millions of lives, provoking a radical decline in the belief among Indians that Britain could successfully help develop their country (see Chapters 1 and 2).

Dialogue between Indians and their rulers increased during the last three decades of the nineteenth century. Throughout the subcontinent, Indians established local and regional organisations. During the 1880s, a hundred local associations were established in Madras alone. The Poona Sarvajanik Sabha (Poona's Public Society), established by Ranade and a group mainly consisting of mathematics teachers, promoted peasants' legal rights. Allan Octavian Hume (1829–1912), an imperial official who had seen the Indian Mutiny, along with Naoroji, Banerjea, Ranade and Wacha, established the Indian National Congress in 1885. The Congress was the first major organisation to house different professionals, including economists, teachers, lawyers, traders and merchants. It created a space for the Indian middle and elite classes to voice concerns about, and raise prescriptions for, the country's numerous problems. The seventy-two delegates that attended

THE FIRST INDIAN NATIONAL CONGRESS, 1885.

Figure 1.1 First session of the Indian National Congress, 28–31 December 1885, Bombay. Allan Octavian Hume is sitting in the middle (third row from the front) with Dadabhai Naoroji to his right, and Gopal Krishna Gokhale sits in the second seat to his left.

the first meeting in Bombay were all founders and leaders of modern institutions, and among them were members of the first generation of modern Indian economists (Figure 1.1).

By the early twentieth century, the Indian economists' political agitation against existing political economy education and laissez-faire imperial policies compelled the imperial administration to better understand the country's social and economic conditions. Consequently, courses on Indian Economics started being offered at the imperial universities as of the beginning of the century, along with the first textbook on Indian Economics.[11] The first complete history of Indian Economics came in 1966 when Bipan Chandra provided an overall picture of this first generation of modern Indian economists and their attempts to produce a body of works that theorised and modelled 'economic nationalism'.[12]

Until at least the early 1970s, however, scholars maintained that although Indian Economics identified British rule as a barrier to economic development, it did not offer solutions to the problem of

---

[11] Khodaiji, 'A Nationalistic Framework for Political Economy'.
[12] Chandra, *The Rise and Growth of Economic Nationalism in India*, 1.

generating economic growth, nor did it create alternative tools for analysing economic development.[13] The scholars seem to focus on the discursive and material constraints imposed upon the Indians. For instance, the research often concludes that there was little space for Indians to think outside of the norms and claims of European knowledge, as they were taught a European curriculum.[14] The Indian economists were subsequently critiqued for only regurgitating existing thought. Moreover, India's extreme poverty is said to have led its intellectuals to become preoccupied with urgent political and economic needs, rather than knowledge creation.

Studies from the late 1970s shifted the rhetoric. Birendranath Ganguli's and Christopher Bayly's analyses showed that late nineteenth-century Indian intellectuals were able to create new definitions of existing concepts and theories that reconciled the Indian context with dominant ideas within political economy.[15] Norbert Peabody examined how Indians harnessed, redirected and shaped parts of economic knowledge that emerged during the imperial encounter, establishing that the Indian actors formed a part of this knowledge.[16] Benjamin Zachariah found that Indian actors pushed for developmental theory to include an Indian element from 1930 to 1950 – a factor that he labels the 'indigenist' theme.[17] Jayasankar Krishnamurty published a book about twentieth-century Indian writers such as Bhimrao Ramji Ambedkar and Radhakamal Mukerjee, concluding that Indians anticipated many development debates emerging post-Second World War.[18] Goddanti Omkarnath briefly zoomed in on three periods of Indian development thinking: namely, Kautilya's ancient *Arthasastra* from the second and third centuries, economic nationalism in the late nineteenth century and post-independence Indian development thought.[19] These studies started to 'decolonise knowledge' by bringing India's discourses to the fore.[20]

---

[13] See, for example, Gopalakrishnan, *Development of Economic Ideas in India*; Chandra, *The Rise and Growth of Economic Nationalism in India*; Chandra, 'Reinterpretation of Nineteenth Century Indian Economic History'.
[14] Seth, *Subject Lessons*, chap. 1.
[15] Ganguli, *Indian Economic Thought*, 85; Bayly, *The Birth of the Modern World*, 323.
[16] Peabody, 'Knowledge Formation in Imperial India'.
[17] Zachariah, *Developing India*, 293.
[18] Krishnamurty, *Towards Development Economics*.
[19] Omkarnath, 'Indian Development Thinking'.
[20] See, for example, Apffel-Marglin and Marglin, *Decolonizing Knowledge*.

Partha Chatterjee and Manu Goswami contributed further to a growing consensus that late nineteenth-century Indian nationalists merged discourses from several European and North American thinkers, resulting in new knowledge to do with nationhood. Chatterjee offered one of the first detailed analyses of Indian thinking on nationalism. He found that it followed English utilitarianism, French positivism and Classical Political Economy in the mid-nineteenth century, while by the end of the century the discourse in Indian Economics had shifted to follow Friedrich List (1789–1846) and the German Historical School, becoming critical of Classical Political Economy.[21] Goswami was able to situate nationalistic discourses in India from around 1857 to 1920 within their political and socio-economic context by adopting a geographical–historical perspective.[22] She found that Indian intellectuals, including the Indian economists, constructed a nationalist imagining of a bounded national space and economy.[23] In their studies, however, Chatterjee and Goswami considered the Indian intellectuals principally as activists and thinkers in the nationalist movement, not as economists.[24]

This book places these economists into the history of economics and offers economic historians new sources on the Indian economy at the end of the nineteenth century. Each chapter zooms in on different aspects of this generation's thinking and work. They were part of the first batch of students to attend the imperial universities established in the mid-nineteenth century, graduating with degrees in history, mathematics and political economy. It was in 1870 that Naoroji presented the first study from this generation to an audience in London. He had done a back-of-the-envelope calculation to find India's national income per capita, and the result shook the London elite. Naoroji estimated India's national income per capita at 27 shillings – compared to Britain's £33 per capita income. India, lectured Naoroji, was undoubtedly poor, but the more pertinent question was whether India's poverty was increasing or decreasing (see Chapter 4). The studies by Naoroji's peers that followed started with the same overarching question. This

---

[21] Chatterjee, 'The Social Sciences in India', 487–8.
[22] Goswami, *Producing India*, 27–30.   [23] Ibid., 5, 215.
[24] Chatterjee, *The Nation and Its Fragments*; Chatterjee, *Nationalist Thought and the Colonial World*; Goswami, *Producing India*; Ganguli, *Indian Economic Thought*; Zachariah, *Developing India*; Bayly, *Indian Society and the Making of the British Empire*.

first generation of modern Indian economists saw poverty all around them and argued that they needed to better understand its evolution and its causes to find more appropriate solutions. In so doing, they could perhaps convince their British rulers to implement an effective plan for development that would bring forth much-needed progress.

The Invention of Progress and Development

There was and is, however, little consensus on what progress and development mean. Some say development defies definition. Indeed, there are as many definitions as there are researchers, if not more. Nevertheless, in the nineteenth century a useful distinction existed between inevitable processes that occurred automatically without intervention – progress or regress – and intentional plans to harness progress – development.[25] However, the terms were still, on occasion, used interchangeably. Ranade, for example, wrote about a 'dynamical progress or development'.[26] What was certain was that development was a positive intervention in society, often performed by the state, to limit negative change and bring about positive change. The negative changes, regress, for the Indian economists included increasing poverty, inequality and deaths during famines. The positive, progress, included increasing access to education, higher income levels and political participation.

Social scientists and historians quarrel over when the idea of development was invented. In economics, students are taught that it was invented after the Second World War,[27] while several historians place the beginning of development in the interwar period of the nineteenth century, when state development took hold more strongly.[28] A study cutting across history and economics, though, convincingly proves it started much earlier in Europe at the beginning of the nineteenth century.[29] Almost all of the studies, however, begin and end in

[25] Cowen and Shenton, *Doctrines of Development*, 22.
[26] Ranade, *Essays on Indian Economics*, 10.
[27] Arndt, *Economic Development*; Boianovsky, 'Beyond Capital Fundamentalism'.
[28] Cooper, 'Writing the History of Development'; Coquery-Vidrovitch, 'La mise en dépendance de l'Afrique noire'.
   For periodisations of the history of development, see the introductions of Unger, *International Development*; Macekura and Manela, *The Development Century*; Hodge, Hödl and Kopf, *Developing Africa*.
[29] Cowen and Shenton, *Doctrines of Development*, chap. 1.

Europe.[30] Imperialism and European industrialisation produced a European dominance in all things, giving rise to the belief that Europe had what the rest of the world lacked.

Progress was said to have spread from Britain to other European countries, then to European settlements in America, eventually reaching Russia and Japan by the end of the nineteenth century. Development is often confined to European industrial progress and that region's specific experience with progress. The idea of development itself is said to have originated in Europe and spread across the world like the material processes of progress. Development is thus extensively founded on European ways of knowing.

And yet, as Zachariah has written, ideas have no borders. Ideas spread with no rigid or final form; they exist within certain contexts and time periods, ever unstable. Zachariah has suggested considering 'a model of ideas gravitating towards each other', rather than pulling out individual words.[31] He found, for example, the terms 'progress', 'development', 'modernisation', 'industrialisation' and 'backwardness' in texts from early twentieth-century India.[32] In the chapters that follow, I show how ideas around development started to dominate the research agendas of the first generation of modern Indian economists some fifty years prior to the end of the Second World War. The idea of development can thus be found in places other than where historians usually look and earlier than economists think.

My intention here is not to define development a priori but to use development as an overarching focus to tease out the concepts, theories, models and policy prescriptions that the first generation of modern Indian economists studied and disseminated and to bring these Indian economists into the global debate around what progress and development mean.[33] By relocating development economics to another time and space, I uncover new variations on the idea of development.

[30] There are two exceptions, both published in 2020: Trincado, Lazzarini and Melnik, *Ideas in the History of Economic Development*; Decker and McMahon, *The Idea of Development in Africa*. The first includes one chapter on India in the interwar period, so a later period than my focus. The second looks at Africa and concludes that the idea of development was predominantly European or Western in Africa due to imperialism.

[31] Zachariah, 'Moving Ideas and How to Catch Them', 135.   [32] Ibid., 139.

[33] As Eric Helleiner has done in his books that trace the deep and global intellectual roots of International Political Economy. Helleiner, *The Neomercantilists*; Helleiner, *The Contested World Economy*.

Redefining Development

There are several examples of redefinition and hybrid theories in Indian Economics. Take Ranade's stadial theory of civilisation. The stadial theory had become popular in the eighteenth century to explain the differences between regions. Countries were different, according to the stadial theory, because they were in different stages of their development. To a large degree, Ranade's stadial theory looked like the existing four-stage model that had become widely accepted in the course of the late eighteenth-century Scottish Enlightenment. Nevertheless, he remade the theory by adding a lower imperial stage to which India had regressed due to imperialism. Ranade redefined a time in India's past as one where the country had been at a higher stage, enjoying greater progress than it was experiencing in the late nineteenth century. Ranade and his peers could thus refute the idea that India could not now skip to a higher stage of civilisation because they had already experienced a period of great progress in the past. India did not need to wait to progress or gain independence, like the stage theorists from Europe argued (see Chapter 3).

In this way the Indian economists of the late nineteenth century were the first to conceptualise a dependent imperial economy. Such an economy relied on its foreign rulers for demand, development, politics, infrastructure and education. In the case of India, dependence had ruralised the economy and drained the nation's resources. It had no chance of developing – as promised through the imperial ruler's civilising mission – because British domestic tariff barriers discouraged Indian textile exports, and tax payments drained Indian wealth. The Indian economy could and would not behave like other non-imperial territories (see Chapter 6).

Ranade also redefined universal development. For Europeans, David Ricardo's (1772–1823) theory of comparative advantage, which advocated for a global division of labour that assigned raw material production to Asia and industrial production to western Europe and North America, became irrefutable. Even List, who prescribed universal free trade once all countries had industrialised, denied the possibility of Asian progress. Industrialisation was thus only for Europe and, at best, North America. Theorists like List, who came from a country that was industrialising after Britain, argued that their countries should and could industrialise like Britain, but that the same did not hold for

Asia.[34] Seeing their economy – chiefly reliant upon agricultural production and exports – deindustrialise and become increasingly poor, the Indian economists did not believe there were benefits to such an international division. But while the Indian economists could not imagine a world without an industrialised western Europe, the British could imagine a world without an industrialised India (see Chapter 6).

The Indian economists could, however, imagine an industrialised India. Their rereading of Indian history, which resulted in the redefinition of the stadial theory where the country had been at a higher stage of civilisation before imperialism, enabled Indian Economics to reimagine the global political economy of development. If all countries industrialised, capital accumulation and global aggregate demand would increase. The resultant increase in exchange would enable still greater investment in industrial growth, thanks to higher levels of capital accumulation. Previous theories associated with Classical Political Economy, such as Ricardo's, were Eurocentric, justifying a zero-sum world-view that enriched Europe while impoverishing the rest of the planet. Global industrialisation would be win–win for everyone (see Chapter 6).

Relocating Development Economics: An Approach

Some historians who study knowledge production in imperial contexts have convincingly argued that knowledge was dominated by Europeans and their experiences under imperialism. They stress that we cannot ignore the impact that the hegemony of European and imperial discourse had on the intellectuals among their imperial subjects.[35] Others call for deprovincialising narratives where we can expose how dominant narratives, like development, came from certain times and spaces.[36] Global historians insist that there is little to no space for Indian thinking as long as the Empire existed, due to the interconnectedness of India, and other imperial territories, with its rulers.[37] Another group of historians has

---

[34] Helleiner, 'Globalising the Classical Foundations of IPE Thought', 992; Boianovsky, 'Friedrich List and the Economic Fate of Tropical Countries', 658–62.

[35] See, for example, Patel, 'Towards Internationalism'; Seth, *Subject Lessons*; Guha, *Dominance without Hegemony History and Power in Colonial India*.

[36] See, for example, Escobar, *Encountering Development*; Daston, 'Whither Critical Inquiry?'

[37] See, for example, Kapila, *An Intellectual History for India*; Sartori, *Bengal in Global Concept History*.

successfully shown that the spread of ideas from Europe to India was not a simple diffusion – the receivers transformed, adapted and refracted the ideas that came to them.[38]

We are then, as Kapil Raj noted, presented with a dilemma. Either modern science is a product of western Europe that spread to the other societies as they encountered European capitalism, or modern science is made up of competing national narratives, each claiming their thought is most applicable to their national context. One way around the dilemma is to see modern science as dehumanising and alienating because it imposed a foreign framework of rationality on non-European regions. Gyan Prakash has shown, for instance, how a group of Indians produced 'another reason' in imperial India.[39] The knowledge produced, according to this view, can only be applied locally in direct contradiction to the supposed originators of modern science, who always considered it to be universal. Several scholars, nevertheless, now agree that modern science is not universal. Western Europeans produced various iterations of modern science; it is far from a unified entity.[40] Modern science does not have its own logic of development based on a formal set of propositions. It is not innately universal, nor is it always forcibly imposed on others. In his analysis of the role of European and Indian exchange in the making of modern science, Raj thus proposed that we relocate it to other, non-European spaces.[41]

I use Raj's relocating approach to situate the Indian economists within their specific space and time. European imperial officials imposed modern science on the colonies through big, small, formal and informal institutions, arguing that it was the only universal way to understand and explain the world. The European curriculum employed in schools and universities in the imperial territories entrenched a hierarchy of knowledge where the European was held to be superior to all others. Indian scholars who went through that schooling system were often convinced themselves that Indian graduates and intellectuals were only regurgitating existing knowledge rather than producing anything original.[42]

---

[38] See, for example, Washbrook, 'Intimations of Modernity in South India'; Stein, *A History of India*; Bayly, *The Birth of the Modern World*.
[39] Prakash, *Another Reason*.
[40] Porter and Teich, *The Scientific Revolution in National Context*.
[41] Raj, *Relocating Modern Science*, 6.   [42] Seth, *Subject Lessons*, 28.

The first generation of modern Indian economists were rarely regarded as economists. For example, a 1902 newspaper review of Romesh Chunder Dutt's widely read volume on Indian history stated:

The literary skill and research which he has devoted to his object, prove Mr. Dutt to be capable of writing history if he could for a moment put his politics aside. But the work before us is not a history, it is merely a collection of historical arguments for the use of a political sect.[43]

Similar conclusions remained commonplace until the early 1970s.[44] Placing the Indian economists within their context is important to understanding whether and how they could voice their concerns and perspectives on the world and how their arguments were regarded.

This generation was struggling to be heard in a complex, and at times dangerous, milieu. It was thus challenging for them to contribute to economic knowledge. Censorship was a reality in imperial India. Propaganda, manipulation and domination challenged and constrained knowledge production. Ranade had his scholarship funding suspended for stating that the Mughal Empire had been better for India than British rule.[45] Surendranath Banerjea was found guilty of contempt and sentenced to two months in prison for publishing an editorial in the *Bengalee* on 2 April 1883 in which he compared Judge Norris with Jeffreys and Scroggs, British judges from the seventeenth century who were notorious for their infamous conduct, because Norris had been involved in a dispute regarding a family idol, a *saligram*, at the Calcutta High Court.[46]

Yet, by the turn of the century, this group of Indian economists was recognised as activists and leaders of the independence movement, their texts being used by other political activists, mainly those part of a widespread and successful Swadeshi (home manufacturers) movement (see Chapter 5). One key example is Sakharam Ganesh Deuskar's *Desher Katha* (Story of the Country), published in Bengali in 1904. Deuskar (1869–1912) summarised the work of Ranade, Naoroji and Dutt in popularised form as he advocated for the use of handlooms in

---

[43] Reprinted in Gupta, *Life and Work of Romesh Chunder Dutt*, 294.
[44] Gopalakrishnan, *Development of Economic Ideas in India*; Chandra, *The Rise and Growth of Economic Nationalism in India*; Chandra, 'Reinterpretation of Nineteenth Century Indian Economic History'.
[45] *Mahadev Govind Ranade: His Life and Career.*
[46] Ramos, 'Contesting the Imperial Gaze', 242; Banerjee, *Studies in Administrative History of Bengal*, 151–5.

the textile industry to increase employment and compete with Lancashire cloth, rather than large capital investment in Indian textile factories. The imperial administration proscribed the text in 1910 when it had already sold over ten thousand copies, been summarised in a pamphlet, *Krishcher sarbanash* (Ruin of the Peasantry), inspired Swadeshi street plays and become mandatory reading for an entire generation of Swadeshi activists.[47] When in 1892 Naoroji became the first Indian to be elected as a Member of Parliament in Britain, he was hailed the Grand Old Man of India, a counterpart to the United Kingdom's Grand Old Man, William Gladstone, then serving as prime minister for the fourth time. Naoroji was recognised as the representative for the whole of India and the undisputed leader of the entire independence movement.[48] In Figure 1.2 he is drawn as a colossus with one foot in India and another in Britain, hailed as the voice of India. Naoroji had bridged the gulf between India and Britain with patriotism and perseverance.

Figure 1.2 Cartoon depicting Dadabhai Naoroji's two roles as British MP and Indian Representative.

[47] Goswami, *Producing India*, 246.   [48] Patel, *Naoroji*, 190.

Despite the challenges of producing economic knowledge, there will always be space for contribution and change – as Raj demonstrates in his book *Relocating Modern Science*. My relocation of development economics shows how the Indian economists' national and international context left room for imagining a new configuration of global development. They were Indians who travelled and studied in other countries, especially Britain. The historical, political and socio-economic context offered the discursive possibility necessary for them to rearticulate and redefine existing economic thinking, rather than only reproduce prevailing economic theories. As many historians of ideas theorise, ideas are necessarily transformed in dialogue.[49]

My relocating approach thus incorporates the idea that existing knowledge can both constrain and facilitate social actions. Our field of perception is limited by what we learn and know, but that knowledge simultaneously offers meaning and understanding of our context.[50] The late nineteenth-century Indian economists were taught concepts, frameworks and tools of analysis by their imperial university education and existing literature, which were primarily based on another regional context.[51] They used these imported and imposed ways of knowing to understand different regional circumstances in the South Asian subcontinent, speaking and publishing in diverse spaces where their legitimacy and ability to be heard varied substantially.[52]

My relocation of development economics happens on two fronts. First, development economics is relocated to another time. As previously noted, contrary to other economists I find that development economics predates the Second World War, going back to the late nineteenth century. Second, development economics is relocated to another space, India, where historians of economics have rarely gone before. In this way, I seek to offer a new perspective on the history of development economics.

At the end of the nineteenth century, Romesh Chunder Dutt declared that 'the East must produce its own thinkers, its own historians, its own

---

[49] Goswami, *Producing India*; Zachariah, 'Moving Ideas and How to Catch Them'; Sartori, *Bengal in Global Concept History*.

[50] Bakhtin, *The Dialogic Imagination*; Zachariah, 'Moving Ideas and How to Catch Them'.

[51] Govindarajan, *G. Subramania Iyer*; Ranade, *Essays on Indian Economics*, 2.

[52] For a more detailed discussion of my method, see Bach, 'Positive Discourse Analysis'.

economists'.[53] What follows is the story of how the first generation of modern Indian economists did just that. Indian Economics is a body of literature that used existing economic, philosophical and political thinking to better understand the Indian economy. In the process, it produced a refracted idea of development that illuminates the imperial economy and prescribes a more equal and prosperous global economy. But before dealing with their ideas of progress and regress, and their plan for development, I flesh out the intellectual, political and socio-economic context (in Chapter 1) and describe the beginnings of Indian Economics (in Chapter 2).

---

[53] Reprinted in Gupta, *Life and Work of Romesh Chunder Dutt*, 388.

1 | *The Context*

India experienced several turbulent decades after the official takeover by the British Crown, following the Indian Mutiny, in 1858. Becoming an official territory of the British Empire came with promises of progress. Already by the 1870s, though, the promises seemed hollow. The textile industry, once a flourishing sector that supplied fabrics to most of the world, was dwindling. The average Indian was sinking into deeper poverty. And millions died in the three largest famines of India's history between 1873 and 1901.

It goes without saying that India's large territory, rich history and its dependent position within the British Empire rendered its context dense and complex. India was extensively linked to the global economy and had a long history of trading in the subcontinent, primarily in textiles during the Mughal period, and later as one of the main suppliers of raw materials to the growing textile industry in Manchester in northern England. This chapter aims to contextualise the first generation of modern Indian economists by identifying the major trends and events affecting India in the last four decades of the nineteenth century.

1860s: Ramifications of the Indian Mutiny, 1857–8

The year 1858 marks a shift in precisely who held power over India. The soldier revolt of 1857–8 triggered the formal imperialism of India, when the British East India Company handed the reins to the British Crown. Historians have already studied this event in depth, identifying a range of different causes and effects.[1] The year 1858 is significant here because it marks the start of a period in which British control over the

---

[1] Almost 300 studies have been written on the Indian Mutiny with little to no consensus on why it happened. National bias – British versus Indian accounts – can partly explain the disagreements. But the varied accounts also stem from the fact that the event was widespread and complex. In terms of causes, the main four theories to emerge in the twentieth century are the nationalist interpretation, the

Indian economy dramatically increased. Now that the Crown ruled India, Indians saw the British as a permanent fixture, and increasingly they were forced to find ways to cooperate with them.

At the same time, the Indian Mutiny had put British rule in question, as imperial officials were forced to justify their presence in the subcontinent. The well-known idea of the civilising mission was concocted, as an afterthought, to legitimise their intervention. India's chaotic and poor population needed enlightened Europeans in order to progress and eventually learn how to rule themselves. The imperial administration disseminated the myth of its civilising mission primarily through James Mill's *History of British India*, first published in 1817, which became a core text for all Indian civil servants. Imperialism, J. Mill (1773–1836) claimed, would edify the half-civilised natives of India, simultaneously justifying British rule.[2]

Yet, J. Mill's narrative of India's chaotic and brittle legal structure and social relations was based on accounts written by imperial officials, specifically judges, revenue collectors, clergymen and surveyors, who complained of disorder and the ways in which British rule was vulnerable. J. Mill used, for instance, Francis Buchanan's account of Kanara on the south-western coast of India after the Anglo-Mysore War when writing about Indian agriculture, and his understanding of Indian property rights came from a judicial official in Bengal. The accounts were written in moments of crisis during, for example, disputes over revenue collection or arguments in court. J. Mill failed to see that these were moments of chaos and disorder, not necessarily the norm, and that British actions intensified the disorder.[3] Although they perhaps did not always intend to do so, the British thinkers created the discourse necessary to give legitimacy to the Empire.

The revolt of 1857–8 brought about two particularly important prescriptions for progress. It underlined the need for improvements to

---

Marxists' analysis, the mutiny as traditionalist rebellion and the explanation based upon studies of local uprisings. Recent research has found one reason common to all rebel statements: the rebels felt like the British East India Company was trying to make all Indians eat the same food, which, according to many Indians, corroded the essence of Indian life. The rebels opposed the idea that India shared a common culture or nationality and fought for Indian plurality. For more discussion, see, for example, Adas, 'Twentieth Century Approaches to the Indian Mutiny of 1857–58'; Wilson, *India Conquered*, 244.

[2] Mill, *The History of British India*, i, 177, 332.

[3] Wilson, *India Conquered*, 202.

public infrastructure and the legal system, and shifted the overall imperial approach from one based on universal assumptions concerning progress and development to one that considered India's local conditions. While war was raging in India in 1858, John Stuart Mill (1806–73), son to J. Mill and a senior examiner for correspondence for the British East India Company in London, drafted an essay advocating for keeping the Company in power. His 'Memorandum of the Improvement of the Administration of India during the Last Thirty Years' conveyed how British rule was 'improving the physical and mental condition of the inhabitants'.[4] Circulated to Members of Parliament, the essay argued that the Company had benefited India through three main developments: low and fair taxes, achieved by limiting the government's right to extract resources from Indian society; the maintenance of law and order; and by improving public infrastructure. J. S. Mill employed a laissez-faire rhetoric where low taxes and a legal system were sufficient to secure industrial profits and incentivise people to work. Yet, like his father, J. S. Mill argued that India was too poor to construct the necessary infrastructure through private enterprise, as was possible in Britain. Instead, they required British support. The emphasis on public-financed infrastructure in India marked a peculiarity of liberalism during this time.

J. S. Mill's memorandum on the Company's achievements in India formed the basis of the imperial approach to follow. As of 1861, the government published the *Moral and Material Progress* periodical, detailing the physical improvements in India. Each report included a list of new laws passed, and some information on finance, the post office, telegraphs, steamships, public works and the Indian geological department. The order of importance seemed to go from physical infrastructure and public works to education, which was not high on the list of priorities. The first report stated that ₹1,032,021, or £68,800, had gone to education in Bengal, which was about the same as the amount given to the army barracks. With little access to statistics on the Indian economy, progress was equated to the official transactions made by the imperial administration – such as expenditure on roads, irrigation and army barracks, and the pace of railway construction. Even doubling the number of letters delivered by the post office between

---

[4] Mill, *Memorandum of the Improvements in the Administration of India during the Last Thirty Years*, 1.

1855 and 1860 was marked as an achievement.[5] The imperial administration started to both minutely record their expenditure on public works like irrigation, railways and the legal system, and increase their investment in such projects.

These reports, read by the Indian economists, set the tone for how progress and development was seen and dealt with on the subcontinent. This was, of course, affected by the aforementioned shift in Britain's overall approach to imperialism – from a strategy based on universalist assumptions of progress and development to one that was supposed to adapt to India's local conditions. Prior to the 1857–8 revolt, Britain's approach had to some extent centred on the belief that they could and should help Indians to assimilate their progressive ways. However, the events of 1857–8 had the British questioning why their subjects were unsatisfied with imperial rule. Rather than consider whether their mission had failed, they claimed that the uprising had been caused by Indian resistance to modernity, universal norms of civilisation, progress and development. Imperial rule was now viewed as necessary to rejuvenate native society and protect it from dissolution, rather than to civilise according to Britain's experience of progress. India was seen to be suffering from exposure to modernisation and internal conflicts. Deemed irrational and politically and economically static, India was not seen as ready for progress and development. From 1858 until the 1910s, the imperial officers put aside, to a certain degree, the idea of improving India to prepare it for independence, aiming instead to preserve Indian society the way it was.[6]

Henry Maine's *Village-Communities in the East and West*, published in 1871, was the most significant text within the shift. Maine (1822–88) was a highly visible member of the imperial administration, a famous scholar of Indian law and society, and one of the most important thinkers on imperial ideology. An earlier text by Maine, *Ancient Law*, published in 1861, theorised an inherent link between society and law. To sustain progress, he claimed, law should be harmonised with the state of society. Maine's theory was based on a new history of property rights. Whereas preceding scholars divided societies into those with communal property rights and those with

---

[5] Wilson, *India Conquered*, 288–9; Nayar, *Colonial Voices*.
[6] Cain, 'Character, "Ordered Liberty", and the Mission to Civilise'; Mantena, *Alibis of Empire*, 9–15.

private, he conceptualised a historical sequence where property was originally communal, eventually being divided to be owned by individuals. According to Maine's reading, private property rights were inherently progressive. All societies started with communal property rights and then transitioned, thanks to progress, to private property rights. The timing, however, of when ancient customary laws became written had a substantial effect on legal progress. Maine argued that the progress required for the transition, or more concretely the codification of law, was not immanent or inevitable; it depended on a political transformation or revolution that shifted power from the divine kinship to aristocracies. Successful codification therefore became the factor that distinguished progressive from stationary societies. The transition from communal to private property rights had failed to emerge in India because Hindu law had been written too late.[7]

Village-Communities in the East and West theorised that private property emerged out of communal property. Village communities were at the centre of Maine's analysis. Maine, as well as earlier members of the imperial administration such as Sir Charles Metcalfe, Thomas Munro and Mountstuart Elphinstone, was keen to understand why and how Indian village communities were disintegrating at the beginning of the nineteenth century. Societies, according to Maine, were first organised around status and then eventually they adopted the more progressive contractual form of organisation. The Indian village community structure, organised according to status, was therefore an example of an earlier mode of society – meaning that their disintegration held the key to the question of how and why a society moved from status to contract. Ancient society was held together, apolitically, by status or stable bonds of customs and structures of kinship, whereas modern society was held together by formal contracts. Maine's theory was essentially dualistic, labelling some societies as traditional and others as modern.[8] Although the breakdown of such regressive socio-economic structures was inevitable, Maine concluded that the 1857–8 revolt proved that the dissolution had been wrongfully accelerated by imperial rule.[9]

---

[7] Maine, *Ancient Law*, 18.
[8] Ibid.; Maine, *Village-Communities in the East and West*, 1–19.
[9] Maine, *Village-Communities in the East and West*, 39.

Maine's discourse portrayed a model of distorted and arrested development in which a religious aristocracy had managed to impose traditional and customary order. The imperial administration had prioritised the most ancient interpretations of the Hindu code: when they imposed the British judicial system onto the Hindu legal system, the subsequent legal code overemphasised the importance of native rules and customs. Ritual formalities and adherence to religious texts were incorporated into the code, establishing irrational norms and practices, such as caste. 'Native rules hardened', wrote Maine, 'and contracted a rigidity which they never had in real native practice'.[10] Maine therefore prescribed preserving native society until India was ready to shift to the progressive contractual law.

Maine's new interpretation of legal progress initiated a discursive shift, arguing that India, as well as countries like Ireland, could not yet accommodate universal forces of progress such as private property rights. The discourse essentially undid the ideology that underpinned Classical Political Economy. While J. S. Mill's earlier *Principles of Political Economy* had prescribed private property rights for India, because customary or status law hindered progress, Maine's discourse spread the idea that the principles of political economy ignored the multifaceted local factors of obstruction found in India.[11] Maine's reinterpretation of India's needs came at a time when there was a conscious call for a new approach to imperialism on the subcontinent. The mutiny had exposed the limits of imposing law and order on a foreign population, and Maine brought a needed theory to better understand Indian society, providing the only solution to managing the colony without triggering another revolt.[12] As a result, dominant figures, including J. S. Mill, Sir Charles Wood (1800–85), the president of the Board of Control of the British East India Company, and Sir George Campbell (1824–92), the lieutenant-governor of Bengal from 1871 to 1874, now identified custom, the peculiar logic of India, as the new axiom of imperial policy.

By 1870, the difference between India and Europe had essentially become synonymous with the difference between custom and private property. Maine's thesis thus shifted the course of imperial policies. India was no longer ready for modern institutions. The queen's

[10] Ibid., 44.   [11] Mill, *Principles of Political Economy*, 229–37, 325.
[12] Hadjigeorgiou, 'The Legacy of Sir Henry Maine in the 21st Century', sec. 4.

proclamation of 1858 declared a principle of non-interference in native religious beliefs and customs, and the policy debates that followed centred on whether private property rights should be implemented in rural areas.

1870s and 1880s: Indian Famines and the Long Depression

India was hit by two of the worst famines of its history in the 1870s. The Bihar famine of 1873–4 started due to a drought in the province of Bihar, affecting the neighbouring provinces of Bengal, the North-Western Provinces and Oudh. The newly appointed lieutenant-governor of Bengal, Sir Richard Temple (1826–1902), organised a successful relief effort. He oversaw, for instance, the import of 450,000 tonnes of rice from Burma, which helped to keep the mortality rate low. The story was dramatically different in the famine that followed in 1876–8. A drought in 1876 resulted in a crop failure in the British-administered presidencies of Madras and Bombay, as well as the princely states of Mysore and Hyderabad. By 1877, the famine affected regions in the north, including the Central and North-Western Provinces and a small area in Punjab. Some 8 million people died, while the viceroy of India, Lord Robert Bulwer-Lytton, continued to oversee wheat exports to Britain at record levels.

That second famine hit during a time when the imperial administration wanted to reduce their expenditure on welfare. Temple, who had been criticised for excessive spending in dealing with the Bihar famine a few years earlier, was cautious not to invite the same when crisis struck once more. Now famine commissioner for the imperial administration, he opted for a laissez-faire approach. He implemented relief work for those who could work, including children, and organised handouts to small children, the elderly and the poor. The large death toll triggered debates questioning how India was ruled. One consequence of these debates was the Famine Commission of 1880, which instituted the Indian Famine Codes. The codes consisted of famine scales, including three levels of food insecurity – near-scarcity, scarcity and famine. The commission, with the help of the scales, was tasked with famine prevention.[13] Another consequence was the establishment of the Indian National

---

[13] Davis, *Late Victorian Holocausts*, 58.

Congress by Allan Octavian Hume, along with other imperial officers like William Wedderburn (1838–1918) and many of the Indian economists, less than a decade later in 1885. The Congress was set up to voice, among other things, their concerns with the way the British were ruling India. It would serve as a key platform for the first generation of nationalists, including the Indian economists (see Chapter 2).

At the time of the famines, distress among the peasants was particularly visible in Bengal and Maharashtra, with uprisings occurring in the first half of the 1870s. The first uprising started in 1873 in the Pabna district in eastern Bengal, when the Agrarian League was established to raise funds for poorer peasants and organise rent strikes. In 1874, a second riot started with a social boycott against the moneylenders in the districts of Deccan in Maharashtra. Both riots pushed the imperial administration to pass acts to appease the peasants. Based on the high number of famine mortalities during this period and distressing accounts of rural life, it is safe to say that these were pacifying measures at best (see Chapters 4 and 5).

Meanwhile, the global economy, but especially Europe and North America, was suffering from an economic recession. The Long Depression, as it has come to be known, was sparked by a global financial panic in 1873. This came after the end of the American Civil War in 1865 and the German-Franco War of 1870–1, when there had been an investment boom, particularly in railways. The downturn lasted at least until the end of the 1870s, but historical records of global output show a significant slowdown in growth until 1896.

It was not, however, a simple economic standstill; employees saw their real living standards increase, as the price of products decreased. It was rather the growth of capital and labour productivity, and the rate of capital accumulation, that slowed significantly, notably in Britain. While new technology and innovation, especially in Germany and North America, enabled others to gain the upper hand against older industries in Britain, significant debt built up. Capital investments in Britain thus slowed, as demand for British goods decreased and profits shrunk. Lower rates of investment meant that British productivity and consumption slumped, which threatened the structure of world trade due to Britain's pivotal role in the global market. British imports and investment could boost growth in many regions of the world. And a lack of British investments and demand caused economic downturns.[14]

Indian peasants were roped in to restore Britain's previous dominance of the world market. On a global level, India's large trade surplus became a key component in sustaining capital accumulation in the City. Britain earned huge surpluses in its trade with India and China, helping it to maintain deficits with the United States, Germany and the white dominions. Britain's surplus with Asia enabled, to a certain extent, its free trade policy and its trading partners' high rate of industrialisation. It also allowed North America and industrial Europe to retain their tariff barriers.[15]

In India, agricultural production grew by 1 per cent every year from 1870 to 1900, and the cultivated land area increased by 30–40 per cent between 1870 and 1946. As a result of commercialisation in, primarily, wheat, rice, cotton, jute, groundnut and sugar cane, growth rates in the agricultural sector were positive in most regions. Employment in the sector rose from 60 per cent to 65 per cent in the late eighteenth century, and to 80 per cent at the end of the nineteenth century. The value of exports, of which at least half consisted of primary products, increased 4 per cent each year from 1876 to 1913. More than half of India's exports were agricultural goods such as grains, seeds, raw cotton and raw jute.[16] During this period, total agricultural exports doubled, spurring the creation of new towns that employed merchants, artisans and service workers. Expansive railway construction reduced transportation costs and subsequently increased international demand for Indian agricultural products, incentivising peasants to expand and intensify cultivation. Aggregate commercialisation was,

[14] Washbrook, 'The Indian Economy and the British Empire'; Heilbroner, 'The Paradox of Progress'.

[15] Latham, *The International Economy and the Undeveloped World*, 70; Park, 'Depression and Capital Formation', 511, 516; Davis, *Late Victorian Holocausts*, 57; Arrighi, *The Long Twentieth Century*, 262.
  This is only a part of the story. Berrick Saul shows that global trade networks are not quite as straightforward and do not represent a zero-sum system. India's surplus could not simply be said to have transferred wealth to Britain and its trade partners. Britain's use of India's trade surplus may only partly explain India's agricultural commercialisation. Saul, *Studies in British Overseas Trade*.

[16] Washbrook, 'The Indian Economy and the British Empire', 63; Roy, *Economic History of India*, 90; Balachandran, 'Colonial India and the World Economy', 86–7.

however, rather small. Production rose mainly because more land was being used, not because the sector had become more efficient; the average growth rate of crop output, for instance, was only 0.37 per cent.[17]

As Britain became more economically reliant on India during the Long Depression, it met with another wave of imperial critique when several of its leading thinkers condemned the cost and violence of its colonial presence on the subcontinent. In the 1870s and 1880s, Britain was spreading itself thin with wars in Afghanistan and Burma, triggering another round of debates over the Empire's legitimacy. The criticism came to the forefront during the 1880 general election when William Gladstone campaigned against the Conservative government's dangerous and impractical imperial policy.[18] This resulted in the Empire being rebranded as the *Pax Britannica*, a term that literally means British peace. It denotes a period of relative peace between the major global powers and emphasises Britain's role as a global police force from the end of the Napoleonic Wars in 1815 to the beginning of the First World War in 1914.[19]

Historians have often mistaken the *Pax Britannica* label as a sign of British confidence during a flourishing period of imperial rule. However, there are several examples that show British uncertainty and weakness in the subcontinent. Temple described the various major problems and responsibilities faced by the imperial project in his book *India in 1880*, where he listed fifty-three threats to British rule in India, focusing on Indian 'dissatisfaction', 'discontent' and 'hostility' towards the colonising power.[20] Sir William Hunter (1840–1900), a member of the Indian Civil Service, claimed that Britain was on trial again in his book *England's Work in India*, published in 1881.[21] *Pax Britannica* was yet another attempt on the part of the imperial officials to justify and hence maintain British power over India. Imperialism turned out to have a circular logic – the purpose of imperial power was just to sustain imperial power, not to civilise India or bring about global peace.

---

[17] Roy, *Economic History of India*, 104–5; Chaudhary et al., *A New Economic History of Colonial India*, 103, 108.

[18] *The Times* (London), 26 November 1879, 10.

[19] Wilson, *India Conquered*, 296.   [20] Temple, *India in 1880*, 207, 62, 355.

[21] Hunter, *England's Work in India*.

1890–1905: Further Famines, Deindustrialisation and Border Disputes

There were two more severe famines around the turn of the century. The first started in 1896 in the mountainous region in central and northern India, affecting the United Provinces, the Central Provinces, Bihar and Berar, parts of the Bombay and Madras Presidencies, Punjab and the princely states of Rajputana, Central India Agency and Hyderabad. Despite the British administration following the Famine Code established in the early 1880s, the mortality rate was high at some 1 million people, as the guidelines failed to offer relief to all those in need. In the Central Provinces, for example, there were tribal groups who did not want to work for public works to earn food rations and others who simply did not qualify for relief. The second famine to affect the whole subcontinent in this period began in 1899 with the failure of the monsoons over western and central India. It hit the same regions as the previous famines, so population numbers had barely recovered. Estimates vary, but up to 4.5 million died due to crop failures across the subcontinent.

Indian famines and rising poverty resulted from modernism rather than a lack of it. Wheat production expanded drastically and cereal was exported in high quantity during the last quarter of the nineteenth century, when India experienced the worst famines in its history. Between 1875 and 1900, annual grain exports increased from 3 to 10 million tonnes, equivalent to the annual nutrition of 25 million people. The opening of the Suez Canal and the invention of the steam ship reduced transport costs, encouraging the Empire to increase exports from the subcontinent. Farmers and landowners were then incentivised to grow monocultures for the international market. To supply enough raw cotton for the mills in Manchester, the Cotton Supply Association, part of the Manchester Chamber of Commerce, decided to set up cotton monocultures in Berar and Nagpore. More cash crops, monocultures and food exports meant India was no longer self-sufficient when it came to feeding its population.[22] The 1899–1900

---

[22] Sen, *Poverty and Famines*; Singh, *From Naoroji to Nehru*; Dyson, 'The Historical Demography of Berar, 1881–1980'; Hardiman, *Peasant Resistance in India*; Beckert, *Empire of Cotton*; Davis, *Late Victorian Holocausts*; Satya, *Cotton and Famine in Berar*; Wilson, *India Conquered*.

famine caused 143,000 Beraris to starve to death, while thousands of bales of cotton were exported.

All of this meant that famines spread ever quicker and with greater intensity. There is little evidence that rural parts of pre-imperial India suffered from famines to the degree that they did under the British East India Company and the Crown. Forced to be economically subservient to its rulers, imperial India was no longer able to act in its own best interest. As Britain industrialised and India became more closely integrated into the global market, the imperial power flooded its subject with cheap textiles, causing unemployment in India to rise. British textile exports to India increased from 60 million yards of cotton goods in the 1830s to 968 million yards in 1858, bypassing a billion by 1870.[23]

While Indian peasants were roped in to sustain British industrialisation, Indian capitalists went out of business. In a trend often referred to as India's deindustrialisation, there was a general decrease in aggregate industrial employment and production. The small-scale textile industry, historically successful at exporting its products the world over, was worst hit. A study using census data found that the level of employment by manufacturers stagnated at around 14.8 million at the end of the nineteenth century.[24] Additional research calculates that industrial employment declined from 20 to 13–15 million from 1881 to 1931 and that the population dependent on industry decreased from 18 per cent to between 8 and 9 per cent, during which time there was a dramatic decrease in employment among cotton spinners and weavers.[25] In Gangetic Bihar in eastern India, the percentage of employment in cotton went from 62.3 per cent in 1809–13 to 15.1 per cent in 1901.[26] India's share of global output also declined sharply, falling from 17.6 per cent in 1830 to 2.8 per cent in 1880 and then to 1.4 per cent in 1913.[27] In the case of yarn exports to Japan, these dropped from 8,400 tonnes in 1890 to almost nothing in 1898.[28]

[23] Satya, *Cotton and Famine in Berar*, 50, 155, 281–2, 296; Davis, *Late Victorian Holocausts*; Wilson, *India Conquered*, 321.
[24] Thorner and Thorner, *Land and Labour in India*, 70–1.
[25] Roy, *Economic History of India*, 150, 163, 172; Bagchi, 'De-industrialization in India in the Nineteenth Century'; Bagchi, 'Deindustrialization in Gangetic Bihar 1809–1901'; Clark, *The Conditions of Economic Progress*.
[26] Bagchi, 'De-industrialization in India in the Nineteenth Century', 139–40.
[27] Bairoch, 'International Industrialization Levels from 1750 to 1980', 272–83.
[28] Maddison, 'The Historical Origins of Indian Poverty', 68.

Deindustrialisation, nevertheless, spread unevenly across the small-scale industries. The indigenous industry produced different goods: intermediate goods (e.g., cotton yarn and dyes), tools for peasants (e.g., ploughs or hand implements), consumer goods for the poor (e.g., coarse cloth, pottery for daily use, grain milling) and commodities for well-off consumers or export markets (e.g., decorated cotton cloth, silk, brassware, carpets, leather goods). British industrialisation significantly damaged the viability of the first three product groups because these goods could be produced much more cheaply with machines. However, the fourth group of products did not experience significant competition. The sari, for example, was made of silk and other fibres, which the mechanised factories did not use. The silk textile industry experienced no decline and the size of the cotton industry only shrank by 28 per cent. International competition came only from coarse medium cotton cloth and printed and bleached cotton cloth.[29]

Deindustrialisation also spread unevenly across regions. Some towns prospered thanks to railways that increased access to global markets, while small-scale textile producers in rural and interior towns had to close because they were outcompeted by foreign imports arriving via those same railways. Long-distance trade in both wool and woven products expanded. Sheep rearing was relocated to areas with easier grazing conditions that could support better breeds, meaning Rajputana became specialised in wool production, whereas United Provinces and Punjab developed as major weaving centres.[30]

One of the biggest causes of deindustrialisation was capital scarcity. General poverty dampened the vitality of the domestic market, causing a low aggregate demand. Deindustrialisation pushed industrial employees out of work and deprived them of income. And as they migrated to rural areas, they demanded even less goods as their farms provided them with their needs. What is more, Indian exports had to compete with growing industrial

[29] Roy, *Economic History of India*, 164–7, 175–6; Chaudhary et al., *A New Economic History of Colonial India*, 62; Sarkar, *Modern India*, 29; Wilson, *India Conquered*, 267–8, 278–9, 285–6.

[30] Roy, *Economic History of India*, 164–7, 175–6; Chaudhary et al., *A New Economic History of Colonial India*, 62; Wilson, *India Conquered*, 267–8, 278–9, 285–6; Sarkar, *Modern India*, 29.

competition from other nations – not just Britain but also
Germany, Japan and France.[31]

An additional cause of deindustrialisation was mechanisation.
Artisans were increasingly forced to deal with segmented markets,
globalisation and increasing wage-employment, as opposed to self-
employment. Income per worker increased in small-scale industry
faster than in large-scale factories. In the indigenous textile industry,
employment fell as income increased. Decreasing employment in the
indigenous industry was thus partly due to increased mechanisation or,
put differently, an increase in efficiency. New tools such as the fly-
shuttle slay were being used in handloom textiles (accounting for
a third of employment in small-scale industry), and the frame-
mounted loom, the jacquard, dobby, drop box and synthetic dyes
were imported from Europe. Productivity rose due to technological
change and a shift from household to wage workshops, increasing the
average number of hours worked per labourer.[32]

Amid this period of monumental change, there were two border
disputes affecting imperial India. The first occurred in
December 1903 when the British Indian Armed Forces invaded Tibet
in order to establish diplomatic relations and resolve the dispute over
the border between Tibet and Sikkim in north-eastern India. Lord
Curzon (1859–1925), the viceroy of India from 1899 to 1905, wanted
to counter the Russian Empire's advances in central Asia, fearing the
eventual invasion of British India. Russia assured the British government that they had no interest in Tibet in April 1904, but Lord Curzon
continued his mission. By August, the British forces had made it to the
capital, Lhasa, and forced the Tibetans officials to sign a treaty that
gave the British further economic influence in Tibet. The treaty recognised the Tibet–Sikkim border and prohibited Tibet from establishing
relations with any other foreign power. In spite of the latter proviso, the
British later recognised Chinese sovereign control over the region.[33]

The second border dispute came in 1905 and concerned the Bengal
Presidency in north-western India. On 19 July, Lord Curzon
announced that the imperial administration would divide the region

---

[31] Kumar and Desai, *The Cambridge Economic History of India*, 2:598–9;
      Washbrook, 'The Indian Economy and the British Empire', 64; Roy, *Economic
      History of India*, 80.
[32] Krishnamurthy, 'De-industrialisation Revisited', 158–60.
[33] Wilson, *India Conquered*, chap. 12.

in two, separating the largely Muslim areas in the east from the pre-dominantly Hindu areas in the west. This partition had huge ramifica-tions for the nationalist movement. The Early Nationalists, including the Indian economists, saw it as a challenge to Indian nationalism in the east and a deliberate attempt to divide Bengal on religious grounds. The Hindus in the east worried that they would become a minority, while the Muslims took it as an opportunity to organise themselves.[34] A mere six years later the split was undone, in response to the Swadeshi (home manufacturers) riots fighting for Indian industrialisation. The Swadeshi movement was a boycott against textile imports and encour-aged people to buy Indian-made cotton (see Chapter 5). The partition of Bengal, a textbook divide-and-rule policy with many twists and turns, is beyond the scope of this book. Suffice it to say that it had huge ripple effects for the nationalist movement, of which the Indian economists were founding and leading figures, that would eventually lead to an independent India and Pakistan in 1947.

The first generation of modern Indian economists started their car-eers in these stormy decades when British rule was supposed to bring progress to their subcontinent. Instead, the British brought higher levels of starvation, deindustrialisation, economic crises and border disputes. It was against this bleak background that the Indian econo-mists set out to discover why their country was so poor and what could be done to reverse such worrying trends. In the following chapter, I dive into their educational backgrounds and the founding texts of Indian Economics.

---

[34] It eventually led to the split of the Indian National Congress into two factions: the extremist and moderate. For more discussion, see Argov, *Moderates and Extremists in the Indian National Movement.*

2 | The Beginnings of Indian Economics

In the 1870s, a generation of economists was born amid a troubling reality in India. As outlined in the previous chapter, the country faced many crises around this time – suffering some of the worst famines in its history, having an imperial administration that struggled to balance its budget, and the crumbling of its textile industry, to name but a few. Dutt wrote of 'almost universal poverty', Ranade talked about the 'phenomenal Poverty', and Naoroji analysed how India was 'sinking in poverty'.[1] Indian Economics, argued its founder, Ranade, in 1892, would create economic knowledge that explained India's distinct problems and would find appropriate solutions.

Indian Difference

There was wide consensus that the Indian context was different. As it was put in one newspaper in 1870, 'the condition of India is in many respects peculiar and the same law which holds good in other countries may not hold good here'.[2] Ever since the British East India Company had to legitimise the peculiar monopoly it had set up in India, its governors and supporters had used the argument that India was different. As early as 1682, Heneage Finch – the lawyer defending the Company in the Sandys trial to protect its monopoly rights, rather than follow the common English practice of free trade – pushed the idea that free trade could only work between people of the same religion. Europeans could trade with each other because they shared the same civil society based on their common Christianity. Non-Christians did not share the same civil laws and moral codes, and so were enemies. The British East India Company was in constant war with the Indians

---

[1] Dutt, *Speeches and Papers on Indian Questions*, 87; Ranade, *Essays on Indian Economics*, 205; Naoroji, *Essays, Speeches, Addresses and Writings*, 160.
[2] Printed in the *Amrita Bazar Patrika* on 1 December 1870.

and could only protect its trade through a monopoly. Despite resistance to the idea, Finch and the governors ultimately persuaded the London elite and England's new king, James II, to support the Company's monopoly rights.[3]

A century and a half later in 1817, when the Company had gained control over much of the subcontinent, one of its officers, J. Mill, who never set foot in India, published *The History of British India*. Mill's widely read book, which later became a core text for all Indian civil servants, took the argument of difference to a whole new level. Mill described India as a country with chaotic and disorderly institutions of government, law and religion, nothing like those in Britain and Europe.[4] In 1857 one popular publisher declared that the book marked 'the beginning of a sound thinking on the subject of India'.[5] The British East India Company had successfully spread a narrative of how India was different. The imperial administration that took over from the British East India Company in 1858 continued to legitimise its rule by declaring India different in the negative sense. India was regressive and inferior to Britain; the British had a civilising mission there (see Chapter 1).

The first generation of modern Indian economists had been convinced that India was different. But they used their difference for other ends. By contrast, they intended to prove India's difference in such a way as to render its economy, institutions and people visible. As scholars such as Robert Young, Allan Luke and Homi Bhabha explain, imperialism makes its subjects both invisible and different. If you declare another population inferior, then you render them less worthy, less visible, and thus legitimise treating them differently. This produces a paradox: Indians were both absent and present.[6] If the Indian economists then had to choose whether to be invisible or different, an obvious choice of survival was to be different. From this paradox of imperialism, Indian Economics was born.

---

[3] Howell, *A Complete Collection of State Trials and Proceedings for High Treason*, 484–6.
[4] Mill, *The History of British India*, 332.
[5] Knight, 'The English Cyclopædia', iv, 231.
[6] Young, *White Mythologies*; Luke, 'Text and Discourse in Education'; Bhabha, *Nation and Narration*.

Imperialist Education in India

Starting in the 1850s, when most of the Indian economists were children, the imperial administration implemented an education system that spread what the British officials labelled 'European knowledge'.[7] Despite the nuances and differences within European knowledge, at the time the imperial officers saw it as a body of thought that shared core prescriptions, categories and background assumptions. Sanjay Seth's history of Indian education of this period finds that it is possible to bundle together the components of European knowledge – what he labels Western knowledge – because they share those common characteristics.[8]

A heated debate around education in India had started some two decades before in the 1830s between the so-called Anglicists and Orientalists. The Anglicists argued that schools should teach in English and spread European knowledge, while the Orientalists advocated for vernacular language and Oriental forms of knowledge instruction. The Anglicists, who ultimately won the debate, claimed that English and European education would civilise native Indian society. Thomas Babington Macaulay (1800–59), the secretary to the Board of Control under Lord Grey from 1832 to 1833, and a leading reformer in transforming the Indian education system, led the group. While serving on the Supreme Council of India in the 1830s, he claimed to have seen that European education had started to produce positive effects among the population.[9] His *Minute on Indian Education* of February 1835 argued that only English should be used in schools and that they should concern themselves only with useful learning – synonymous with, according to Macaulay, European education. The imperial administrators followed his recommendation. As of 1835, schools in India conducted classes in English 'in which the alphabet was taught under the same roof with classes reading Shakespeare, the Calculus, [Adam] Smith's *Wealth of Nations*, and the Ramayana'.[10] The Ramayana is an ancient Indian epic poem, so education was to consist of the dissemination of European, if not predominantly British,

---

[7] Wood's 1854 despatch, quoted in Seth, *Subject Lessons*, 2.
[8] Seth, *Subject Lessons*, 3.
[9] Parliament of Great Britain, *Hansard's Parliamentary Debates*, XIX: 522.
[10] 'Report of the Indian Famine Commission', 18.

knowledge with a few examples of Indian sources. The 1835 educational reform was only the start of the Europeanisation process.

In 1854, Charles Wood, the president of the Board of Control of the British East India Company, sent a despatch to Lord Dalhousie, the then governor-general of India, suggesting that universities and schools extend European education beyond the elite Indian classes. 'The education which we desire to see extended in India is that which has for its object the diffusion of the improved arts, science, philosophy and literature of Europe; in short, European knowledge.'[11] Another despatch in 1859 added that vernacular language instruction was necessary pre-university, while English instruction and European knowledge should dominate university degrees. Imperialism became a pedagogic enterprise.

The imperial educational reform set in motion the establishment of India's first three universities, in Bombay, Calcutta and Madras, between 1856 and 1857, which were soon followed by others. While the colleges were tasked with teaching students, the universities examined the potential graduates at the end of their degrees. The first matriculation examinations passed 219 graduates in 1857–9, rising to 2,778 in 1881–2.[12] The 1850s and 1860s saw the first generation of Indian graduates trained in European knowledge that would ultimately form the members of the growing intellectual groups, like the first generation of modern Indian economists, and political institutions.

As a generation that grew up under imperialism, the late nineteenth-century Indian economists were educated in schools, colleges and universities that the foreign rulers had established. Some of them, such as Dutt and Banerjea, went to Britain to continue their studies. Horace William Clift's (1852–1901) *Elements of Political Economy* and J. S. Mill's *Principles of Political Economy* were among the set texts for history, law, politics and economics students at least until the end of the nineteenth century.[13] J. S. Mill was particularly popular with the Indian economists because he prescribed industrialisation with free trade, but only once a country had industrialised. He was, argued

---

[11] Wood's 1854 despatch, quoted in Seth, *Subject Lessons*, 2.

[12] Calcutta University had 162 in 1857, Bombay University had 21 in 1859 and Madras University had 36. Nurullah and Naik, *History of Education in India during the British Period*, 218–36.

[13] Khodaiji, 'A Nationalistic Framework for Political Economy'; Nurullah and Naik, *History of Education in India during the British Period*, 227.

Ranade, more nuanced in his analysis of the needs of India because he understood that countries like India needed protection for their nascent industries to industrialise, a process synonymous with progress (see Chapters 3 and 5).[14]

The Indian economists left university having been taught particular ways of meaning and discursive practices that came essentially from Europe.[15] As well as Clift and Mill, another major economist whom they studied was the German Friedrich List. Dutt wrote that '[t]he contributions of the German race to modern civilisation and modern thought are of a very high order'.[16] Most of the Indian elite would have learned German, although Dutt admitted that '[he] never learnt German well enough to read the great works of modern German historians in the original'.[17] But there is enough evidence to confirm that the Indian economists were aware of List's ideas (see Chapters 5 and 6), as List and the German Historical School were cited in several of their texts.[18] Many studies find a strong resemblance between the works of nationalists like List, Giuseppe Mazzini (1805–72), an Italian politician, Otto von Bismarck (1815–98), a Prussian statesman, and Indian Economics.[19] Moreover, List's *National System of Political Economy* was translated into English as early as 1856. (It was first translated into an Indian language, Bengali, Dutt's mother tongue, by Benoy Kumar Sarkar in 1932.[20]) Several of the Indian economists travelled widely, at least all over Europe, which would have exposed them to these ideas and allowed them access to other books not found at home. The Indian economists were also encouraged to read widely. Dutt, for instance, had been taught that you should '[n]ever trust what

---

[14] Ranade, *Essays on Indian Economics*, 96–7.
[15] Gallagher, Johnson, and Seal, *Locality, Province, and Nation*, 10; Wilson, *India Conquered*, 309; Bayly, *Recovering Liberties*; Sartori, *Bengal in Global Concept History*; Seth, *Subject Lessons*.
[16] Quoted in Gupta, *Life and Work of Romesh Chunder Dutt*, 148–9.
[17] Quoted in ibid., 384; see also 155.
[18] See, for example, Dutt, *The Economic History of India under Early British Rule*, 1:300; Dutt, *Speeches and Papers on Indian Questions*, 123–4; Ranade, *Essays on Indian Economics*, 20–2.
[19] Chatterjee, *The Nation and Its Fragments*; Goswami, *Producing India*; Singh, *From Naoroji to Nehru*; Ganguli, *Indian Economic Thought*; Bach, 'What Laws Determine Progress?'; Bach, 'A Win-Win Model of Development'; Gupta, *Life and Work of Romesh Chunder Dutt*, 148–9; Dasgupta, *A History of Indian Economic Thought*; Gopalakrishnan, *Development of Economic Ideas in India*.
[20] Mukherjee, *Benoy Kumar Sarkar*, 34; Kapila, *An Intellectual History for India*.

one nation tells you' and was urged to read the writings in all the three great modern languages – English, French and German – and 'judge for yourself'.[21]

There was a consensus among the Indian economists that European education was a welcome progressive force in India. It was, they argued, the most important and valuable institution implemented by the imperial administration. Their only complaint was that Indians did not get enough European education. Syed Mahmood (1850–1903), a high court judge in north-western India, wrote that the imperial education was 'one of the most significant episodes, not only in India, but in the history of the civilised world'.[22] The Indian economists were happy to acquire many discursive resources from their European education in India and, for some, in Britain.[23] As this book shows, they cited extensively European and North American thinkers. In other words, the Indians themselves started to disseminate European knowledge.

The Indian economists recognised that the European thinkers they read were diverse and offered varied epistemologies, theories and policy prescriptions. Ranade and Iyer's goal in forming Indian Economics was to debunk British orthodoxy. They argued that the likes of Ricardo, J. Mill, Adam Smith (1723–90) and T. Robert Malthus (1766–1834) were inappropriate for countries like India and instead made the case for using theories from later British economists and economists from continental Europe and North America.

Criticising British Orthodox Economics

Once the first generation of modern Indian economists had graduated and began producing studies and writings of their own, they fought against the very assumptions, theories and conclusions that their Eurocentric education had taught them. 'I saw the limitations of those doctrines', wrote Dutt, 'and perceived how the greatest European writers failed to grasp the economic conditions of Eastern life.'[24]

---

[21] Quoted in Gupta, *Life and Work of Romesh Chunder Dutt*, 384.
[22] Mahmood, *A History of English Education in India*, 1.
[23] For more information on textbooks and what was taught to this generation and later generations, see Khodaiji, 'A Nationalistic Framework for Political Economy'.
[24] Gupta, *Life and Work of Romesh Chunder Dutt*, 388.

What followed intertwined modern and traditional thought. In the inaugural speech of Indian Economics, Ranade argued for an 'enlarged view' to accommodate and explain Indian specificities.[25] Our 'teachers and statesmen', lectured Ranade,

seem to hold that the Truths of Economic Science, as they have been expounded in our most popular English textbooks, are absolutely and demonstrably true, and must be accepted as guides of conduct of all time and place whatever might be the stage of National advance.[26]

Ranade believed this had led to a lack of understanding as to why India had 'phenomenal Poverty'.[27] Orthodox political economy, according to Ranade, 'condemns the poor to grow still poorer'.[28] Likewise, Iyer, the author of the other founding text, wrote that the 'leading principles of the orthodox economic science, as expounded in English textbooks, have to be modified when applied to the conditions of this country'.[29] He reasoned that 'India's economic interest considerably suffers from a too blind adherence to the doctrines of Ricardo and [J.] Mill on the part of our rulers'.[30]

The orthodox economics tradition, according to Ranade, did not take into consideration the 'relative differences in Civilisation, or the possession of natural advantages, or disadvantages, in matters of situation, climate, soil, National aptitudes'.[31] The lack of such modification meant that 'great problems are approached in this extremely narrow frame of mind'.[32] The founding texts of Indian Economics then outlined and commented on the development of the European science. Both Ranade and Iyer concluded from their retrospectives that the truths of economics were not universal, even though countries often went through stages of growth that seemed similar across the world (see Chapter 3).[33] India needed its own economic thinking, theories and concepts because the troubling socio-economic conditions in India and elsewhere seemed to disprove the idea of principles such as free trade and comparative advantage that could be universally applied. As a result, there was a need for a new school of thought that reflected

---

[25] Ranade, *Essays on Indian Economics*, 23.   [26] Ibid., 2.   [27] Ibid., 25.
[28] Ibid., 6, 27.
[29] Iyer, *Some Economic Aspects of British Rule in India*, app. 1, p. 1.
[30] Ibid., app. 1, p. 3.   [31] Ranade, *Essays on Indian Economics*, 2.
[32] Iyer, *Some Economic Aspects of British Rule in India*, app. 1, p. 3.
[33] Ibid., app. 1, p. 4; Ranade, *Essays on Indian Economics*, 11.

the realities of India's current economic situation, namely imperialism and the poor socio-economic state.

Indian Economics was founded on the idea of Indian difference. Indian society, wrote Ranade and Iyer in the founding texts, was 'fundamentally different and, in many respects, backwards', still based on 'custom instead of competition' and 'status over contract'.[34] Both Ranade and Iyer used the common perception of India as different to push for an Indian Economics that would offer a better understanding of their country and develop more appropriate policies to effectively transform it into a modern society. Together with their fellow Indian economists, they agreed with the British that India was regressive and poor, but they denied that regress prevented progress. In contrast, Indian Economics, to Ranade and Iyer, opened up a hope for future progress, if the imperial administration would implement effective development policies and eventually grant India independence (see Chapters 5 and 6).

Ranade argued that Indian Economics would explain their economy more adequately because it would employ a local, historical and global perspective; he favoured the historical-institutional approach of the German Historical School, which 'regards ... Universalism and Perpetualism in Economic Doctrine [as] both unscientific and untrue'.[35] This methodological basis would reflect the necessary historical experience, practical observations and social reality. 'The Method', lectured Ranade, 'to be followed is not the Deductive but the Historical Method, which takes account of the past in its forecast of the future; and Relativity, and not Absoluteness, characterizes the conclusions of Economical Science', which is a 'Social Science ... best studied historically'.[36] In his conception, theory was a practice, and so to determine and test a theory, they had to analyse practices within a particular economy.

Ranade and Iyer preferred turning to the continental Europeans, North Americans and the later British economists. The economists of Ranade and Iyer's day understood that economics of '*a priori* conclusions based on individual self-interest and unrestricted competition',[37] or 'the assumption of the existence of the so-called

[34] Iyer, *Some Economic Aspects of British Rule in India*, app. 1, pp. 2, 4; Ranade, *Essays on Indian Economics*, 24.
[35] Ranade, *Essays on Indian Economics*, 22.   [36] Ibid., 22–3.   [37] Ibid., 23.

"economic man" being influenced' only by 'acquiring wealth' and 'around exertion' did not reflect the real economy or real economic practices.[38] Iyer and Ranade recognised J. S. Mill and John Elliot Cairnes (1823–75), an Irish economist, as having modified aspects of this doctrine, but 'the subsequent fresh conceptions', wrote Iyer, 'and the modernisation of the Science are mostly the work of German and French writers'.[39]

Iyer understood that List had a 'dislike of English predominance', which influenced the American political economist Henry Charles Carey (1793–1879).[40] List and his German peer Adam Muller (1779–1829), and later Carey, saw 'the obstacles to the progress of younger communities created by the action of older and wealthier nations'.[41] British dominance over economic thought and territory was impoverishing late industrialisers. Iyer also cited the French-speaking Swiss economist Jean-Charles-Léonard de Sismondi (1773–1842), who was among the first to critique what he labelled laissez-faire economics, which left an economy and its people to their own devices. Iyer drew upon Sismondi to explain how Europeans had started to become dissatisfied with earlier British thinkers that did not sufficiently take 'account of the material and moral well-being of the nation' and 'well-being of individuals' (see Chapter 6).[42] Ranade, for his part, wrote how

the authority of writers of Political Economy forget that Political Economy, as a hypothetical *a priori* Science, is one thing, while Practical Political Economy as applied to the particular conditions of backward countries is a different thing altogether. Americans, Australians, and Continental Political Economy, as applied to practice, permit many departures from the *a priori* positions of the abstract Science.[43]

Compared to the older, so-called classical, or orthodox, British economists, these new thinkers offered more realistic explanations of economic change and viable solutions for harnessing progress.

Indian Economics also offered a much-needed global perspective. Ricardo's theory of comparative advantage advocated for an international division of labour that assigned industrial production to Europe and raw materials to the rest of the world. Ranade realised

---

[38] Iyer, *Some Economic Aspects of British Rule in India*, app. 1, p. 13.
[39] Ibid., app. 1, p. 13.   [40] Ibid., app. 1, p. 16.   [41] Ibid.
[42] Ibid., app. 1, p. 14.   [43] Ranade, *Essays on Indian Economics*, 96.

that the levels of value added were different for raw materials than for manufactured goods.[44] Low rates of profits associated with agricultural production meant low increases in capital accumulation in just those regions where it was most needed. Under such a global division of labour, India would remain unindustrialised and regressive, condemned to perpetual poverty. Indian Economics' critique of the comparative advantage model would form a major part of its contribution to economic knowledge (see Chapter 6).

The First Generation of Modern Indian Economists

From the 1870s there had been an increase in the number of Indians studying and informing their imperial rulers about conditions in the country. This first generation of modern Indian economists started to study their economy from new perspectives. Ranade's and Iyer's founding texts bundled the studies that started to come in the 1870s with a common goal of progress and placed future studies under the intellectual umbrella of Indian Economics.

Around the same time, several town and regional organisations were formed in the 1870s and 1880s. These new spaces for dialogue would have helped to enable further research and exchange among elites and the middle class from different Indian states. The biggest and most significant was undoubtedly the Indian National Congress, established in 1885, which housed many different professionals, including political economists, teachers, lawyers, traders and merchants, who held a variety of political viewpoints. The Congress, which institutionalised the emerging nationalist movement, was founded by the retired civil servant A. O. Hume. In 1883, Hume had written a letter to graduates of Calcutta University outlining his idea to build a body that would represent Indian interests. He organised a series of secret meetings with Naoroji, Banerjea, Wacha and Ranade, among others, to establish a formal organisation that could push their demands for reform.

During the last few days of 1885, the first Indian National Congress was held at Gokuldas Tejpal Sanskrit College in Bombay. Hume had initially planned to have it in Poona, but an outbreak of cholera forced them to change the location at the last minute. The seventy-two members in attendance were all founders and leaders of modern institutions,

[44] Ibid., 23–30.

and among them were members of the first generation of modern Indian economists. Naoroji, Banerjea, Gokhale, Ranade, Wacha, Iyer and Telang sat alongside fellow Indians, mostly lawyers, and British civil servants like Hume and Wedderburn. Joshi and Dutt went to later meetings. The majority of members were Hindu, but there were also Muslims and Parsis in attendance during this first period of the Indian National Congress. Several of the Indian economists served as president of the Congress – Naoroji in 1886, 1893 and 1906, Banerjea in 1895 and 1902, Dutt in 1899, Wacha in 1901 and Gokhale in 1905. The Congress became a central nodal point for building the Indian nationalist movement and a key space for the first generation of modern Indian economists to share, present and debate their ideas across state lines and religions.

The first generation of modern Indian economists was composed of nine individuals. Ranade, Naoroji, Wacha, Telang and Gokhale were from Bombay, the prosperous city located in the western region of Maharashtra with a bustling maritime trade and commerce. Joshi was born in Poona, which was the cultural and educational centre of Maharashtra in the nineteenth century. Gokhale spent some time studying at Deccan College in Poona, where Ranade delivered the inaugural speech of Indian Economics. Naoroji, Telang, Ranade, Wacha, Gokhale and Joshi all studied at some point or other at Elphinstone College. One of the oldest colleges in the country, it was named after Mountstuart Elphinstone, the departing governor of the Bombay Presidency in the 1820s, who was responsible for establishing a system of higher education in Bombay. It had first started as an English-language school for Indian students in 1824, later becoming a high school following a resolution in 1827, and a large donation by the public, that declared the school would teach Indians the English language as well as the arts, science and European literature. Naoroji, Telang, Ranade, Wacha, Gokhale and Joshi did not study at Elphinstone at the same time, but some of them, like Naoroji and Ranade, returned there to teach subjects like mathematics, history and political economy.

The college would certainly have served as another nodal point for these western Indian economists, though it was far from the only point of exchange in Bombay. Ranade, Gokhale, Wacha and Telang, for example, were nominated members of the Bombay Legislative Council that helped the imperial administration to obtain advice and assistance. The Indian Council Act of 1861 had set up an advisory board empowering the provincial governor to nominate four non-English Indian members to the council. The nominated members could move their own bills and vote on bills, but they could not see the budget, question the executive, move resolutions or interfere with laws passed in the Central Legislature. At least for Naoroji, we know from private correspondence that some of these economists conversed regularly and intensely with each other about the pressing issues of their time.[45] Overall, however, there remains but a small trace of the dialogues that took place (see the introduction).

Dadabhai Naoroji (1825–1917) was the first of the modern Indian economists to be born, growing up in a poor Gujarati Parsi family of priests in Bombay. In 1845 he finished his studies at Elphinstone College. He then proceeded to start a newspaper at twenty-five, help establish a political association in Bombay at twenty-seven, and be appointed to the mathematics and philosophy chair of Elphinstone College at twenty-nine. At the age of thirty, he moved to England to set up a branch of the company he worked for in India. He later established his own cotton-trading firm there and went on to teach Gujarati as a professor at University College London.[46] Naoroji pursued political roles and integrated himself into progressive social milieus in Britain rather than in India because he believed that the British public would be more likely to respond to his arguments and could more easily be persuaded to reform the imperial structure. During his thirty years in England, he became a key point of contact for Indians coming to study law in London. He, along with Banerjea, Wacha and Ranade, was a founding member of the Indian National Congress, established in 1885. Of those who attended the first Congress, a number had been first introduced to each other by Naoroji in London. Naoroji held several political roles in India and was the first Indian to be elected as a member of the British Parliament in 1892 (Figure 2.1).[47] These roles helped to make him the voice of India (Figure 1.2).

Another Parsi economist was born some twenty years later, Dinshaw Edulji Wacha (1844–1936), to middle-class parents. In 1858, like

---

[45] Naoroji, *Dadabhai Naoroji: Selected Private Papers.*
[46] Wilson, *India Conquered*, 335.
[47] On two other occasions he ran unsuccessfully. *Dadabhai Naoroji: A Sketch of His Life and Life-Work.*

Figure 2.1 Portrait of Dadabhai Naoroji, circa 1892, when he became a British MP.

Naoroji before him, he joined Elphinstone College, but he had to withdraw four years later to work for his father's mercantile business. Under his father, he learned his first lessons in finance, eventually becoming a great statistician – as his biography relates, 'figures are Mr. Wacha's forte'.[48] And it was in finance that he forged a career, joining the Bank of Bombay, where he was trained to manage one of its branches, and then the only public accountants in Bombay, Messers, Brodie and Wilson, where he helped wind up a dozen bankrupt estates and some banks and financial associations that had collapsed due to the American Civil War of 1861–5. In 1874, he invested his fortunes into the cotton industry and managed the Morarji Gokuldas and Sholapur Mills. In those years, he became more engaged in politics, starting, for example, to first contribute and then edit the English columns of the

[48] *Dinshaw Edulji Wacha*, 2.

Kaiser-i-Hind (Emperor of India), a weekly Gujarati newspaper with a nationalist stance.[49] Wacha typically wrote on financial issues like army expenditure, land revenue policy, salt taxes and various duties. Some of the rare evidence of dialogue still available between this group of Indian economists comes from his letters to Naoroji between 1884 and 1917.[50] Like many of the other Indian economists of this generation, he was the president of the Indian National Congress in 1901 (Figure 2.2).

Mahadev Govind Ranade (1842–1901) was born in Bombay into a middle-class family of Marathi Brahmin government officials. He also attended Elphinstone College and was among the first graduates from Bombay University in 1859. A student with much potential, his MA exam was sent to the University of Edinburgh to serve as model.[51] Although he then worked at Elphinstone College in various research capacities, Ranade is most well known for serving as a judge at the High Court

SIR D. E. WACHA.

Figure 2.2 Portrait of Dinshaw Edulji Wacha as the seventeenth president of the Indian National Congress in Calcutta in 1901.

---

[49] Ibid, 5.
[50] Naoroji, *Dadabhai Naoroji Correspondence: Correspondence with D.E. Wacha, 4-11-1884 to 23-3-1895*; Naoroji, *Dadabhai Naoroji Correspondence: Correspondence with D.E. Wacha, 30-3-1895 to 5-4-1917*.
[51] Brown, *The Nationalist Movement*, 39.

between 1892 and 1901 – the highest legal position that could be achieved by an Indian at that time. Several eminent British authorities and his Indian contemporaries thought of Ranade as a reformer who spoke of the social, political and economic injustices he witnessed in India. He was described as being tolerant of all religions and classes, willing to cooperate with anyone, and firmly believing in a common platform for the Indian nation. Ranade held that the people of India were first Indians and then Hindus, Muslims, Parsis and Christians, and he wished for progress for all (Figure 2.3).[52] Many of Ranade's contemporaries found his critique of British orthodox economics useful in seeing how and where its theories could not apply to India's economic reality.

Figure 2.3 An oil painting showing Mahadev Govind Ranade reading in the Brahman Sabha Hall in Poona City, Bombay, circa 1900. In religious law, Brahman Sabha refers to a religious and moral court where cases of violation of personal law and religious norms were trialled by learned Brahmins like Ranade himself.

[52] *Mahadev Govind Ranade: His Life and Career.*

Ganesh Vyankatesh Joshi (1851–1911) was Ranade's right-hand man, born in the same state, Maharashtra. His father was a treasury officer in the state of Miraj, and his grandfather had fought alongside the Peishwas against the British in the early nineteenth century. Joshi started his studies at a vernacular school at Tasgaon but quickly joined the British schooling system at Poona High School. In 1873 he graduated from Elphinstone College with a degree in logic and moral philosophy, with history and political economy as his minor subjects. He then became a teacher at Ahmednagar High School, a position he had to resign four months later due to a misunderstanding between him and the headmaster and some domestic issues. Fortunately, he was able to find another posting relatively quickly, and eventually he became headmaster of Sholapur High School, 1890–8, and later of Poona High School, 1904–7 (Figure 2.4). In 1896 Bombay was struck by the Bubonic plague, and from 1897 to 1904 Joshi joined the effort to combat it, first as a ward inspector and then as

Figure 2.4 Portrait of Ganesh Vyankatesh Joshi as headmaster of Satara High School in the Indian state of Maharashtra in the first few years of the nineteenth century.

superintendent of the Potepur Plague Camp. The Bombay government conferred upon him a title of honour, Rao Bahadur,[53] in 1898 for his faithful service to the Empire during the epidemic.[54]

Kashinath Trimbak Telang (1850–93) was born into a middle-class Hindu family in Bombay. He was an apt student, winning several prizes and scholarships throughout his studies. He earned his BA and MA in 1867 and 1869, respectively, and qualified for the legal profession in 1872. He later became the third Indian ever to be appointed judge, after Bal Mangesh Wagle and Ranade. At the time, the legal profession was dominated by Europeans, making it 'uphill work'.[55] Nevertheless, he quickly impressed those in the profession with his competence and was seen to perform as well as his European colleagues. He established the Hindu Union Club in 1875 to foster good relations between different groups within the Hindu community through meetings where they could exchange views and work together to build a better future. The club held lectures and debates on the leading questions of the day, attracting many educated men to its weekly meetings. Telang was later elected president of the Asiatic Society and appointed as vice chancellor of Bombay University in 1892 (Figure 2.5).

Gopal Krishna Gokhale (1866–1915) was born into a poor family in the Bombay Presidency. He gained a university degree, thanks to his elder brother who earned enough money to pay for his studies. Gokhale went to Rajaram College in Kolhapur and Deccan College, Poona, where he became an educationalist along with other members of the Deccan Education Society, which aimed to educate the poor. Notably, the society had been set up by Ranade in 1884, and the following year had established Ferguson College, where Gokhale became a professor in the 1890s, first teaching mathematics and then history and political economy. Gokhale worked closely with Ranade, taking up the secretaryship of Ranade's Poona Sarvajanik Sabha and the editorship of its journal, the *Quarterly of the Sarvajanik Sabha*. In 1902, Gokhale left teaching to enter politics (Figure 2.6).

---

[53] 'Rao Bahadur' was a title of honour given to members of the Indian community for outstanding service to the Empire. Translated, Rao means 'prince', and Bahadur 'brave' or 'most honourable'. The title 'Rao Bahadur' was given to Hindus, while 'Sardar Bahadur' was the equivalent title for Sikhs, and 'Khan Bahadur' the equivalent for Muslims and Parsis.

[54] Joshi, *Writings and Speeches of G.V. Joshi*, i–iii.

[55] Naik, *Kashinath Trimbak Telang*, 30.

Figure 2.5 Portrait of Kashinath Trimbak Telang.

Alongside Bombay, another significant nodal point in India at this time was the capital of the north-western Bengal Presidency, Calcutta. Calcutta, which had been experiencing rapid industrial growth in the cotton and jute industries from the 1850s, was the capital city of India at the time. Dutt and Banerjea, who were both from Calcutta, met when they attended university there. The pair quickly became friends, travelling to London in 1869 to sit the Civil Service exam. Iyer was from a town not far from the third key nodal point of Madras, in the south-eastern Madras Presidency; he studied at a college in Tanjore but did some training at Madras University. Madras had become home to a major naval base and was the administrative centre for the British in southern India. Once the railways started to connect Bombay, Calcutta and Madras in the late nineteenth century, communication and exchange between these

GOPAL KRISHNA GOKHALE

Figure 2.6 Portrait of Gopal Krishna Gokhale from 1909.

economists would become easier – although much of the evidence of dialogue has been lost.

Romesh Chunder Dutt (1848–1909) was born into a Bengali family of British East India Company employees who were well known for their literary and academic achievements. Just two years after graduating from Calcutta University in 1866, he left India with Banerjea for Britain to study at University College London before sitting the Indian Civil Service examination in 1869. He was successful and became the second Indian to be appointed an Indian civil servant, being employed as an assistant magistrate and collector.[56] In 1893, he became the first Indian to be appointed district magistrate serving in Burdwan and Orissa. After retiring from the Civil Service, he became a professor of Indian history at University College London in 1897 (Figure 2.7). From 1898, he was a regular contributor on famine and tariff debates in the internationally recognised newspaper *The Manchester Guardian*, known for publishing alternative perspectives.

---

[56] The first Indian to be appointed to the Indian Civil Service was Satyendranath Tagore (1842–1923) in 1863. Born in Calcutta, he was also a poet, composer, writer, social reformer and linguist.

Figure 2.7 Portrait of Romesh Chunder Dutt, circa 1911.

Dutt's friend and travel companion Surendranath Banerjea (1848–1925) was educated at Doveton College and graduated from Calcutta University in 1868. Along with Dutt, he passed his Civil Service exam in 1869 but was barred owing to a claim that he had misrepresented his age. He was later cleared because according to Hindu custom you count your age from the date of conception, not from birth. Following this, he took his final exams and returned to India in 1871. However, he served only two years as an assistant magistrate in Sylhet before the government forced him to resign due to a judicial error. He returned to England to submit an appeal, but it was denied, according to him, as a result of racial discrimination. Thousands of people took to the streets in his home state Bengal to protest the charges, but he was never to return to the Civil Service. It is said that this was the major reason he became a leading figure in the nationalist movement. After the Civil Service, Banerjea worked for some time as a teacher, starting at a school in Calcutta. In 1878, he took over the editorship of the *Bengalee*, an English-language newspaper based in Calcutta with an extensive circulation. Two years earlier, Banerjea had founded the Indian National Association – the first avowedly nationalist organisation of the imperial era. The association, which later merged with the Indian National Congress, aimed to promote the advancement of the people of India. It attracted educated Indians and activists from all over the country and was a key forum for the then nascent independence movement. A dedicated journalist and nationalist, he was often referred to as 'Surrender not' Banerjea – a play on his first name, Surendranath (Figure 2.8).[57]

The final economist in this first generation, Ganapathy Dikshitar Subramania Iyer (1855–1916), grew up not far from Banerjea and Dutt. From the state of Tamil Nadu in south-eastern India, he studied art at Saint Peter's College in Tanjore, graduating in 1873. He then attended a teacher's training course in Madras, 1874–5, after which he worked as a teacher for some years until he was appointed headmaster of the Triplicane Anglo-Vernacular School in 1879 (Figure 2.9). He also became a leading journalist to change public opinion, educate the masses and

Babu Surendranath Banerjea

Figure 2.8 Portrait of Surendranath Banerjea.

[57] Banerjea, *Speeches by Babu Surendranath Banerjea*, 7.

o. Subramaniya Iyer

Figure 2.9 Portrait of Ganapathy Dikshitar Subramania Iyer.

ignite the independence movement. In 1878 he founded *The Hindu*, an English-language newspaper, to offer a contrasting voice on the appointment of T. Muthuswamy to the bench of the Madras High Court, which was being opposed by the Anglo-Indian press. *The Hindu* eventually became a daily newspaper and is currently India's national paper.[58] Sometimes Iyer's explosive writings caused him trouble. His partnership with *The Hindu*'s managing director, Veeraraghavachariar, would crumble when they disagreed over how critical they could be of Hindu traditions. Veeraraghavachariar warned Iyer that publishing anti-orthodox views could cause them to lose readers and face defamation suits. Yet Iyer did not wish to compromise. He believed that the only way forward was through change, reforms and progress;[59] conservatism would lead only to stagnation and ruin. The solution to India's problems lay in European training and independence.

The first generation of modern Indian economists belonged mostly to the middle classes and lived in urban or semi-urban

[58] He founded another newspaper in the Tamil language, *Swadesamitran*, in 1882.
[59] Muthiah, 'Willing to Strike and Not Reluctant to Wound'.

areas. In the second half of the nineteenth century, 60 per cent of the educated made up just 20 per cent of the population and came mostly from higher castes such as Brahmins, Vaishyas and Kayasthas.[60] The educated were thus from a relatively privileged strata of society, educated in English, and not representative of the population. They were passionate advocates for the poor, nevertheless. Dutt, for example, was the first economist to interview and survey the poor rural peasants, to understand what caused poverty and what to do about it. Ranade and Joshi sent agents to check on famine-affected areas so they could tell the imperial administration where relief was in urgent need. The journalism of Wacha, Iyer and Banerjea aimed to educate the masses, combat regressive social norms and ignite the independence movement to bring progress to the whole nation. Gokhale taught the poor. Naoroji calculated India's per capita income and cost of living in the early 1870s to prove to the British that the average Indian was poor (see Chapter 4). These men fought on the behalf of the poor for much-needed progress in a country that they believed was becoming ever poorer.

In the 1870s, this group of prolific writers, journalists, political activists and congressmen started debates on Indian progress and development, as well as the need for a better understanding of India's unique conditions to emerge. They made speeches and published newspaper and journal articles and books. Although most are lost, they also wrote letters, some daily, to fellow Indians, imperial officials and anti-imperialists. Among the first publications of this generation is Naoroji's paper entitled 'The Wants and Means of India', presented in July of 1870 at a meeting of the Society of Arts in London. In the paper, Naoroji concluded that India was not able to produce enough goods to supply all its needs. The paper spurred an intensive investigation into the poor economic conditions in the country and resulted in economic issues dominating all newspapers, political literature and academic lectures. Naoroji then published *The Poverty of India* in 1876, and Ranade founded the Poona Sarvajanik Sabha's quarterly journal in the late 1870s to spread a better understanding of India's poverty. The economic inquiry into India's regressive state

---

[60] Kamerkar, 'Impact of British Colonial Policy on Society', 380.

and Britain's role in creating such poverty essentially hit a peak with Dutt's two-volume *Economic History of India*, published in 1902 and 1904, respectively.

The Indian economists asked: Why was India backwards? Why was India still far away from transitioning from a backward to a modern, developed nation? Why had the economic distance between India and Britain widened instead of narrowed? Why did the Indian economy not generate progress when those of America, France, Germany, Canada, Italy, Russia and even Japan did? The answers, the Indian economists hoped, would result in the implementation of better imperial development policies that would bring about much-needed progress.

The whole first generation of modern economists were convinced that the existing imperial policies were regressing India. Their plan to reverse this trend included industrialising India's economy through a policy framework of balanced growth (see Chapter 5). There were, nevertheless, nuances in perspective and focus among them. Ranade and Iyer, who wrote the founding texts of Indian Economics, argued that India needed its own economic principles and theories. Along with Joshi and Naoroji, Ranade was a member of the Bombay strand of the first generation, which concentrated on imperial finance, banking and exchange in general. Other economists such as Naoroji and Dutt argued that India would be able to abide by universal economic norms as soon as they became independent. Under the yoke of imperialism, however, Naoroji concentrated on the economic draining of India's various resources. The Bengal strand of the first generation, which included scholars such as Dutt, focused on land revenue, rural relations and peasant indebtedness and particularly emphasised indigenous institutions and practices. Much like India's modern-day slogan 'unity in diversity', Indian Economics was united without always sharing the same research focus, approaches, ideology or discursive practices.[61]

Indian Economics would explain the extreme levels of poverty that seemed to be misunderstood by imperial officials. This first generation of modern Indian economists believed that if the imperial rulers were properly informed, then they could be persuaded to implement more progressive and less extractive policies. The following chapters show

---

[61] Cohn, *Colonialism and Its Forms of Knowledge*, 111.

how Indian Economics conceptualised a stadial theory of civilisation (Chapter 3) and an idea of regress (Chapter 4) that would emphasise India's progressive past and explain its regressive present. They could then identify an effective development plan both for their home (Chapter 5) and the world (Chapter 6) that would account for India's unfortunate peculiarities and global developments.

3 | *Stages of Civilisation*

A consensus had formed in the nineteenth century whereby the differences between Europe and the rest of the world could be explained by stadial theory. Different regions were distinct because they were in different stages of civilisation. Stadial theory conveniently created a narrative that legitimised imperialism by critiquing irrationality and poverty in the rest of the world. Located in a subcontinent over 7,000 kilometres from their foreign rulers, Ranade and Dutt saw another stadial theory. They tweaked the European version to fit their understanding of India's history and current reality in the late nineteenth century.

In his study of some late nineteenth-century Bengali intellectuals – not the same as those covered in this book – Dipesh Chakrabarty explained that these intellectuals practically rejected the European stadial theory because they were against the idea that India had to wait to become independent and industrialise. As Chakrabarty outlined, stadial theory implied that India would and should remain at a lower stage of civilisation.[1] At the same time, the Bengali intellectuals in question still employed stadial theory in their studies to explain how society changed. Ranade and Dutt, however, remade the theory by including a lower stage to which India had regressed due to imperialism and an earlier, higher stage of civilisation where India had enjoyed greater progress than it did in the late nineteenth century. Ranade and Dutt, along with their fellow Indian economists, could thus refute the idea that India could not skip to a higher stage of civilisation because they had already experienced great progress in the past. They did not need to wait to progress and to gain independence, like the stage theorists from Europe argued.

---

[1] Chakrabarty, *Provincializing Europe*, chap. 1.

Europeans Theorising Change through Stages

Around the turn of the eighteenth century, the work of Adam Smith, John Millar (1735–1801) and Adam Ferguson (1723–1816) converged, and there emerged a widely accepted four-stage theory of societal change that accounted for differences through time in terms of changing economic conditions, social customs and institutions.[2] These economists selected sources to make comparisons and found causal regularities from which they deduced common characteristics that could apply to different stages of civilisation. The most clearly defined stadial theory comes from Smith and is also seen in Millar. Both theorised that human sustenance is the primary need of society. In the first stage of civilisation, humans were hunters and gatherers, focused only on finding what they needed to survive. As this need was common to all humans and as humans were all relatively similar physically, the development of diverse modes of subsistence occurred universally across all societies. 'The similarity of his wants', wrote Millar, 'as well as of the faculties by which those wants are supplied, has everywhere produced a remarkable uniformity in the several steps of his progression.'[3]

In each successive stage, a different method was employed to secure subsistence: hunting, herding, agriculture and then commercial industry. Hunters became ever more accustomed to herding animals, transforming the hunters into shepherds. They gradually acquired knowledge of the crops required to feed animals, eventually leading them to forego their nomadic way of living and to acquire more agricultural skills. Settled accommodation led to division of labour and commercial industry. Each stage included the features of the previous; the old mode simply ceased to be the sole method by which subsistence was provided. Change from one stage to the next occurred, thanks to the discovery of new skills and technology, as well as the division of labour. The latter was primarily spurred by growth in population – Smith and Millar assumed that humans desire both to survive and procreate, hence the greater aggregate need for food.[4]

---

[2] Smith, *Adam Smith's Political Philosophy*, 23–4; Burrow, *Evolution and Society*, 10–11.

[3] Cited in Smith, *Adam Smith's Political Philosophy*, 49.

[4] Ibid., 48–50; Burrow, *Evolution and Society*, 14; Meek, 'Smith, Turgot, and the "Four Stages" Theory', 14.

Stadial theory was used to explain why countries like India were poorer than others. India, however, had not always been perceived by Europeans as poor. According to the Indian economists, European travel accounts from the fifteenth to seventeenth centuries showed how impressed visitors were with the subcontinent. Europeans had seen India as a prosperous region when the various East India Companies arrived in the seventeenth and eighteenth centuries. At the beginning of the nineteenth century, however, the perception shifted. J. Mill, a colonial civil servant, blamed previously optimistic views on the orientalist and Sanskrit philologist Sir William Jones (1746–94), who argued that Asia was a source of wisdom.[5] Along with Maine and Herbert Spencer (1820–1903), Mill now argued that Indian society was at a low stage of civilisation.[6] The reach of Spencer's conception, in particular, went global, claiming to be a grand theory that explained historical transformation.[7] Given India was at a lower stage, argued the imperial officials, it had many stages left to go through and had to wait to industrialise and become independent.

Although the four-stage theory seems more widely known, there existed a three-stage theory in the nineteenth century. Turgot had a three-stage theory with a suggestion of a fourth stage when a society reaches the commercial stage. As the Indian economists lived in a commercial society, or at least regarded Britain as being in that stage, it is not surprising that they would have seen progress within a four-stage model. Finally, a clarification on Auguste Comte is necessary here. Comte theorised three stages: theological, metaphysical and positive. Contrary to Mill, Smith, Ferguson and Millar's economic stages of progress, Comte, however, theorised intellectual stages of progress. Indian Economics focused not on intellectual progress but on economic and political progress.

[5] Mill, *The History of British India*, 367, 431.
[6] Burrow, *Evolution and Society*, 227.
[7] As of the 1890s, Spencer became very open about his anti-imperialist opinions. He found the state a regressive force, so for him the strong imperial government in India only showed how dangerous imperialism could be. Spencer was referring to the Indian Mutiny as an inevitable result of a government that was too strong. His anti-imperialism grew out of his belief in non-universalism: The British would never be progressive for India because they could not run India successfully using their own experience from Britain. Countries evolved on their own terms with unique local conditions, meaning a foreign entity imposing its rule on a country would, in so doing, always create a disconnect from this natural evolution. Kapila, *An Intellectual History for India*, 102–3.

Social Evolutionary Theory

The stage theory of civilisation became part of a larger trend in the nineteenth century of using evolutionary theory to understand how societies changed. Around the time Charles Darwin's (1809–82) work on evolution was published in 1859, thinkers started to see social institutions as arranged in an evolutionary series. Spencer, Maine, J. S. Mill and John William Draper (1811–82) – all cited by several of the Indian economists[8] – employed metaphors and analogies from the natural sciences to explain societal change which, according to them, adhered to an order and to certain stages.[9]

Social evolutionary theory, like stadial theory, was attractive because of its unifying aspect. It explained that the differences between peoples were the result of them being at different stages in the same process. The theory provided a justification for social theorists to understand racial differences in terms of environmental variance over long periods of time, rather than ignoring disparities. Finding reasons for the differences helped to explain why, for instance, utilitarianism, which assumed that all men acted and reacted rationally to maximise their own self-interest, did not seem to hold in India. Social evolution helped to explain how context could affect different societies. It attempted, like stadial theory, to answer the question of why populations in Asia seemed to behave irrationally.

Finally, natural selection within social evolutionary theory offered up the idea of survival of the fittest to explain any societal changes or processes. After reading Darwin's essay, Spencer coined the expression 'survival of the fittest' in his *Principles of Biology*, published in 1864.[10] The transfer of discursive practices from evolutionary to social evolutionary theory was, however, limited. As social theorists like Maine and Spencer understood, the ideas of survival of the fittest and universal

---

[8] A few examples: Draper's *A History of the Intellectual Development of Europe*, in Naoroji, *Poverty and Un-British Rule in India*, 51–2; J. S. Mill's *Political Economy*, in Naoroji, *Poverty and Un-British Rule in India*, 55–7, and Dutt, *The Peasantry of Bengal*, 184–6; Spencer, in Naoroji, *Dadabhai Naoroji Correspondence: Correspondence with D.E. Wacha, 4-11-1884 to 23-3-1895*, 1:288; Maine, in Dutt, *Indian Famines*, 188, and Ranade, *Religious and Social Reform*, 109, 112.

[9] Burrow, *Evolution and Society*; Nisbet, *Social Change and History*; Reinert, 'Darwin and the Body Politic'; Tilly, *Big Structures*; Bury, *The Idea of Progress*.

[10] Spencer, *The Principles of Biology*.

change explained away too much complexity. Instead, social evolutionary theory employed historical and comparative analyses of specific societies to trace the history of local human institutions.[11]

Indians Theorising Change through Stages

Ranade and Dutt's stage theory looked like the existing four-stage theory. Ranade described India as being on a chain that ran from the lowest to the highest forms of life.[12] There were 'many stages of growth', theorised Ranade, and the imperial rulers could not treat India the same as Britain because it was at a different stage.[13] Comparisons across regions, wrote Dutt,

have their use; and they show us how the same historical laws rule the destinies and the progress of nations at the farthest ends of the globe, and how the same great historical causes often affect and control the march of events, simultaneously in the east and the west.[14]

Regions across the world could be compared because they changed in similar ways. Like the Europeans before them, Ranade and Dutt thought that dividing an area's history and future into stages helped explain how change had happened and what would happen in the years and decades to come.

First came a simple stage of civilisation.[15] As conceptualised by Dutt, that initial stage took place at the

dawn of civilisation, on the small beginnings of progress and knowledge, for which the enlightened and mighty nations of the modern world are indebted to the early shepherds and cultivators of Egypt and Babylonia, of China and India ... The history of civilisation, of the infant civilisation of mankind, belongs to these four countries.[16]

In this 'simple stage of civilisation ... communities lived by agriculture and by pasture ... [and] division into classes was little known'.[17] Civilisation in this stage had self-sufficient structures, which Dutt labelled

---

[11] Burrow, *Evolution and Society*.
[12] Ranade, *Religious and Social Reform*, 43; Healy, 'Social Change', 31–2.
[13] Ranade, *Religious and Social Reform*, 28.
[14] Dutt, *Epochs of Indian History*, 11.
[15] Dutt, *The Economic History of India in the Victorian Age*, 2:21.
[16] Dutt, *Epochs of Indian History*, 3.   [17] Ibid., 21.

'Village Communities'.[18] Within the system, Ranade described how the local power was strong because despots were only engaging in expanding territory, rather than developing their existing territory. There was little communication between the local communities and the ruling elite, who sought not to develop their existing territories and their populations but to expand their political and economic power over new areas.[19] Production on a large scale was impossible, thought Dutt, as 'society was yet in its infancy'.[20] The village served as the nodal point of civilisation, where families would provide for themselves their minimum needs.

A higher stage included industrialisation because, as Joshi wrote at the time, industrialisation was 'a superior type and a higher stage of civilisation'.[21] Ranade and Dutt argued that India had been a global supplier of goods in the past and that regions of the country with progressive regimes had united different religious groups and pushed for lower levels of inequality and poverty.[22]

Assumptions of Change

Ranade and Dutt used social evolutionary theory to explain how Indian society had changed. Maine's work, which also employed social evolutionary theory, spread widely in the nineteenth century (see Chapter 1) and was cited by both men.[23]

Society, assumed Ranade, never remained stationary; societal change was the 'natural growth of things'.[24] He held that change spread across society because, like organs, its parts were interdependent, each serving a certain function for the whole. The parts were then ordered according to their level of importance. Ranade attributed this thinking to another economist of his generation, Telang, who understood that

[y]ou cannot develop the chest without developing your other organs; you cannot starve yourselves and yet desire that your muscles shall grow and your

---

[18] Ranade, *Essays on Indian Economics*, 233; Dutt, *The Economic History of India under Early British Rule*, 1:119–20, 346–8; Dutt, *Speeches and Papers on Indian Questions*, 6; Iyer, *Some Economic Aspects of British Rule in India*, 218.

[19] Ranade, *Rise of the Maratha Power*; Dutt, *The Economic History of India under Early British Rule*; Dutt, *A History of Civilization in Ancient India*.

[20] Dutt, *Epochs of Indian History*, 21.

[21] Joshi, *Writings and Speeches of G.V. Joshi*, 616.

[22] Ranade, *Rise of the Maratha Power*; Dutt, *Epochs of Indian History*.

[23] Ranade, *The Miscellaneous Writings*, 31; Dutt, *The Peasantry of Bengal*, 177.

[24] Ranade, *Religious and Social Reform*, 97.

nerves have the same elasticity as before. There is an interdependence between the parts, so that it is not possible to do justice to one without doing justice to the other also.[25]

Society, like a human body, could not be 'broken up into separate spheres of activities'.[26] The social system would not properly function if political rights were dysfunctional. Nor could a society have proper political rights if the social system was unjust and unreasonable. The economy could only work if the social system worked, too. The same went for the religious sphere, and so on. 'This interdependence', lectured Ranade, 'is not an accident but is the law of our nature.'[27]

In the same vein, Ranade used the metaphor 'body politic' to theorise the interdependence of societal parts.[28] A body's eyes, skin and organs, like society's social, economic and political spheres, were connected. Change in one part of society then led to a change in another. This dynamic would be fundamental in understanding how to bring about progress. Ranade could understand and explain how India had changed, and how she would change, if he identified the parts of society, their connections and interdependence. The body politic, as well as other biological metaphors, were widely used as exploratory tools during the nineteenth century.[29]

Led by social evolutionary theory, Ranade focused on the function of each societal part: universal education enlightened the people, the agricultural sector fed the people, the political body led the people and so on. His focus on the function of organs and societal parts meant that more comparisons could be made across species and societies. India, theorised Ranade, would benefit from law and order, and universal education because the relevant societal institutions operated similarly in India and Britain, accommodating local conditions when needed. Ranade compared, for instance, the imperial industrial policies in Java and India. He concluded that Java was able to progress more quickly than India thanks to the Dutch system.[30] 'A civilised European Power', wrote Ranade, 'was entrusted with the rule of vast Territories inhabited by a comparatively barbarous people, and the experiment was ... a success, by the side of which the comparative failure of the

---

[25] Ibid., 152. The address, entitled 'Commemoration Address: The Telang School of Thought', was delivered at the Hindu Union Club, Bombay, in 1895.
[26] Ibid., 281. [27] Ibid., 282–3. [28] Ibid., 247.
[29] Reinert, 'Darwin and the Body Politic'.
[30] Ranade, *Essays on Indian Economics*, 70–104.

British Rulers presents a very suggestive contrast.'[31] Aware that Java's population was smaller and more homogenous than India's, he nonetheless determined that

after making all allowance for these differences, there remains a sufficient substratum of common conditions, which justifies the assurance that an experiment undertaken in the same spirit here, with the necessary adaptations to suit local conditions, has a reasonable chance of attaining at least qualified success.[32]

When Java was returned to the Dutch government in 1814 (the British had conquered the territory in 1811), the Dutch had 'abolished free trade' and 'substituted Differential Duties in imports from foreign parts'.[33] They also 'abolished the *Ryotwari* system of small Holdings at fixed cash rates, and reverted to the ancient Native method of Joint Village Responsibility'.[34] They 'steadily adhered to the Native model of Government', limiting 'foreign Agency to the work of inspection and report'.[35] The difference was radical, according to Ranade: 'the British Indian system' was 'Conservative and Protective', and the Dutch was 'based on modern ideas of equality'.[36]

Ranade described in detail how Java's production was organised in a way that 'all three parties who worked the system, the Government, the Contractor, and Peasants, benefitted by it'.[37] The government borrowed money at low rates of interest, as it was easier for a government to borrow, to pay the contractors in advance for the produce they raised. The village labourers were thus paid throughout the year and could pay taxes without themselves having to borrow money. The system paid for itself, as the government bought produce at low prices to make a 'large margin of profit on sale in Europe'.[38] Using the Java example, Ranade built an argument that India was capable of progressing if only it had modern institutions that pushed industrialisation and decreased poverty and inequality.

Ranade and Dutt ordered the functions of societal parts according to their relative importance, some institutions having a more pivotal role than others. They explained how social and educational elements, for instance, had the ability to change other spheres, like the political or economic ones.[39] Ranade analysed how movements in the

---

[31] Ibid., 72–3.   [32] Ibid., 73.   [33] Ibid., 75.   [34] Ibid.   [35] Ibid., 78.
[36] Ibid., 78–9.   [37] Ibid., 82.   [38] Ibid.
[39] Ranade, *Rise of the Maratha Power*, 4; Dutt, *The Economic History of India under Early British Rule*, 1:13.

sixteenth century like the Protestant Reformation in Europe and the Maratha revolution at the turn of the seventeenth century had preceded any substantial economic progress.[40] Social movements that altered the status quo, and education, or what Dutt labelled 'moral advancement', were more important than economic or political changes.[41]

Focusing on the functions of societal parts meant, however, that their explanations ignored certain processes and mechanisms. Functional explanations indicate what a thing does, but not why or how it exists in the first place. For example, Ranade and Dutt's assumption that moral improvements like liberal ideas would inevitably spread explained that liberal ideas would bring about progress but not how or why these ideas emerged in the first place. Ranade and Iyer defined liberal ideas as a process that broke down rigid caste structures, allowed women more freedom, and led to more equality and democratic institutions. But they ignored why they came about. This was common during the nineteenth century. When something like moral improvement was identified and its function understood, further explanation was seldom sought.[42]

Ranade and Dutt thought of progress as gradual. 'Every nation', wrote Dutt, 'has had slowly to progress.'[43] Ranade explained that 'the process of growth is always slow, where it has to be sure growth'.[44] In other words, sustainable progress inevitably takes time,[45] and the interdependence of parts explained why. 'Growth is structural and organic', theorised Ranade, 'and must take slow effect in all parts of the organism, and cannot neglect any, and favour the rest.'[46] Moreover, humans, theorised Ranade and Dutt, and Europeans like Millar and Smith before them, preferred gradual rather than sudden

[40] Ranade, *Rise of the Maratha Power*, 4.
[41] Dutt, *Indian Famines*, 63.
   Naoroji also ordered the function of different societal parts. He observed how education had 'produced natural effects', promoting civilisation, independence of character and creative thinking. Naoroji, *Essays, Speeches, Addresses and Writings*, 549.
[42] Healy, 'Social Change', 6.   [43] Dutt, *The Peasantry of Bengal*, 182.
[44] Ranade, *The Miscellaneous Writings*, 117.
[45] Dutt, *Speeches and Papers on Indian Questions*, 161; Ranade, *Religious and Social Reform*, 168.
[46] Ranade, *The Miscellaneous Writings*, 117–18.

change.[47] Societies would not change quickly, just as animals mutate only slowly from one generation to the next. Societal change was thus conceptualised as an evolutionary and not a revolutionary process.

Social evolutionary theory defined progress, positive change, as when society moved from chaos to order. Ranade and Dutt, and the likes of Maine and Spencer, argued that history showed that society had moved from barbaric and chaotic to ordered and civilised.[48] Ranade's history of the *Rise of Maratha Power* in the western state of India has a chapter entitled 'How Order Was Brought Out of Chaos', describing how the Maratha were able to harness progress through fostering order.[49] Adopting Maine's popular thesis that customary law preceded contractual law, Ranade, in an 1892 speech entitled 'Social Evolution', outlined how society progressed from 'from status to contract, from authority to reason, from unorganised to organised life'.[50] India was still dictated by the law of status, argued Ranade, and had not reached the progressive law of contract, contrary to Britain and other advanced western European countries.[51] Similarly, as Maine theorised in his research on Indian village communities (see Chapter 1), Dutt found that the relationship between *zamindars* (landlords) and *ryots* (peasants) was governed by status, as opposed to contract.[52] India was thus chaotic and progress needed to be harnessed to create order. To harness progress, a country needed a plan for development (see Chapter 5).

Like many thinkers before them, Ranade and Dutt used stadial theory to explain the differences between civilisations. If Indian civilisation was different than Britain's, it was because it was in a different, lower stage. Ranade and Dutt adopted the assumptions of change associated with social evolutionary theory. In the pages that follow, I show how Ranade and Dutt deviated from the stadial theory they were taught and read about.

---

[47] Ranade, *Religious and Social Reform*, 168, 170; Dutt, *Indian Famines*, 147, 321; Dutt, *England and India*, 47; Dutt, *The Economic History of India under Early British Rule*, 1:xviii; Dutt, *Speeches and Papers on Indian Questions*, 14; Naoroji, *Essays, Speeches, Addresses and Writings*, 21; Smith, *Adam Smith's Political Philosophy*, 63–4.
[48] Burrow, *Evolution and Society*, 159, 190.
[49] Ranade, *Rise of the Maratha Power*, 87–96.
[50] Ranade, *The Miscellaneous Writings*, 116–17.
[51] Ranade, *Essays on Indian Economics*, 24.
[52] Dutt, *The Peasantry of Bengal*, 56, 177; Dutt, *Indian Famines*, 188; Maine, *Village-Communities in the East and West*.

Bidirectional Stadial Theory

Ranade and Dutt's key point of departure from the existing stadial theory was how societies could regress down or progress up the chain of stages. Ranade described an ebb and flow of 'growth and decay'.[53] Progress and regress came and went for these Indian economists. Some European scholars dealt with regress in terms of economics and politics in the nineteenth century,[54] but they tended to theorise regress as something that could potentially happen after the last stage of progress. Karl Marx (1818–83) and Ferguson, for instance, held that the commercial age led to decadence, overconsumption on luxury and a decrease in the civic spirit necessary for progress.[55] They both used the example of the fall of Rome to illustrate how overspending on luxuries led to regimes dissolving. The fall of Rome, a regression, pushed Europe into a new stage of civilisation. The nineteenth-century European stadial theory dealt with regress but rather as a distinct stage of civilisation. Regress, to Ranade and Dutt, could happen to society at any point in its passage through the stages; it was not a distinct stage but a process that pushed societies down to lower stages.

In the past, India had been at a higher stage of civilisation, with a prosperous handicraft industry supplying markets around the world. Ranade called for India to be restored to its previous position as a global supplier of goods.[56] India needed to re-establish its former 'proud position as the garden and granary of the world'.[57] Gokhale referred to this as its 'natural position',[58] while Naoroji urged India to be 'restore[d] it to its former health'.[59] Iyer wrote:

The people of India showed great aptitude for commerce, and the fact that, notwithstanding the facilities for trade that modern civilisation, under the

---

[53] Ranade, *Religious and Social Reform*, 28.
[54] Outside of the disciplines of economics and politics, Daniel Pick's work analyses the many discourses around degeneration at the same time. Nevertheless, his work centres on criminality and eugenics, focusing on biology rather than economics and politics. Pick, *Faces of Degeneration*.
[55] Ferguson, *Principles of Moral Political Science*; Marx, *Capital*; Heilbroner, 'The Paradox of Progress'; Hill, 'Adam Ferguson and the Paradox of Progress and Decline'.
[56] Ranade, *Essays on Indian Economics*, 5, 12, 176; Ranade, *Religious and Social Reform*, 148.
[57] Ranade, *Essays on Indian Economics*, 176.
[58] Gokhale, '21st Indian National Congress, Presidential Address', 10.
[59] Naoroji, *Essays, Speeches, Addresses and Writings*, 36.

auspices of British rule, has introduced, they should have lost their ancient habits of trade, their enterprise and desire for wealth, is a melancholy commentary on the blighting effects of continued foreign dominion.[60]

'Asiatic countries are', he continued, 'poorer than they were two centuries ago.'[61] What has become of the manufactured goods, asked Banerjea rhetorically in a speech at the Indian National Congress, that India used to sell all over the world? 'Vanished', he answered, 'into the inane – they have disappeared into thin air.'[62] There had been a 'retrogression'.[63]

Dutt pleaded for a 'restoration'[64] to the 'equilibrium'.[65] He asserted that India should return to when it was a global supplier of goods.[66] And Ranade and Dutt talked of 'reverses'[67] to explain how and why India had previously been at a higher stage of civilisation but had since regressed down to a lower stage. 'The golden cup was drained.'[68] Some of the Indian economists cited European sources as evidence of India's prosperous past. For instance, Dutt wrote how George Smith (1765–1836), at one point the director of the British East India Company; Munro, an official in the British East India Company; and Francois Bernier, a traveller, described India as a thriving manufacturing country.[69] Iyer wrote of 'Indian cities like Surat, Goa, Calicut, other ports and inland cities, that astonished foreign visitors and attracted the cupidity of foreign plunderers, by their very opulence and magnificence'.[70] Europeans, wrote Naoroji, had conquered India because they saw how India's prosperity could enrich them.[71]

[60] Iyer, *Some Economic Aspects of British Rule in India*, 296.   [61] Ibid., 297.
[62] Banerjea, *Speeches and Writings*, 43.   [63] Ibid., 46.
[64] Ranade, *Religious and Social Reform*, 43; Ranade, *Essays on Indian Economics*, 176.
[65] Dutt, *The Economic History of India under Early British Rule*, 1:92, 202; Dutt, *England and India*, 40.
[66] Ibid.
[67] Ranade, *Religious and Social Reform*, 146–7; Dutt, *The Economic History of India under Early British Rule*, 1:86; Dutt, *Speeches and Papers on Indian Questions*, 158–9.
    Naoroji also wrote: The modern world was indebted to India, so in 'treating India as they were doing they were killing the bird that laid the golden eggs'. Naoroji, *Poverty and Un-British Rule in India*, 651.
[68] Dutt, *The Economic History of India under Early British Rule*, 1:115.
[69] Ibid., 1:100, 259–60; Dutt, *Speeches and Papers on Indian Questions, 1897 to 1900*, 79.
[70] Iyer, *Some Economic Aspects of British Rule in India*, 124.
[71] Naoroji, *Essays, Speeches, Addresses and Writings*, 33.

Explaining how India had devolved, Ranade argued that the 'theory of evolution has, in this country, to be studied in its other aspect of what may conveniently be called devolution'.[72] Ranade defined devolution as degeneration, regress and the opposite of evolution. Devolution was a negative change that had brought India to a lower stage. Ranade was not using the more recent definition of devolution in political economy, which rather refers to the transfer of power from central to local governments. While India, according to the civilising mission of the imperial administration, was supposed to be evolving or progressing, it was in fact devolving or regressing down the stages of civilisation. Ranade was again adapting social evolutionary theory to the Indian context. Though Europe was assumed to evolve or progress constantly, Ranade did not see the same in India.[73]

European thinkers tended to espouse an idea of progress as linear and unidirectional, but for the Indian economists who could point to a more prosperous past, this was not the case. The stadial theory that emerged in Indian Economics offered an opportunity for flexibility in the conception of progress – the stages were linear but a civilisation could progress to a higher level and then regress to a lower one.

India's Higher Past Stage

Ranade and Dutt challenged the prevailing European view of Indian history, pointing towards a higher stage of Indian civilisation in the past when the British had not yet imperialised their subcontinent. In this higher stage, India had a strong industrial and exporting economy with pockets of progressive regimes. This was from around the fourth to the seventeenth century, when India had a flourishing economy with an internationally competitive and successful handicraft industry, mostly in textiles, that saw them trade with many corners of the world. Ranade and Dutt argued that Indian civilisation had then been at the highest stage.[74] The 'stationary East', stated Ranade, was a popular fallacy.[75]

---

[72] Ranade, *Religious and Social Reform*, 27.
[73] For further analysis on the use of devolution in the idea of progress, see Burrow, *Evolution and Society*.
[74] Dutt, *The Economic History of India in the Victorian Age*, 2:3, 8, 35, 95; Dutt, *Speeches and Papers on Indian Questions*, 61; Ranade, *Religious and Social Reform*, 99.
[75] Ranade, *Religious and Social Reform*, 26.

In this long period, India had been the most developed country in the world in all spheres of society – economic, political and intellectual. Economically, Ranade gave the example of the Indian iron industry that had been able to meet all local demand, as well as exporting manufactured goods to foreign trade partners such as Britain.[76] Politically, at this stage relative peace had been established, thanks to unification. Ranade showed how the Maratha power in the western state of Maharashtra in the seventeenth century had unified the Indians, leading to a progressive state. In ruling the state, the Maratha emperor between 1674 and 1680, Shivaji, had not distinguished between class or caste.[77]

There were self-sufficient village communities in this higher stage. They contained 'in miniature all the materials of a State within themselves, and are almost sufficient to protect their members, if all other governments are withdrawn'.[78] Their structure, argued Dutt, was a good protection against poorly run governments because it largely prevented bad governance at a national level from affecting the everyday lives of villagers. A community's internal ruling structure ensured peace and efficiency, and their production provided for their minimum needs. 'I cannot but think', uttered Dutt, 'that this ancient land system of India is better than your modern English system; for the soil in India belongs to the nation, and not to a few individuals.'[79] In Britain, the landlord owned the land and leased it to the cultivator. In India, it was the cultivator who virtually owned the land (inheriting it from his father) and could sell or mortgage at his will, then handing it down to his sons. Sometimes the cultivators paid rent to a landlord; sometimes they paid a land tax direct to the state. If he paid the tax, he could not be evicted. If there was a landlord, the Indian cultivators paid rent to him, and the landlord then passed a portion to the state and kept some as his salary and some to pay for communal projects like the maintenance of roads and wells in the village.[80]

Ranade referred to this as the 'Joint Responsibility System of the Village' in Java[81] and observed how effective it was where it had been preserved by the Dutch. In the system, the cultivators paid one-fifth of

[76] Ranade, *Essays on Indian Economics*, 171–2.
[77] Ranade, *Rise of the Maratha Power*, 26.
[78] Dutt, *The Economic History of India under Early British Rule*, 1:346.
[79] Dutt, *Speeches and Papers on Indian Questions*, 91.   [80] Ibid., 71.
[81] Ranade, *Essays on Indian Economics*, 76.

their output in rent. Labourers paid rent in time and offered the mandatory one day of work a week to help build roads, canals and other public works. Each household had to volunteer one adult male for such work, but later on villagers were able to hire workers for these projects. Ranade had seen that labourers were generally paid higher wages in Java than in the imperial system in India. Banerjea showed with official statistics that labourers were better paid within the earlier self-sufficient village system than at the end of the nineteenth century.[82] The British had destroyed the village communities, which brought regress to the subcontinent.[83]

The period here is vast, stretching across about a millennium with changing religions, institutions, rulers and societal structures. Yet Ranade and Dutt start a historical consensus that this was the golden age of India's global domination over trade and civilisation.[84] J. Mill's

[82] Banerjea, *Speeches and Writings*, 34–45.
[83] There was and is an ongoing debate on the feudalism question in Indian history. Much like Ranade and Dutt, the studies show the differences and similarities between western European and Indian feudal systems. Feudalism was a mode of distribution of means of production and appropriation of surplus. While India had thriving trade networks, the economy was predominantly agricultural where feudalism was often found. The feudal structure consisted of landlords and servile peasants. The landlords extracted surplus by exploiting the land and its workers. In east India, for instance, Buddhist monasteries controlled the land. In the south, there were temples that became estates. Moreover, Brahmins had owned land in the upper and middle Gangetic basins, central Asia, the Deccan and Assam. Non-religious landlords also existed. In Orissa, for instance, tribal chiefs became landlords. In other areas, administrative officials collected taxes from peasants. The degree of servility of peasants varied across regions. What can be generalised perhaps is that in India, in contrast to western Europe, kings made land grants to collect taxes from the surplus. The grantees then collected the taxes from their tenant peasants, who could be evicted and subjected to forced labour if they failed to pay the rent. In western Europe, feudal lords granted land to their serfs for their own land to be cultivated. Sharma, *Early Medieval Indian Society*.
[84] The period, referred to as the early medieval period in more recent literature, has been studied extensively since the late nineteenth century. Most of the studies focus on the vast and extensive trade networks, often referred to as the Silk Road, and show goods travelling long distances to rich communities. Christopher Beckwith's work forcefully disputes the notion of Central Eurasians as barbaric nomads, showing that the agrarian and urbanism were both part of the steppe empires. The two sectors were deeply connected through trade: 'The trade of luxury goods [along the Silk Road] constituted a very significant part of the internal economy within Central Asia.' Beckwith argues that the cornerstone of the Central Eurasian society was the heroic lord and his war band and friends, *comitatus*, that swore to defend him to the death. The system was successfully maintained through trade, rather than raiding (which only happened when

and Maine's widely read texts published in the first half of the nineteenth century pushed a narrative of India as backwards and at an early stage of progress (see Chapter 1), clouding India's history. The idea that Europe was the first to progress due to its superiority in all things ignored the fact that India had been strong in intellectual progress, industry and trade. Notably, that version of history also ignored the role that India and others from the region played in constructing Europe.[85] Ranade and Dutt were the first to gain traction with this alternative version of global history by rejecting the dominant idea that the world continuously progressed with the inevitability of a human growing.

Ranade and Dutt's rereading of Indian history debunked the dominant reading of global history where progress originated in Europe and would then spread to the rest of the world. That history assumes that (a) Europe is the birthplace of progress, modernity, capitalism, industrialisation or enlightenment, making it superior to the rest; (b) progress was constructed with institutions and practices destined to become universal; and (c) progressive change unfolds in stages.[86] As Chakrabarty argues, it was historicism that allowed Marx to argue that the 'country that is more developed industrially only shows, to the less developed, the image of its own future' and enabled historians such as Phyllis Deane to identify English industrial growth as the first industrial revolution.[87] The dominant reading of global history created a timeline that measured the assumed cultural distance (at least in institutional progress) between Europe and the rest, legitimising imperialism. All countries would reach the same end point, but some would get there earlier than others.

As active members of the nationalist movement, Ranade and Dutt were naturally using their rereading of a glorious past as a tool to unite Indians and fight against imperial rule. India's prosperous past enabled

exchange was impossible). Trade was the only way, reasons Beckwith, for the lord to acquire the goods necessary for his and his *comitatus'* survival. Beckwith, *Empires of the Silk Road*, xii.

[85] For more recent discussion on this other version of global history, see Hobson, *The Eastern Origins of Western Civilisation*; Chatterjee and Hawes, *Europe Observed*; Said, *Orientalism*.

[86] Matin, 'Redeeming the Universal', 354; Ferguson, *Ferguson: An Essay on the History of Civil Society*; Fukuyama, *The End of History and the Last Man*; Mill, *The History of British India*; Rostow, *The Stages of Economic Growth*.

[87] Quoted in Chakrabarty, *Provincializing Europe*, 7.

Ranade, Dutt and their fellow nationalists to theorise that India had the necessary resources and capabilities to rise to the highest stage of civilisation.[88] As Naoroji argued, 'India is capable, under natural circumstances, of providing twice, three times or more the expenditure, as the improvement of the country may need, in attaining all necessary progress.'[89] Describing a progressive past was and is a vital part of nationalist movements throughout global history.

Nevertheless, Ranade and Dutt's rereading of Indian history debunked the idea that Britain was ahead of the rest even before the Industrial Revolution because it pointed out that the narrative ignored India's and China's previous progress. The Indian and Chinese economies were superior to many others up until the end of the eighteenth century, during which time Britain imported Indian textiles in return for gold and silver looted from America. Moreover, Akbar, the sixteenth-century Indian emperor, spoke of rights for women and tolerance for all religions (*sulah kul*) in the same period that Prince Philip II of Spain was part of the Spanish Inquisition.[90] History is more complicated than what the dominant reading portrays. It is too simplistic to uphold the idea that progress started in Europe.

India's ruralised economy, wrote Dutt and Ranade, meant that industry was in 'its infant stage' or 'rudimentary stage'.[91] Deindustrialisation in the textile industry caused mass unemployment and pushed ever more people into the rural areas as they looked for ways to earn a living. There were, consequently, increasing numbers of landless poor in the rural areas. Moreover, in the agricultural sector the system had become semi-feudal, which made the peasants poorer. Imperial land reform had disintegrated the self-sufficient village communities that had existed earlier in Indian history.[92] The village structure had been inherited from the initial stage of civilisation but should have stayed because it harnessed progress; Dutt agreed with Smith and Millar that certain components remained in higher stages. The agricultural sector had

---

[88] Ranade, *Essays on Indian Economics*, 5, 12, 176; Naoroji, *Poverty and Un-British Rule in India*, 401; Dutt, *Speeches and Papers on Indian Questions*, 37.

[89] Naoroji, *Poverty and Un-British Rule in India*, 365.

[90] Mukherjee, 'Empire'; Hobson, *The Eastern Origins of Western Civilisation*; Chatterjee and Hawes, *Europe Observed*.

[91] Dutt, *Epochs of Indian History*, 520; Ranade, *Essays on Indian Economics*, 46.

[92] Dutt, *The Economic History of India under Early British Rule*, 1:120; Dutt, *England and India*, 72; Dutt, *The Peasantry of Bengal*, 188.

once again become the dominant sector, and Indian exports were now mainly made up of raw materials, rather than manufactured goods, as had been the case in India's past higher stage. A dominant agricultural sector belonged generally to the lowest stage of civilisation but had now returned to India. Here was India's current stage of civilisation, a stage specific to India, lower than the one it had experienced before the British took over their subcontinent.[93]

Ranade and Dutt did not reject the existence of stages of progress but rather critiqued the order or sequential understanding of those stages that placed India at a lower stage and did not let it pass to a higher level. Ranade and Dutt's reformulation of the existing stadial theory is pertinent because the European version was problematic. That stadial conceptualisation reinforced the idea that history tells an inevitable story of constant improvement and progress. Located in India, the Indian economists could not agree with the irreversibility or inevitability of progress. Their country had been progressing and was currently regressing.

---

[93] Ranade, *Essays on Indian Economics*, 350; Dutt, *The Economic History of India in the Victorian Age*, 2:3, 10; Naoroji, *Poverty and Un-British Rule in India*, 581–624; Naik, *Kashinath Trimbak Telang*, 28, 54.

4 | *Regress*

In that distant territory within Britain's large empire, there was a group of economists that pushed at the boundaries of how the British and their European neighbours theorised societal change. India was not simply at a lower stage of civilisation. It had been at a higher stage before the British came to their shores. Countries could go through periods of both progress and regress, meaning that they could fall in and out of a role of economic superiority. Ranade and Dutt's stadial theory widened the perspective on how civilisations could change in different ways. As Dutt's history of ancient India narrated, the earlier stages looked similar across regions, 'but the parallel closes with the eleventh century, since then the history of Europe is one of independence, progress, and civilisation; that of India is one of foreign subjection, and consequent degradation and decline'.[1] Since India had been controlled by the British, it regressed to a lower stage (see Chapter 3).

Poverty had been a lived reality for Indians, including for some of the Indian economists, since the late seventeenth century. Some, like Naoroji, came from previously prosperous families that had since lost their riches due to falling regimes and the strong British East India Company, who had been able to monopolise the lucrative economic activities in some areas.[2] Then in 1861 the American Civil War broke out and changed the dynamics in the Indian economy. While some cotton merchants, including Naoroji, benefited from the increased demand for Indian raw cotton due to the disturbance in production in war-stricken America, weavers in rural India could no longer afford the higher-priced raw cotton (see Chapter 1). When the Civil War ended in 1865, the price of Indian cotton plummeted, and many cotton merchants went bankrupt. Naoroji was only one example: he went to England in the 1850s to set up his own cotton-trading firm that later went bankrupt.[3]

---

[1] Dutt, *Epochs of Indian History*, 152.   [2] Patel, *Naoroji*, 15.
[3] Beckert, *Empire of Cotton*, 91–5; Patel, *Naoroji*.

A second, much grimmer, crisis came quickly thereafter. A drought on the eastern shores of India in 1865 led to a severe famine in the Orissa region. The governor refused to provide much-needed emergency grain, and by 1867 a third of the population had died. Four additional famines then touched the entire Indian subcontinent between 1873 and 1901 (see Chapter 1). The Indian economists felt these crises sweeping their cities and villages. Naoroji and Dutt would spend most of their adult lives examining the regress that they saw in India. They would explore how it could be measured, how it varied from region to region, and its causes.

Measuring Regress

When looking at poverty and its narratives in the second half of the nineteenth century, there is a confusing contradiction. On the one hand, most British policymakers and the public saw India as different, convinced by the civilising mission that India needed to be imperialised. On the other hand, it was hard to convince the British that India was poor. Poverty, to the Briton who had never been to India, was not possible in a land that produced luxury products bought in shops all over the country. A poor nation could not produce the kinds of rich and educated, elite and middle-class men that arrived ever more frequently in London – men like Naoroji and Dutt.[4] The British nation saw India as rich and prosperous, and the famines were only anomalies caused by Indian laziness or fecundity. Moreover, the imperial administration only fuelled the picture of prosperous India with their annual *Moral and Material Progress Reports*, first published in 1861. To prove that the British were civilising the Indians, the reports used official statistics to show significant improvements in social and economic progress (see Chapter 1).

Naoroji read these reports and many other documents, thanks to some imperial officials such as Erskine Perry and Mountstuart Grant-Duff who gave him access to the India Office Library in Whitehall, London, in the 1860s and 1870s. Naoroji would spend many hours assiduously combing through the various reports, memoirs, parliamentary debates and other sources to prove the increasing poverty in India. Grant-Duff later came to regret this, as Naoroji mobilised the imperial

[4] Patel, *Naoroji*, 52.

officials' own words to prove his point.[5] In February of 1871, Naoroji stood in front of a London audience and spoke of the various 'fallacious statements' made in a recent India Office return given to Parliament that included a paragraph on 'General Prosperity'.[6] The report had found a surplus of Indian exports, stating that there had been a 188 per cent increase in exports along with a 227 per cent increase in imports in the 1840s and 1850s. Naoroji found several instances of misleading statements that 'led to the almost universal belief that India is rich and prosperous, when it is not so'.[7] Naoroji thought he needed to push against an imperial administration that was, according to him, construing facts into their preconceived theory of India.[8] Naoroji understood the internal logic of the civilising mission: to maintain its legitimacy, the imperial officials had to spread an optimistic view of how India was faring. He feared, however, that the narrative was preventing a true understanding of India's condition.[9]

Naoroji was the leading figure articulating growing concerns about India's extreme poverty and how the imperial rulers were to blame. Born into a poor Gujarati Parsi family of priests in Bombay, he had made it out of poverty and finished his studies at Elphinstone College in 1845 at the age of twenty. At thirty, he moved to Britain to work in the cotton industry and teach Gujarati as a professor at University College London.[10] He then joined the Liberal Party and in 1892 became the first Indian to be elected as a British MP. In a rather personal, although

---

[5] Ibid., 56. [6] Naoroji, *Essays, Speeches, Addresses and Writings*, 112.
[7] Ibid., 114.
[8] Ibid., 19, 41; Naoroji, *Poverty and Un-British Rule in India*, 179; Naoroji, *Dadabhai Naoroji Correspondence: Correspondence with D.E. Wacha, 30-3-1895 to 5-4-1917*, 2:323, 388, 502, 510.
[9] There were several more examples of the British spreading incorrect statements about India. Naoroji wrote to one of his contemporaries, Wacha, complaining of several imperial reports circulating that showed poverty decreasing in India and which were wrongfully trying to deny that there was any cause for concern. English newspapers, wrote Wacha to Naoroji in 1889, wanted to mislead Parliament by stating that the British had 'achieved wonders in 30 years and it is idle to talk of investigating into the faults of an administration which has performed miracles'. In another exchange in 1893, they corresponded about how a single officer was assigned to write a report on the condition of each province, but the reports were not openly distributed, and no independent experts were appointed. Naoroji, *Dadabhai Naoroji Correspondence: Correspondence with D.E. Wacha, 30-3-1895 to 5-4-1917*, 2:170.
[10] Wilson, *India Conquered*, 335.

brief, autobiography, Naoroji thanked his mother for instilling in him progressive ideas.[11] Naoroji's main thesis was that India had the potential to elevate and ameliorate its socio-economic condition. He aimed to bring progress to India by exposing how Britain was draining its wealth.

In the early 1870s, Naoroji started by calculating the national income of India to counteract the imperial officials' poor understanding of what was really going on in his country. He wanted to prove the existence of extreme poverty by measuring per capita income – what he defined as total production divided by population. Naoroji's aim of comparing standards of living across regions and time was facilitated by his decision to reduce economic welfare to a single index that would provide him and his fellow economists with a solid quantitative argument. At the meeting of the Society of Arts in London in July of 1870, he presented his findings. The Society of Arts had a goal of finding solutions to pressing social challenges like improving and expanding manufacturers. Through events, funding and prizes, the organisation strove to improve scientific understanding and refine art, and to alleviate poverty and lower unemployment. 'I propose', started Naoroji, 'the following question: Is India at present in a condition to produce enough to supply all its wants?'[12]

With limited and poor data, Naoroji made a 'rough estimate' by taking the land revenue that the imperial administration had collected for 1870–1.[13] On average, Indian farmers were taxed one-eighth of total produce, so Naoroji inferred that the gross product of India per annum was around £168 million. To that figure, he added the gross revenue from opium, salt, forest products, coal production and revenue from appropriated land, arriving at a conservative figure of £200 million. Dividing the number by India's 170 million people gave him 27 shillings per person, which he rounded up to 40 shillings to account for industry and manufacturing, which he thought negligible. Here was the first ever national income, or rather gross production, estimate for British India. Naoroji believed that he could persuade the imperial officials to remedy the increasing poverty by showing them facts. If he put his findings in a rigorous scientific format, facts could act

[11] *Dadabhai Naoroji: A Sketch of His Life and Life-Work.*
[12] Naoroji, *Essays, Speeches, Addresses and Writings*, 97.
[13] Naoroji, *Poverty and Un-British Rule in India*, 2. It was only published in 1876, with the title 'Poverty of India'.

as his 'armour'.[14] Fellow economists like Banerjea and Iyer agreed that Naoroji's figure showed how poor Indians really were,[15] and indeed the 40 shillings figure caused a scandal in London. By comparison, average income per head in the United Kingdom was around 33 pounds.

The outrage caused by Naoroji's small national income estimate in 1870 pushed imperial officials to react. Lord Ripon, who later became viceroy of India in 1880, ordered Evelyn Baring (1841–1917) to calculate the first imperial estimate of India's gross production. Baring, the future Lord Cromer, found an income per head of 27 rupees. Much like Naoroji, he concluded that the Indian population was exceedingly poor. Naoroji was pleased by the response and saw it as an acknowledgement of Indian poverty from the British. He asked to see the calculations, but Baring declined, and the imperial administration never published the full estimate.[16]

Naoroji presented a perfected estimate in 1873 to the Select Committee on East Indian Finance.[17] Although he dismissed the imperial statistics as incomplete and at times completely wrong, he realised that the raw data in the imperial reports could be used to further credit his claims of a poor India. In this estimate, he incorporated the production of other sectors, not just agriculture, like he had done in 1870. This time he defined annual national income as the sum of total domestic material production (agricultural, manufacturing, mining and fisheries) and external profits from foreign trade. He processed a large amount of data on commodity prices, patterns of land cultivation,

---

[14] Naoroji, *Dadabhai Naoroji Correspondence: Correspondence with D.E. Wacha, 30-3-1895 to 5-4-1917*, 2:61; Naoroji, *Dadabhai Naoroji Correspondence: Correspondence with D.F. Wacha, 4-11-1884 to 23-3-1895*, 1:433; Naoroji, *Dadabhai Naoroji: Selected Private Papers*, 260–2.

Naoroji was nevertheless careful to assert that facts were always statements of truth. In a passage citing Jeremy Bentham, Naoroji explained that facts needed interpretation, meaning researchers had to make value judgements about those facts. Additionally, he realised that humans can only observe a small number of those facts. There was, argued Naoroji, always a necessary element of belief when using scientific reports, which was an issue in India, where frequent errors led to distrust. Naoroji, *Essays, Speeches, Addresses and Writings*, 11.

[15] Banerjea, *Speeches and Writings*; Iyer, *Some Economic Aspects of British Rule in India*, 27–31.

[16] Naoroji, *Poverty and Un-British Rule in India*, 311. [17] Ibid., 4, 220.

crop patterns and crop yield, and acreage under irrigation to derive total production estimates for each province. He found India's total production to be no more than £340 million – equivalent to 40 shillings, or 20 rupees, per capita. During famine years, the figure would be closer to 30 shillings per head, not much different from his initial estimate of twenty-seven.[18]

Several debates followed between Naoroji and other individuals tied to, or working in, India. On the evening of 24 July 1876, a meeting was organised at the Bombay branch of the East India Association at the Framjee Cowasjee Institute, where many had come forward to criticise Naoroji's estimate.[19] Naoroji spent half of his speech attempting to disprove James Mackenzie Maclean's critique. Maclean (1835–1906) was a British journalist who owned and edited the *Bombay Gazette*, a major English-language newspaper in India at the time. He would have moved in the same circles as Naoroji in both India and England, serving as a Conservative politician in the House of Commons from 1885 to 1900 and going to events at the several societies that discussed British and Indian relations and issues.

Maclean's most significant criticism was Naoroji's underestimate of the Bombay cotton industry. Maclean had asked Naoroji 'to add £15,000,000 for Cotton manufactures'.[20] But Naoroji took Maclean's own data from his *Guide to Bombay* and proved that the additional figure to be added could not exceed £3 million, much less than the £15 million Maclean put forward.[21] Naoroji's calculations showed that the Bombay cotton industry was insignificant. He added that Maclean had failed to provide a single element of the calculation that had led him to the figure of £15 million. The different ways that Naoroji and the British presented their work shows their unequal footing. Naoroji cited where he obtained his data and explained his calculation and how he rounded up 'to leave a wide margin'.[22] The British critics either failed to debate, like Baring, or offered corrections without citing the source or detailing the calculation that gave them such a figure, like Maclean.

---

[18] Ibid., 25.
[19] Ibid., 141; Naoroji, *Essays, Speeches, Addresses and Writings*, 276.
[20] Naoroji, *Poverty and Un-British Rule in India*, 126.
[21] Maclean, *A Guide to Bombay*.
[22] Naoroji, *Poverty and Un-British Rule in India*, 126–7.

Later critiques came from Frederick Charles Danvers (1833–1906), a public works official at the India Office, in 1879 and 1880. According to Danvers, Naoroji had failed to include 'railway wealth',[23] but Naoroji was not sure what he meant by this:

Suppose 100 maunds of wheat exist in the Punjab, and its cost to the producer, say, is Rs. 100 – suppose that this wheat is carried by railway to Bombay, and its value at Bombay is Rs. 125; does Mr. Danvers mean that this circumstance has *added* Rs. 25, or anything at all, to the existing wealth of India?

If so, then no such thing has happened. The 100 maunds of wheat existed in the Punjab, and the Rs. 125 existed in Bombay, before the wheat was moved an inch. After the movement, the only result has been change of hands.[24]

In this hypothetical example, the wheat had travelled to Bombay where the sale price, which was divided between the railway owners and workers and the merchant, was 25 rupees higher than the production cost. Neither grain nor money, however, was added to what already existed in India. 'Such "railway wealth" does not exist,' concluded Naoroji.[25] Anyone familiar with the physiocrats from eighteenth-century France will see how Naoroji seems to agree with François Quesnay (1694–1774), the leader of the physiocrats, that earth was the one and only source of wealth.[26] Naoroji argued that railway figures such as associated profits should not be included in a national income estimate because they only distributed goods around a country.[27]

While it is hard to know what exposure Naoroji would have had to Quesnay's works, Ranade and Iyer cited them in the founding texts of Indian Economics (see Chapter 2).[28] Naoroji may therefore have been taught the French economists' ideas at Elphinstone, where Ranade also

---

[23] Ibid., 180.   [24] Ibid., 180–1.   [25] Ibid., 181.

[26] Quesnay, 'Analyse de la formule arithmétique du tableau économique'.

[27] There were other critiques that Naoroji discussed at length in various forms, published in his *Poverty and Un-British Rule*. One other example of a specific critique came from James Caird (1816–92), an agricultural expert who served on the Indian Famine Commission 1878–9. He criticised Naoroji's estimate for ignoring several productive and significant agricultural sectors, to which Naoroji responded in detail. For further discussion on the critique, see Patel, *Naoroji*, 59–60.

[28] Ranade, *Essays on Indian Economics*, 16; Iyer, *Some Economic Aspects of British Rule in India*, app. 1.

studied; he may also have been exposed to them during his thirty years living in England. More concrete links between Naoroji and others analysing the effects of railways exist. At the turn of the century, Naoroji corresponded with Edward Atkinson (1827–1905), who studied the effects of railways on the economy.[29] Atkinson was a Boston-based businessman, notably the president of the Boston Manufacturers' Fire Insurance Company as of 1877. In 1898, he was a founder of the American Anti-Imperialist League, appalled by the expansionist policies of the US government first in Cuba in 1898 and a year later in the Philippines. Sometime earlier, in the 1880s, Atkinson, much like Naoroji, had analysed the 'potent causes of permanent change in respect to the production and distribution of the necessary articles pertaining to the subsistence of the people'.[30] The two men agreed that profits, wages and taxes came from the conversion and sale of the annual product – in other words the total product.

The similarities stopped there. While Naoroji admitted that railways had an 'indirect means of increasing the material production of any country', the means was 'fully and completely included in the estimate of the actual annual production of the country'. Therefore, he reasoned that nothing more than the 'actual material production of the year' should be added to find the annual income.[31] Atkinson collected data on railway mileage and grain production in the United States and found a positive correlation between the two. Arriving at the opposite conclusion to Naoroji, he argued that cheaper transportation meant that grain production could increase as the market expanded. Without railways, argued Atkinson, America's grain surplus would either not have been produced or it would have been wasted. Moreover, the cheap transport led to lower food prices, and thus it freed up time for some labourers to do work other than in subsistence agricultural production. Another economist familiar to Naoroji, Michael Mulhall (1836–1900), reached a similar conclusion. Mulhall was an Irish economist and newspaper editor who collected a large amount of statistics on the world's arts, agriculture, commerce, manufactures, education, railways and public health. He found a correlation between increasing production and exports and railway mileage in India. 'Previous to the

[29] Patel, *Naoroji*, 231.
[30] Atkinson, 'The Railway, the Farmer and the Public', 1.
[31] Naoroji, *Poverty and Un-British Rule in India*, 181.

making of railways and canals,' wrote Mulhall in 1880, 'the products and trade of India were stagnant, but the progress of the last twenty years is marvellous.'[32] Naoroji did not agree that the railways brought progress in India.

The difference, according to his peer Ranade, lay in how and where railways were built in India. When Ranade wrote on the Dutch Java (see Chapter 3), he discussed how

the Railway policy pursued … killed our local indigenous Industries, and made people more helpless than before, by increasing their dependence and pressure on Agriculture as their only resource. The policy adopted by the Dutch Government sixty years ago has produced the opposite effects, and made Java export four times less Raw Produce and four times more Manufactured Produce than has been the case in British India.[33]

Railways could be progressive (see Chapter 5), but they were not in India under British rule.

While Naoroji was convinced of his 20-rupee figure, which excluded railway data, he still preferred to use the more widely accepted British figure of 27 rupees and with that prove India's extreme poverty. Naoroji noted that the difference between twenty-seven and twenty was marginal.[34] Similarly, Iyer argued that even if the imperial figure was higher than Naoroji's, it was not a source of celebration, rather the opposite: 20 rupees was the minimum wage for famine labourers, sufficient 'to enable life to remain with the body. It makes no allowance for healthy nourishment and much less for luxury.'[35] The difference was especially irrelevant, according to Naoroji, due to India's skewed income distribution. Some of the Indian masses would not even have had 27 or 20 rupees per year. Iyer pointed out it was an average, 'follow[ing], therefore, that there must be millions upon millions of people who support themselves on a smaller pittance'.[36, 37]

Naoroji could now compare the income per capita with the average cost of living to find out whether Indians had enough income to survive.

[32] Mulhall, *The Progress of the World*, 224.
[33] Ranade, *Essays on Indian Economics*, 97–8.
[34] Naoroji, *Poverty and Un-British Rule in India*, 311.
[35] Iyer, *Some Economic Aspects of British Rule in India*, 28.   [36] Ibid., 28.
[37] While Naoroji was the first to calculate a national account for India, many economists followed. For instance, as of 2023 the most recent study found an income per capita of 31 rupees for 1875. Caruana-Galizia, 'Indian Regional Income Inequality'.

Table 4.1 *Dadabhai Naoroji's national income and cost of living per state, 1867–70.*

Area	Production per head (in Rs)	Three quarters of the cost of living for inmates or cost per head outside of jail (in Rs)
Central Provinces	22	23
Punjab	25	20
North-West Provinces	18	16
Madras	18	42
Bengal	19	23.12
Bombay	40	35

If the cost-of-living estimate was higher than the national income, then India was 'sinking in poverty'.[38] Naoroji returned to the imperial reports to gather data on the costs of shelter, clothing and food for Indian prison inmates and recommended expenses of the same for 'coolie' emigrants who would travel by sea from Calcutta. To extrapolate the cost of living for the general Indian population, he took three quarters of this statistic to account for children, assuming children consumed less than adult inmates and emigrants (Table 4.1). Having calculated the regional averages, he arrived at a national average of 34 rupees.[39]

The cost of living was thus higher than the per capita national income – thirty-four versus twenty-seven. In Naoroji's own words, India's national income did not 'provide the bare necessities of life'.[40]

Comparing Regress across Regions

Comparing poverty across regions was another popular way of understanding how an economy was faring. Since the discovery of Africa and Asia, intellectuals struggled with the observed differences between populations of different regions. Comparing different regions became important in attaining scientific certainty with a universal scope. Maine and the researchers that followed him attempted to theorise how and

[38] Naoroji, *Poverty and Un-British Rule in India*, 188.   [39] Ibid., 501.
[40] Ibid., 31, 326.

why only some countries had industrialised, and this was only possible through comparing those countries' social formations with others. One source for such study was Mulhall's country rankings in his *Progress of the World*, published in 1880, which Naoroji used to understand where India's economy stood compared to others.[41] According to Naoroji, taking Mulhall's statistics for other countries with his Indian figure showed that India was nineteen times worse off than Britain.[42] Naoroji argued that this made India the poorest country in the world.

Dutt found another strategy to compare regress across regions. From a young age, Dutt had travelled around Bengal with his father, who was a collector for the imperial administration, 'and the relocations of those early days are among the pleasantest reminiscences of my life'.[43] His father taught Dutt that travelling was both enjoyable and educational and encouraged him to finish his studies in England.[44] Dutt's own travels were extensive in both India and Europe. He would stay for extended periods of time in England, taking shorter trips to neighbouring European countries, and these travels would eventually serve as a way for Dutt to compare regress across regions, which he had been surprised to see even in Europe.

Dutt was born into a Bengali family of British East India Company employees in Calcutta well known for their literary and academic achievements. In 1868, after finishing his examination at the University of Calcutta and 'obtaining a scholarship of 14 rupees a month', he set off on his first voyage to Europe with his friends Banerjea and B. L. Gupta.[45] They went to England to study with professors at University College London and sit the Civil Service examination of 1869. Dutt wrote in his travelogue that they ran away at night without permission from their guardians.[46] According to his biography, there seems to have been a conflict based on some misunderstanding between his uncle, Rai Bahadur Shoshee Chunder Dutt Bahudur, who had been his guardian ever since his parents had passed away, and his cousin, Suresh Chunder Dutt, Rai Babu's son. Ultimately, 'the hazardous step he had taken' paid off because Dutt

---

[41] Mulhall, *The Progress of the World*.
[42] Naoroji, *Dadabhai Naoroji: Selected Private Papers*, 246; Naoroji, *Essays, Speeches, Addresses and Writings*, 310, 367; Naoroji, *Poverty and Un-British Rule in India*, 384, 564.
[43] Gupta, *Life and Work of Romesh Chunder Dutt*, 12.   [44] Ibid., 14, 152.
[45] Ibid., 14.   [46] Dutt, *Three Years in Europe*, 1.

succeeded in becoming the second Indian to be appointed an Indian
civil servant in 1871, being employed as an assistant magistrate and
collector.[47]

Like many of his contemporaries privileged enough to travel to
Europe, Dutt saw the need to observe progress or modernity to better
understand it. 'For us', wrote Dutt, 'who are born and educated in India,
it is also of incalculable advantage to see with our own eyes and to study
with care the results of modern civilisation in Europe and America, and
to assimilate what is good in them with our national progress.'[48] This
was not, however, the common way in Europe to go about understanding another region in the nineteenth century. Take Mill's highly
endorsed *History of British India* (see Chapter 1). In the first pages,
Mill stated that he did not need to travel to India to understand its past
or present: 'Some of the most successful attempts in history had been
made, without ocular knowledge of the country, or acquaintance with
its language.'[49] He cited William Robertson (1721–93), who never went
to America and still composed its history.[50] Mill thought he was more
capable of writing India's history because

the man best qualified for dealing with evidence is the man best qualified for
writing the history of India. It will not, I presume, admit of much dispute that
the habits which are subservient to the successful exploration of evidence are
more likely to be acquired in Europe than in India.[51]

Observation was not sufficient: in 'so extensive and complicated
a scene as India, how small a portion would the whole period of his
life enable any man to observe!'[52] Instead, Mill reasoned that he could
use travel accounts along with other materials that were so abundant in
England to write India's history.

Similarly, Marx, who published some articles on India and theorised
an Asiatic mode of production, drew not on first-hand experience but
on Jean-Baptiste Tavernier's *Travels in India* and Bernier's *Travels in
the Mogul Empire*, Mill's *History of British India*, Dutt's *The
Peasantry of Bengal* and M.M. Kovalevsky's writings on the Bengal
Social Science Association, among others.[53] And yet Marx travelled
through France, Belgium and England, as well as Algeria. Why not

[47] Gupta, *Life and Work of Romesh Chunder Dutt*, 7, 17.
[48] Dutt, *Three Years in Europe*, 165.   [49] Mill, *The History of British India*, 9.
[50] Ibid., 9.   [51] Ibid., 10.   [52] Ibid.
[53] Kumar, 'Marx and Engels on India', 493.

India? Advocates of Indian reform at the beginning of the nineteenth century, as Mary Poovey forcefully argues, insisted that the most reliable knowledge about India could not be produced by observations, like in England, but by 'deductive or a priori reasoning, which proceeded from general principles about universal human nature'.[54]

Dutt disagreed. He travelled far and wide, from Naples in Italy all the way to the North Cape in Norway. His journeys in Europe are documented in a travelogue, first published in 1872, based on three of his trips.[55] He took the first to sit his Civil Service exam in 1868–71,[56] the second in 1886 to show his family Europe, and the third in 1893 when he took a furlough from his post to travel the continent as yet another educational endeavour. The travelogue consists of edited extracts from letters Dutt sent home during his trips, including detailed explanations of his experiences, encounters and impressions. He was persuaded to put them in a book by his publisher, who thought it would serve as a good travel guide for Indians going to Europe.[57]

Dutt acknowledged that his travelogue did not meet the standards of typical travel writing but agreed, nonetheless, to publish the letter extracts to fill the gap in the literature of Indian travels to Europe. He was explicit that it 'may therefore serve as a guide-book to Indian youths intending to visit Europe, containing at the same time something more than ordinary guide-books profess to do, –*viz.* the views and opinions of a foreigner for the first time coming in contact with the noble institutions of the West'.[58] Part of the text certainly

[54] Poovey, 'The Limits of the Universal Knowledge Project', 185.
[55] Dutt, *Three Years in Europe, 1868 to 1871*. There are four editions: The third edition was published in 1890 and the fourth in 1896 (I cannot find the dates of the first and second editions). I analyse the latest edition, which is the longest with 377 pages and eleven chapters. The opening four chapters concern Dutt's first trip to Europe and would have comprised the entire contents of the first edition. Chapters five to ten cover his second trip, added for the third edition, and chapter eleven covers his third trip, added for the fourth edition.
[56] After Dutt and Gupta sat their exam in March 1868, they travelled to the south coast of England, visiting towns like Hastings. From July to September 1869, they journeyed to Scotland, going as far north as Inverness, and stopping in the Lake and Peak Districts on the way back down to London. In June and July 1870, they made their way to Ireland and Wales, visiting, among other places, Belfast, Dublin, Limerick, Aberystwyth and Milford Haven. In August 1871, they travelled to France, Germany, Switzerland and northern Italy, stopping in, for example, Paris, Cologne, Baden-Baden, Geneva, Lausanne, Milan and Venice.
[57] Dutt, *Three Years in Europe*, i–ii. [58] Ibid.

reads more like a diary than a travel guide. Dutt weaved in his impressions about fellow travellers on the same boat or excursion, and his thoughts, as well as those of his friends and mentors, on the political, socio-economic and societal context (e.g., he mentions 'two sensational cases' of divorces in the British tabloids).[59] Other parts of the text, most noticeable as of chapter seven, read more like a travel guide, including practical information on things to see in a particular city. Dutt included details about how to get from place to place, sometimes with exact departure and arrival times. He noted where the best sights were located in Paris, historical information on countries such as Belgium and Sweden, and several sections on specific European conflicts, such as the Franco-Prussian War, 1870–1.[60] It was common in this period for Indian travel writing to be a mix of guidebooks, local histories, autobiography and ethnography.[61]

Contrary to Dutt's expectations, he saw poverty in Europe, beginning with his first trip to England as a nineteen-year-old. Europe, according to Dutt, had created 'neat', 'regular', and 'beautiful' spaces, but 'how much more has it yet to do'.[62] 'The lower classes of England are in many respects very far off from what they ought to be.'[63] 'It is really painful to reflect on the amount of suffering of the poor in this country.'[64] The poor lacked education, married too young and had children before they could sufficiently provide for them, and often turned to alcohol and violence. Many people lived in overcrowded housing with limited food, causing some to die from hunger or cold, especially during the winter months. The cold climate, thought Dutt, made the British urban poor worse off than Indians.[65] There were, in fact, few Indian travellers that did not remark on the poverty they saw, especially in Britain.[66] Like Dutt, they saw and wrote about the everyday lives of the lower classes, and some wrote about the inside of working-class homes.[67] What Dutt found was not the utopic modern civilisation that his education had promised him.

By the time of Dutt's second trip, with his family in 1886, the situation had only worsened. Europe was suffering from the Long Depression (see Chapter 1). According to Dutt, there were 2 million unemployed, pushing more people into poverty, alcoholism and

---

[59] Ibid., 150.   [60] Ibid., 204, 376.   [61] Codell, 'Reversing the Grand Tour'.
[62] Dutt, *Three Years in Europe*, 6, 9, 43, 83–4.   [63] Ibid., 26–7.   [64] Ibid., 43.
[65] Ibid., 27–8, 43.   [66] Burton, 'Making a Spectacle of Empire', 134.
[67] Bach, 'Poverty Theory in Action'.

violence. A factory owner that Dutt met in western England during the Colonial and Indian Reception shared his thoughts on the crisis:

Do not think … from the pompous reception we have given you that we are doing well. On the contrary times were never harder than now. Our ships remain in our harbours, our manufactures find no market, our men are unemployed.[68]

There was 'agricultural distress' because farms were becoming less and less profitable as imported corn became cheaper.[69] Putting tariffs on the corn would only worsen the situation, forcing higher prices upon the urban population. On the same trip, Dutt observed that the farmers' labourers were the 'poorest classes in Norway and Sweden'.[70] 'The Swedes are a patient and hardworking but a poor race, and hence large numbers of them emigrate annually to America.'[71] Dutt witnessed a boat leaving the harbour in Christiana, Norway, with about ninety emigrants from Sweden and Norway. The experience 'created a deep impression in [him]'.[72] Poverty was thus a reality in Europe, too.

Dutt's writings on poverty can be contextualised within a growing number of reports on poverty at the time. In the preceding decades, English intellectuals had started to bring forward such observations. For instance, Dutt's work resembles Henry Mayhew's series of articles entitled 'London Labour and the London Poor' in the *Morning Chronicle* of the 1840s.[73] Mayhew (1812–87) used his journalistic skills to interview the working population of London, meticulously observing, documenting and describing their living conditions. There are striking similarities in descriptions of the poor by Dutt and George Sims (1847–1922). Sims published an influential ethnographic study, *How the Poor Live*, in 1883. At the very least, Dutt knew of the work, as it is listed at the end of Dutt's travelogue as suggested further reading. Sims was a journalist particularly interested in reform to better the lives of the poor. He wrote of a room in the slum:

The woman, her husband, and her six children live, eat, and sleep in this one room, and for this they pay three shillings a week. It is quite as much as they

---

[68] Dutt, *Three Years in Europe*, 129. [69] Ibid., 130. [70] Ibid., 193.
[71] Ibid. [72] Ibid., 202.
[73] They were published as a book in 1851, under the title *London Labour and the London Poor; a Cyclopædia of the Condition and Earnings of Those That <u>Will</u> Work, Those That <u>Cannot</u> Work, and Those That <u>Will Not</u> Work*. (The underlined terms appeared in italics, for emphasis, on the book's title page.)

can afford. There has been no breakfast yet, and there won't be any till the husband (who has been out to try and get a job) comes in and reports progress. As to complaining of the dilapidated, filthy condition of the room, they know better.[74]

Dutt describes a family 'huddled together in one uncomfortable room' where the windows are broken and there is 'want of sufficient food, sufficient clothing, and of coal to warm the room'.[75] His description concludes with a comparison to India: it 'presents a sight of misery compared to which the poorest classes of people in our country are well off'.[76]

The poverty debate was later fuelled by Charles Booth's and Seebohm Rowntree's studies on poverty in England. Booth studied poverty in east London in 1887. He categorised four different degrees, including monetary and other sociological issues such as housing and employment.[77] Dutt's travelling could have given him more access to these reports, but there is no way of knowing if he was familiar with them, as he did not cite them in his works.

However, another Indian economist, Iyer, did cite Rowntree's study on 'primary poverty'.[78] Iyer used Rowntree's study to refute an argument made by an imperial official, Mr Pennington, in an article in the *Asiatic Review* on Indian poverty. Like Dutt, Pennington had concluded that there were as many poor people in Britain as in countries like India – Pennington guesstimated around 10 per cent. And, like Dutt, Pennington wrote that the British poor were worse off than Indians because of the relatively colder climate. Iyer disliked this argument. It was 'lamentable that our official class' excuses Indian poverty by referencing the 'poverty that prevails in other parts of the world'.[79] 'Nor', continued Iyer, 'can it be any consolation to these people to be told that they are not the only people suffering from poverty, but, in other parts of the world, there are people who are in a worse condition.'[80] If Rowntree's definition of the poverty line was used, argued Iyer, the proportion of poor in India would be much higher. Quoting Rowntree, Iyer explained how in a family that fell below the poverty line, 'nothing must be bought but that which is absolutely

[74] Sims, *How the Poor Live*, 6.   [75] Dutt, *Three Years in Europe*, 27–8.
[76] Ibid., 28.   [77] Booth, *Life and Labour of the People in London*.
[78] Iyer, *Some Economic Aspects of British Rule in India*, 20.   [79] Ibid.
[80] Ibid., 21.

necessary for the maintenance of physical health, and what is bought must be of the plainest and most economical description'.[81]

Iyer used Rowntree's research to dismiss arguments that the Indian peasant was poor due to his irresponsible spending habits. 'It is absurd to imagine', wrote Iyer, 'that the Indian *ryot* [peasant] [is] so differently constituted from other human beings that he would borrow and entangle himself into the meshes of indebtedness, where there is no need for doing so.'[82] Wedding expenditures in India, continued Iyer, were not overdone, as the British claimed. He explained that guests gave monetary gifts that covered the expenses. Indians did not spend beyond their means. Like Rowntree showed in England, poor people in India were no different than people at their same level of income in other countries.

Data collection on unemployment was starting to come into existence at the end of the nineteenth century. The unemployed were naturally some of the most exposed to poverty. Dutt could have found out about how many people were out of work, thanks to official data collection. The UK's Department of Labour Board of Trade, established in the 1880s, had started to collect data from trade unions on who received unemployment benefits, and an unemployment index was published in their monthly report, the *Labour Gazette*, as of 1893. The report does not include Dutt's figure of 2 million unemployed people that he included in his description of England on his second visit. Nevertheless, the board's index gave an average unemployment rate of 4.5 per cent from 1870 to 1913, which would have been around 1.5 million people.[83]

Dutt used his time in Britain to better understand poverty by comparing Europe with India. The imperial context meant that travelling to the Empire's core became an 'empowering act'.[84] As several scholars have analysed, the travel guides produced by Indian visitors to Britain had more purpose than to serve as touristic handbooks. The travelogues proved that the imperial streets could be possessed by their imperial subjects; the travellers declared themselves free to wander and claim these areas as their own. Furthermore, the Indians showed the British that they could survey and critique Britain as the British critiqued India. By writing about their travels, they were reversing the

---

[81] Quoted in ibid., 23.   [82] Ibid., 13.
[83] Boyer and Hatton, 'New Estimates of British Unemployment'.
[84] Codell, 'Reversing the Grand Tour', 174.

hierarchy of periphery and core.[85] The Indians were welcomed both as
guests and as British imperial citizens. They were not entirely outsiders,
yet their 'guest discourse', as Julie Codell labels it, enabled the travelogues to remain invisible to the imperial power relations that they
ultimately modified.[86] Like Europeans had done to Indians for centuries, Indian travellers studied European subjects. Travelling became
a genre where Indians could reverse the tradition of observing the
other through an ethnographic study and a way to gain authority,
objectivity and credibility by using the scientific method of
comparison.[87]

Dutt's Poverty Theory

Dutt's travelling offered him a way to study regress at home. Through
his travels, he realised that theorising poverty meant he had to observe
it. Both Dutt and Sims described their observations of the poor as
journeys. Sims argued that it was necessary to 'encounter misery that
some good people think it best to leave undiscovered', which was 'as
interesting as any of those newly-explored lands which engage the
attention of the Royal Geographical Society'.[88] The journey to see
'How the Poor Live', wrote Sims, was about giving the poor 'a little
scientific attention' in order to find 'remedies' to cure poverty.[89]
Similarly, after Dutt's first trip to Europe, he headed to rural Bengal
to collect data on rural poverty. Dutt claimed that economists needed
to see the rural poverty to understand and study it. In his first publication on those findings, he took his readers on a journey through the
Bengali countryside. First, he described the 'paddy fields spreading
their sea-like expanse',[90] then he led his readers to places less familiar
to those living in the cities: 'Let us leave the main road, . . . and in about
half an hour reach one of the shady villages.'[91] At the end of the
description of the village, he wrote: 'A spot so secluded seems devoted
to peace and rural happiness; – alas! It is the home of poverty, suffering,

---

[85] Mukhopadhyay, 'Colonised Gaze?'; Harder, 'Female Mobility and Bengali
      Women's Travelogues in the Nineteenth and Early Twentieth Centuries'; Khan,
      Indian Muslim Perceptions of the West during the Eighteenth Century; Burton,
      'Making a Spectacle of Empire', 133.
[86] Codell, 'Reversing the Grand Tour', 186.
[87] Ibid.; Bach, 'Poverty Theory in Action'.   [88] Sims, *How the Poor Live*, 3.
[89] Ibid.   [90] Dutt, *The Peasantry of Bengal*, 60.   [91] Ibid., 61.

and ignorance.'[92] Dutt's studies of the rural poor made him the founder of Agricultural Economics in India. His data collection in the country-side became part of his major contribution to explaining the causes of poverty and famines.[93]

Dutt's theory rejected the imperial discourse that blamed the famines on India's high population growth and dry climate. The Malthusian population trap, used by the British to explain Indian famines, argued that famines occurred as an automatic mechanism to check population growth beyond the means of food production.[94] This was not backed up by the statistics, argued Dutt. Population growth was slower in India than in many other countries, including Britain, which was also far more densely populated.[95] Nor were droughts or lack of food to blame. 'It was not the want of food supply, but it was the want of money to buy food, which caused famines in localities where the crops failed.'[96] Dutt agreed with the imperial famine report that stagnant real wages[97] and rising food prices restricted access to food, especially for farm labourers who were unable to support themselves.[98] In the nine-teenth century, deaths from famines were double the normal rate experienced in India only a century earlier, despite an unchanged climate.[99] From his work, Dutt concluded that droughts or supply shocks did not guarantee there would be a famine but that droughts caused higher food prices and thus reduced access to food for a large group of Indians who then could not afford it.

Dutt found that the lack of access to food was caused by politics and not some natural Indian weakness, whether population growth that was too high or some other reason. There was simply not enough money to pay for food. According to Dutt, India was forced to export grains to Britain, reducing the food supply during a time when grains

[92] Ibid.   [93] Dutt, *The Peasantry of Bengal*; Dutt, *Indian Famines*.
[94] Malthus, *An Essay on the Principle of Population*; Dutt, *The Peasantry of Bengal*, 194–5; Commander, 'Malthus and the Theory of "Unequal Powers"'; Ambirajan, 'Malthusian Population Theory and Indian Famine Policy in the Nineteenth Century'.
[95] Dutt, *Indian Famines*, 17; Dutt, *England and India*, 132; Dutt, *The Economic History of India under Early British Rule*, 1:vi.
[96] Dutt, *Speeches and Papers on Indian Questions*, 23.
[97] 'Report of the Indian Famine Commission'.
[98] Dutt, *Indian Famines*, 15; Dutt, *Speeches and Papers on Indian Questions*, 58.
[99] For reference, the 1876–8 famine reduced Bengal's population by a third (10 per cent of the total Indian population). Maddison, 'The Historical Origins of Indian Poverty', 63.

were needed at home. This pushed up food prices. Moreover, Iyer argued that railways had facilitated the exporting of grain, discouraging storage necessary for dryer seasons. And there were excessive land taxes that caused greater poverty among the rural population (see Chapter 5). In the late twentieth century, Amartya Sen developed his own theory of famines, also based on rural data collection. Like Dutt, he found that Indian famines were caused by a lack of access to food, rather than a lack of supply.[100] What Sen showed is that the imperial structures that Dutt observed lived on almost a century later.

Naoroji and Drain Theory

The general indebtedness and poverty in imperial India were a symptom of the British drain of the country's resources. The drain theory, as it came to be known, gained popularity and support in the late nineteenth century, thanks to Naoroji, who featured it in his writings from 1870 onwards. Not an original contribution by Naoroji, which he himself admitted, it was in fact something that imperial officials had worried about earlier. For instance, John Sullivan, a proprietor of East India stock and a member of the Madras Council, wrote in 1853, 'The little Court disappears – trade languishes – the capital decays – the people are impoverished – the Englishman flourishes, and acts like a sponge, drawing up riches from the banks of the Ganges, and squeezing them down upon the banks of the Thames.'[101]

Naoroji used his time at the India Office Library in the 1860s and 1870s to systematically look through imperial documents. It must have been then that he found evidence that the British themselves worried about the drain of Indian resources. Naoroji was the first to succeed in elaborating upon and successfully spreading drain theory. He argued that Britain was not bringing modernity to India, as the civilising mission promised, but depleting its resources. He spread the idea that India was 'bleeding'.[102] Naoroji insisted that he and his contemporaries needed to

---

[100] Sen, *Poverty and Famines*. It is interesting to note here that Sen included Dutt's works in his list of references but did not cite him anywhere in the text, and Dutt is not cited in his 2009 book *The Idea of Justice*, which is supposed to draw (almost) exclusively upon Indian intellectual thought.

[101] Sullivan, *Are We Bound by Our Treaties?*, 67.

[102] Ranade, *Essays on Indian Economics*, 24; Naoroji, *Poverty and Un-British Rule in India*, 33, 638; Dutt, *Speeches and Papers on Indian Questions*, 62.

spread the truth about the drain because it was detrimental to both India and Britain.[103] Dutt agreed: any other country under such a large drain would also suffer from famines – France, Germany, Britain or America.[104] India would only progress once the drain ceased and it became independent.

Naoroji compiled statistics to measure the drain. The calculations included Indian war repayments for territorial wars that the British imperial administration had decided to fight; unrequited exports; home charges payable to Britain, including imperial officials' pensions; land taxes because they were not spent in India; the absence of protection for India's infant industries; and the negative implications of even constructive efforts like the railways, which deprived many providers of traditional transport services of income and facilitated the import of British-manufactured goods. According to Naoroji, the debt had increased from £118.5 million in 1875 to £220.5 million in 1895.[105] Dutt calculated that while British public debt had decreased, Indian public debt had doubled.[106]

Regress Resulting from a Lack of Capital

Capital played a crucial role in progress. Both Naoroji and Dutt used J. S. Mill's work to argue that the potential for industrial growth was positively correlated to the availability of capital.[107] Naoroji hoped that in doing so they could make the British understand the dire consequences of the drain on India:

Many a time, in discussing with English friends the question of the material drain generally, and the above remarks on railways, irrigation works, etc., I found it a very difficult task to convince. Fortunately, a great authority enunciates the fundamental principles very clearly and convincingly, and I give them below, hoping that an authority like that of the late Mr. Mill, will, on economic principles especially, command attention.[108]

---

[103] Naoroji, *Poverty and Un-British Rule in India*, 641–7; Naoroji, *Dadabhai Naoroji Correspondence: Correspondence with D.E. Wacha, 30-3-1895 to 5-4-1917*, 2:722; Dutt, *Speeches and Papers on Indian Questions*, 62.
[104] Dutt, *Speeches and Papers on Indian Questions*, 62.
[105] Naoroji, *Poverty and Un-British Rule in India*, 13.
[106] Dutt, *Indian Famines*, 13, 15; Dutt, *Speeches and Papers on Indian Questions*, 21.
[107] Naoroji, *Poverty and Un-British Rule in India*, 55–7; Dutt, *Indian Famines*, 59.
[108] Naoroji, *Poverty and Un-British Rule in India*, 55.

Naoroji employed J. S. Mill's discourse of how industry is limited by capital and that capital and industry are interdependent. It followed then that employment was determined mostly by capital and slightly less so by aggregate demand.

The drain essentially explained why India had neither capital nor sufficient demand. In Naoroji's own words, 'the candle burns at both ends'.[109] The theory explained why railways did not increase wealth because these profits were repatriated back to foreign investors, mainly in Britain. Even J. S. Mill, noted Naoroji, had identified the lack of accumulation in Asia, which was required to increase production, as a problem.[110] Dutt explained the need for capital in the rural context. He argued that the Permanent Settlement in Bengal, compared to the other types of landlord and peasant settlements set up by the British, had led to progress through lower taxes, fostering agricultural enterprise and extended cultivation and higher capital accumulation.[111] And capital accumulation was crucial for progress.

Like his income figures, Naoroji's drain statistics were dismissed by the British at first. Naoroji found it was a slow process to get the imperial power to admit that the drain was an issue.[112] He had some success as a member of the Welby Commission, which published a report in 1900 that concluded that Britain charged India too much. The report had been commissioned in 1896 by the British government to investigate wasteful spending in India. Members of the commission included Lord Welby (1832–1915), Lord Chaman (1859–1925) and T. R. Buchanan as parliamentary representatives, and William S. Caine (1842–1903), Wedderburn and Naoroji as representatives of Indian interests. A couple of other Indian economists, Gokhale and Wacha, were brought in a year later in 1897. The authors of the report called for the India Office in London to be made aware of all changes to the charges paid by India and for the payments to be tied to a fixed exchange mission. Wacha wrote to Naoroji in October 1900 congratulating him for successfully proving Indian poverty and subsequently debunking the fallacy that

---

[109] Ibid., 56.   [110] Naoroji, *Essays, Speeches, Addresses and Writings*, 106.
[111] Dutt, *The Economic History of India under Early British Rule*, 1:179; Dutt, *Indian Famines*, 3, 58.
[112] Naoroji, *Dadabhai Naoroji Correspondence: Correspondence with D.E. Wacha, 4-11-1884 to 23-3-1895*, 1:74; Naoroji, *Dadabhai Naoroji Correspondence: Correspondence with D.E. Wacha, 30-3-1895 to 5-4-1917*, 2:718.

India was progressing. Naoroji's 'constant hammering' of the drain of Indian resources, wrote Wacha, had paid off.[113]

Several examples illustrate Naoroji's success. Naoroji and the socialist Henry Hyndman (1842–1921) began a correspondence in 1878 after Hyndman found a copy of Naoroji's *Poverty of India* at a parliamentary bookseller. Reading the book made Hyndman the most vehement critic of British policy in India. Hyndman's *Bankruptcy of India*, published in 1878, drew heavily from *Poverty of India*, describing India as poorer and more famine-stricken than had been admitted in the British press previously.[114] In a later work, Hyndman proposed reducing the drain.[115] In 1881 Hyndman sent a letter to Marx saying that he thought Marx should meet Naoroji. A few days later, Marx sent a letter to a Russian economist, Nicolai F. Danielson (1844–1918), using arguments about the drain of wealth from India that were remarkably similar to Naoroji's. There is no concrete evidence that Naoroji and Marx met, although some like to think they had dinner in London.[116] Hyndman's books persuaded at least the International Socialist Congress that India was worse off under imperialism. Naoroji was invited to the International Socialist Conference in Amsterdam in 1904 where he spoke of India's poverty caused by the British (see Epilogue).

Deindustrialisation

Regress in India was primarily caused by deindustrialisation. The Indian economists experienced how the economy had suffered dramatically after the appearance of foreigners from Europe in the seventeenth century. As cheap textile products flooded the country, thanks to the railways, the Indian textile industry went out of business. The industrial hubs that had previously existed in India during the higher stage, before the British invasion, had disappeared and left a predominantly agricultural economy that contributed to the extreme levels of poverty. India was experiencing, as a recent historian describes it, 'the most severe, long-lasting economic depression in world history'.[117]

---

[113] Naoroji, *Dadabhai Naoroji Correspondence: Correspondence with D.E. Wacha, 4-11-1884 to 23-3-1895*, 1:773.
[114] *Nineteenth Century*, October issue, 1878.
[115] Hyndman, *England for All*, 144.
[116] Patel, *Naoroji*, 84; Goswami, *Producing India*, 227.
[117] Beckwith, *Empires of the Silk Road*, 262.

Iyer used export data to show that there had been a decline in Indian textile exports and an increase in Lancashire imports, which he argued showed a decline in domestic production.[118] Four-fifths of India's population, according to Dutt, now depended on agriculture.[119] Ranade, Dutt and Iyer wrote that between India and Britain, the proportion of raw produce to manufactured goods was four to one, compared to one to four between India and its neighbouring countries.[120] The same area of land, explained Iyer, had to now support more people even though yields had not increased. Land inheritance, in turn, meant that plots were divided more and more with every new generation.[121] Ranade believed that agricultural dependence was 'the weak point of all Asiatic Civilisation',[122] and he described the process of deindustrialisation as the 'rustication' of India's economy.[123]

Deindustrialisation was caused by several factors. Naoroji, Ranade, Dutt, Banerjea and Joshi understood the imperialist pursuits and how Britain's manufacturing sector in Manchester was hurting India's industrial sector. The Manchester Cotton Association lobbyists managed to push for no or low tariffs for imports in India, so that their products could beat the domestic alternatives on price. This prevented Indian infant industries from developing to a stage where they could compete internationally and forced the country to instead specialise in agriculture. At the same time, the Manchester lobbyists fought for protectionist measures for Britain's textile industry, lowering British demand for Indian textile exports. Imperial policies further discouraged modern industrial development in India by discriminating against Indian entrepreneurs through British monopolies of trade. Investors struggled to get access to scarce capital on the subcontinent. The banking sector developed too slowly, leading to high interest rates and a reliance on informal financial institutions.

The studies and dialogue between the Indian economists and the imperial officials had an effect. Towards the end of the nineteenth

[118] Iyer, *Some Economic Aspects of British Rule in India*, 9, 65, 320–78.
[119] Dutt, *Indian Famines*, 3.
[120] Ranade, *Essays on Indian Economics*, 95; Dutt, *England and India*, 124; Dutt, *Speeches and Papers on Indian Questions*, 90; Iyer, *Some Economic Aspects of British Rule in India*, 9.
[121] Iyer, *Some Economic Aspects of British Rule in India*, 66–8, 73.
[122] Ranade, *Essays on Indian Economics*, 94–5.   [123] Ibid., 29, 107.

century, the imperial rhetoric seemed to change, and British officials now agreed that India had increasing poverty. For example, the newspapers of Englishman Robert Knight (1825–90), *The Times of India* and *The Statesman*, started to write about the reality of poverty in India.[124] In a 1900 debate in the House of Lords in response to the Welby Commission report, the Earl of Onslow spoke of 'times [that] have to a large extent altered, and at the present moment India is labouring under a series of calamities which enlist the sympathies not only of every member of your Lordships' House, but of everybody in this country and throughout the Empire'.[125] The current viceroy, Lord Curzon, declared in a presentation in July of 1904, 'Poverty there is in abundance … Misery and destitution there are. The question is not whether they exist, but whether they are growing more or growing less.'[126]

The historian Ram Sharan Sharma wrote in 2001 that 'the concept of modernism is more or less clear to us: it is associated with the advent of capitalism in developed countries and imperialism in "developing countries"'.[127] The confidence in his definition of modernism, in my view, is partly thanks to Indian Economics a century earlier. Ranade and Dutt established a revised history of progress and modernity that described the reality of India and other imperial territories. Naoroji and Dutt measured, compared and studied regress in India to better understand its causes. The Indian economists imagined a future stage of civilisation where their manufacturing industry would be revived, on which Indian prosperity depended. For the short term, they prescribed specific economic policies to attain such a condition (see Chapter 5). In the longer term, India would gain independence by fostering national unity and a national development plan that would cater to both national needs and the changing international landscape. At which point, the Indians could eventually regain their dominant position in the modern industrial world (see Chapter 6).

---

[124] Knight was editor of *The Times of India* and founder of *The Statesman*, two of the most prominent newspapers in India in the nineteenth century. Naoroji, *Poverty and Un-British Rule in India*, 40–1.

[125] 'Indian Expenditure Report of the Royal Commission', 609.

[126] Curzon, *Speeches by Lord Curzon of Kedleston*, 4:58.

[127] Sharma, *Early Medieval Indian Society*, 16.

5 | Developing Balanced Growth at Home

Indian Economics' development plan aimed to harness progress in the two main sectors of the economy – industry and agriculture. The peasants, factory workers and merchants needed specific policies to aid them in growing their crops, manufacturing their products and selling their goods, respectively. India needed agricultural production of raw materials, industrial production using raw materials and distribution of the finished manufactured products. 'A healthy state of things', wrote Dutt, 'is when a large proportion of a nation are engaged in cultivating the soil, while a fairly large proportion of them are also engaged in industries.'[1] Indian Economics prescribed a balanced growth strategy, seen later in India's post-independence five-year plans, the first of which was implemented by Jawaharlal Nehru (1889–1964) from 1951 to 1956.[2]

Balanced growth is more effective than only progressing, say, a nation's industrial sector because the sectors of the economy are interdependent (see Chapter 3). Due to the interdependence, argued Ranade, 'the interplay of those three-fold activities makes a Nation thrive'.[3] The agricultural, industrial and trading sectors all had to flourish to harness progress. According to Ranade, the theory of natural liberty put forward by the English philosophers Thomas Hobbes (1588–1679) and John Locke (1632–1704) wrongly assumed that all wealth was produced only by human labour, giving agriculture more importance than manufacturers in the economy. In the nineteenth century, agricultural work remained predominantly labour intensive, while machines played a large part in manufacturing. Fortunately, as Ranade noted, Smith, J. S. Mill and List had

[1] Dutt, *Speeches and Papers on Indian Questions*, 91.
[2] Dasgupta, *A History of Indian Economic Thought*, 90.
[3] Ranade, *Essays on Indian Economics*, 196.

returned to the idea that an economy is best composed of agriculture, manufacturing and commerce.[4]

Balanced growth was necessary for national insurance because it brought self-sufficiency. Given the devastating famines in the last quarter of the nineteenth century (see Chapters 1 and 3), self-sufficiency was a must, especially as the Indian economists realised that Britain was forcing Indian wheat exports even during famine years (see Chapter 4). India needed food sovereignty in case of naturally low yields caused by droughts. Dutt argued that even Britain should be worried about its reliance on food imports.[5] Telang warned against a country being reduced to a single industry since any change in international demand would then threaten disaster. Balanced growth was a way to hedge against risks.[6] India thus needed policies that harnessed progress in the agricultural and industrial sectors.

Agricultural Policies

The peasants started making their struggles heard at the end of the nineteenth century, with riots breaking out in several parts of India. In the Pabna district in eastern Bengal, for instance, the Occupancy Act X of 1859 meant that peasants could not acquire occupancy rights, while landlords forcefully collected rents. In 1873, an Agrarian League was formed, supported by Dutt and Banerjea. Peasants refused to pay rents and the movement spread across the eastern Bengali districts. The imperial government eventually answered the peasants' demands with the Bengal Tenancy Act of 1885, which granted enhanced occupancy rights. The Indian economists, notably Dutt, who witnessed rural dislocation and distress first-hand proposed several policies to make the peasants better off.

Re-implement the Village Community Structure

Peasants were struggling and discontent because, according to Dutt, their internal self-sufficient village structure was crumbling. This structure had helped insulate Indian peasants throughout history from changing foreign rulers and corrupt governments (see Chapter 3) and

[4] Ibid., 14–17, 20–1.   [5] Dutt, *Speeches and Papers on Indian Questions*, 89–90.
[6] Telang, *Selected Writings and Speeches*, 36–7.

most importantly from high and changing taxes. Dutt claimed that the village community structure should be brought back, as it was more conducive to progress than the centralised structure of the imperial administration: 'A wise Government tries to foster and improve, not to sweep aside, the ancient institutions of a country, when they are consistent with modern progress.'[7] The imperial land reform, argued Dutt, to centralise the judicial and executive powers was regressive because it was destroying the progressive, ancient, self-contained villages.[8] Ranade argued that over-centralisation of rural communities was not conducive to progress.[9] In his lecture on the Dutch imperial system in Java, he contended that the 'Joint Responsibility System in the villages' had led to progress unlike the British land system before the Dutch had regained power over Java in 1816 (see Chapter 3).[10]

Debates on village communities in India can be situated within a wider and earlier discourse on the lack of progressive characteristics in pre-imperialised India with Metcalfe, Munro and Elphinstone (see Chapter 1). The debate was split into two rival schools: the first wanted to invest in the cultivating classes, with the peasantry either as individuals or as village communities, and the second wanted to promote landlord rights or some native aristocracy. The *Fifth Report* of 1812, a British investigation into village communities written primarily by supporters of the *ryotwari* (peasant) system, Mark Wilks and Munro, proved especially authoritative in determining how rent should be decided and who should collect it. Munro was able to implement the *ryotwari* experiment in 1820 with the support of utilitarian reformers. His success challenged Lord Cornwallis and the Permanent Settlement of Bengal (1793), which had given property rights to the *zamindari* to create large estates in the British mode. Munro's *ryotwari* model gave cultivators the property rights and stayed in effect until the Indian Mutiny of 1857–8.[11]

The mutiny reignited the debate, especially following the publication of Maine's *Village-Communities in the East and West*, which concluded that private property emerged out of communal property.

[7] Dutt, *The Economic History of India under Early British Rule*, 1:151.
[8] Ibid., 1:xx, 120, 352, 387–8; Dutt, *Speeches and Papers on Indian Questions*, 72; Dutt, *England and India*, 129; Dutt, *Indian Famines*, 43.
[9] Ranade, *Essays on Indian Economics*, 231–61.   [10] Ibid., 75–6.
[11] Gupta, *Life and Work of Romesh Chunder Dutt*, 331–3; Mantena, *Alibis of Empire*, 12–142.

The change did not lie in who should own the land – cultivators or landlords; Maine argued that both schools of thought were correct. Rather, it led imperial officials to discard the idea that India had had private property rights. Instead, they adopted Maine's view that the country had a communal mode of land ownership and was thus not yet ready for private property rights (see Chapter 1).[12]

Dutt's perspective, on the other hand, was different. He identified reasons why village communities were more progressive than the British land system. Contrary to Maine's assertion that there were no private property rights in pre-imperialised India, Dutt concluded that they existed but were structured differently in India than in Britain. In the Indian village communities, the land belonged to the nation, not to a certain privileged landlord class, which meant that the tenants paid either their share of produce to the community or rent to the tax collectors, who then passed on a share to the government. Dutt favoured the Indian structure of private property rights because it prevented a strong landlord class from accruing too much wealth.[13]

Dutt's idea here seems similar to that of the commons, first proposed by the British economist William Forster Lloyd (1794–1852). Lloyd found that common land tended to be overused,[14] leading Garrett Hardin (1915–2003) to coin the expression 'the tragedy of the commons' a century later.[15] However, that was not Dutt's argument. He found the Indian system, in which *zamindars* could not exploit their tenants, more equitable. In the Indian system, instead of landlords there were tax collectors, who would not only collect taxes but also maintain peace and order. According to Dutt, tax collectors had the incentive to keep peace because collecting taxes was easier during peaceful periods, whereas kings often had the incentive to wage war to accrue more territory. Kings had the incentive to divide their nation because it made it easier to rule – British rule in India being an example.[16] To Dutt, then, common land was not problematic like Lloyd, Hardin and later economists theorised. The common ownership of land in India meant greater equality and that peace was more easily kept.

---

[12] Maine, *Village-Communities in the East and West*, 131.
[13] Dutt, *Speeches and Papers on Indian Questions*, 71, 91.
[14] Lloyd, *Two Lectures on the Checks to Population*.
[15] Hardin, 'The Tragedy of the Commons'.
[16] MacDonald, *Awakening of India*, 159; *British Rule in India: Condemned by the British Themselves*, 49–50, 67.

Moreover, the system Dutt was describing was different from the commons of Lloyd and Hardin. The land in India, which was owned by the nation, was cultivated by one family. It was not a common in the sense of Lloyd or Hardin, who took a grazing field as an example where several farmers grazed their flocks. The risk of abuse that Lloyd and Hardin found with the common ownership was not observed by Dutt in his studies of Indian peasants who cultivated a small plot of land only used by them and their family.

Another advantage of the self-contained village structure was in how it protected peasants from excessive interference from, at times destructive, foreign rulers. The protection meant that taxes stayed at affordable rates. The village community structure, asserted Dutt, was a policy fit for any civilised nation because it let its citizens profit from its own industries 'instead of paralysing their industries by an uncertain and increasing State demand'.[17] Throughout much of imperial India, the structure had been destroyed, leading to extortionate tax rates. Under the imperial land system, tax collectors were paid insufficient salaries, and this often meant that they would ask for higher taxes from tenants to earn enough money for themselves. Moreover, tax collectors were able to charge higher rates because the excessively centralised imperial structure made enforcing a particular tax rate difficult.[18]

Whereas the British generally ruled with as little contact with their subjects as possible, the Mughal imperial officers, when the village community structure had been in place, had moved around India to affirm their presence.[19] The British lack of contact with the population they ruled meant that taxes were often set with little knowledge of the peasants' conditions and yields. Dutt argued that if the British had kept the village community structure, in which those who collected the taxes lived close to the tenants, then the taxes would never have become too high. Dutt's arguments for preserving the village community structure show how he adapted existing ideas to the Indian context. 'Ancient institutions', argued Dutt, that were 'consistent with modern progress' should be kept.[20] Ranade explicitly made that argument in his lecture on the Dutch imperial system. Rulers, whether foreign or not, needed to

---

[17] Dutt, *The Economic History of India under Early British Rule*, 1:94.
[18] Ibid., 1:124.   [19] Wilson, *India Conquered*, 17.
[20] Dutt, *The Economic History of India under Early British Rule*, 1:151.

adapt their policies to local conditions.[21] The Indian economists pushed for progress that was modern yet Indian.[22]

Reduce Land Tax

Lowering land taxes was the most important agricultural policy in Indian Economics. Dutt spent much of his time arguing that lower taxes would solve most of India's problems, including famines, poverty, and capital and investment scarcity. According to Dutt, land taxes in Britain were between 5 and 20 per cent from 1698 to 1798, compared to 90 per cent in Bengal and 80 per cent in northern India between 1793 and 1822. He claimed that the British collected an annual tax revenue of £2,680,000 in India thirty years later, while the last Mughal ruler had only collected £817,533 in the final year of his reign.[23] While the Indian taxpayer, Banerjea recorded, paid 'eight per cent upon an average income per head of 27 Rs a year', the British taxpayer paid 'eight per cent upon an average income per head of £33 a year'.[24] Naoroji wrote:

While a tonne may not be any burden to an elephant, a few pounds will crush a child; that the English nation may, from its average income of £30 a head, be able to pay £2 10s. per head, while, to the Indian nation, 6s. out of 40s. may be quite unbearable and crushing.[25]

British figures agreed that the tax incidence was higher in India than in Britain. Sir William Hunter, a member of the Indian Civil Service, and John Briggs (1785–1875), a British East India Company officer, both agreed that Indians were paying a higher rate than the British. The tax should thus be reduced.[26] Under British rule, tax had increased due to the weakening of the rupee against the pound.[27] The high taxes led to rural indebtedness as peasants were forced to borrow from moneylenders.[28] 'In fact', wrote Iyer, the peasant 'borrows because he is poor, but

---

[21] Ranade, *Essays on Indian Economics*, 70–104.
[22] Ganguli, *Indian Economic Thought*, 85.
[23] Dutt, *England and India*, 134; Dutt, *Indian Famines*, 1–18; Dutt, *The Economic History of India under Early British Rule*, 1:ix, 436–7.
[24] Banerjea, *Speeches and Writings*, 41.
[25] Naoroji, *Poverty and Un-British Rule in India*, 60.
[26] MacDonald, *Awakening of India*, 159; *British Rule in India: Condemned by the British Themselves*, 49–50, 62, 67.
[27] Iyer, *Some Economic Aspects of British Rule in India*, 38–46.
[28] Dutt, *Speeches and Papers on Indian Questions*, 99.

not because he is an extravagant spendthrift'.[29] There was a general lack of savings that exacerbated starvation during famines and prevented peasants from investing in the equipment that would enable them to adopt more efficient agricultural techniques.[30]

Dutt blamed the heavy taxes for transferring to the government all profits from land. Cultivators were left with little incentive or capacity to invest in better techniques, as well as an inability to save for drought years. Dutt observed that in countries where cultivators could keep a share of their profits, there were higher rates of capital accumulation. Aside from discouraging farmers from investing in new machinery, variable tax rates also prevented capital accumulation. Dutt noted that even Adam Smith and Lord Minto, the viceroy and governor-general of India (1905–10), condemned variable land tax.[31] Tax needed to be permanently fixed, as it had been in Bengal under the Permanent Settlement, because if cultivators were certain to keep some of their profits, they were more likely to invest in improving their cultivating techniques to the benefit of the entire society – that is, leading to 'progressive improvement'.[32] Lower and fixed taxes would therefore reduce overall poverty and the death toll from famines and harness progress through increased agricultural productivity and capital accumulation (see Chapter 4).[33]

In the north-western Baroda state, Dutt had gained significant popularity, as exemplified by the fact that Maharaja Sayajirao Gaekwad II, his family and his staff would call him 'Babu Dewan' as a mark of personal respect. Once he retired from the Indian Civil Service in 1897, Dutt was offered the chance to serve as revenue minister of Baroda, which he did from 1904 to 1907 (after serving as a lecturer in Indian history at University College London from 1898 to 1903 and completing his most famous volumes on Indian economic history). In the last two years of his life, 1907–9, he served as Baroda's Diwan. During his years as revenue minister, he implemented 'a model state in India, not only in education and methods of administration ... but also in the

---

[29] Iyer, *Some Economic Aspects of British Rule in India*, 13.

[30] Dutt, *Speeches and Papers on Indian Questions*, 99; Iyer, *Some Economic Aspects of British Rule in India*, 279; Dutt, *Indian Famines*, 118–19.

[31] Dutt, *Indian Famines*, 4, 68; Dutt, *The Economic History of India under Early British Rule*, 1:xi, 183, 368, 374.

[32] Dutt, *Indian Famines*, 149.

[33] Iyer and Banerjea made similar arguments. Iyer, *Some Economic Aspects of British Rule in India*, 38–45, 68; Banerjea, *Speeches and Writings*, 293.

propensity of agricultural people, the briskness of trade and enterprise, the starting of new mills and industries'.[34] Dutt wished to lower, equalise and get rid of some of the excessive land taxes to incentivise the manufacturing of textile products. He abolished some taxes on professions that were mostly paid by the poor and substituted them with an income tax to be paid by the higher classes and imperial officials. In other words, he brought in a progressive tax system. In small towns, he abolished some custom duties on goods brought into the district, lowering the number of customs officers needed. The reduction of duties led to a higher tax revenue because it expanded business and trade.[35]

There was a correlation between high taxes and peasant indebtedness. Increasing agricultural productivity was difficult when peasants were forced to borrow from moneylenders (*bania*) to pay their taxes when their yields were insufficient. In the Bombay Deccan in the nineteenth century, peasants (*ryots*) were forced to borrow money to pay their taxes, so that they could eat from their own harvest. To make matters worse, the moneylenders would buy the crop at half the market price but lend money at interest rates of 38 per cent. The peasants with the necessary capital accumulation to invest in new agricultural equipment were thus instead incentivised to go into moneylending, as it yielded higher profits. There were at least 500,000 moneylenders in India by the 1870s, acting as intermediaries between the village, Calcutta and Manchester. By 1895, a fifth of the land in the Bombay Deccan was owned by moneylenders, mostly indigenous Brahmins and Marwaris from Rajasthan, despite the laws passed by the imperial administration to prevent land transfers. Some historians of South Asia therefore conclude that the high, inflexible taxes prohibited capitalist farming and commercial agriculture from developing.[36]

In the mid-1870s, peasants in some parts of the Poona and Ahmednagar districts in Maharashtra organised a social boycott movement against moneylenders. The Deccan Riots, as they were called, began at Supa, a market village in Bhimthadi Taluka of Poona district, on 12 May 1874. A peasant mob attacked the houses and shops of

---

[34] Quoted in Gupta, *Life and Work of Romesh Chunder Dutt*, 402.
[35] Ibid., 407.
[36] Bagchi, *Private Investment in India*, 6, 38; Davis, *Late Victorian Holocausts*, 64, 67; Guha, 'Raw Cotton of Western India', 27, 70; Washbrook, 'Progress and Problems', 20; Chaudhary et al., *A New Economic History of Colonial India*, 102.

Gujarati moneylenders, seeking to destroy bonds and decrees. Peasants refused to buy from moneylenders' shops or till their land. In 1879, the government attempted to appease the peasants with the Deccan Agriculturists Relief Act, which ensured that farmers could not be arrested and imprisoned if they could not pay their debts.[37]

Dutt and his peers were not against the idea of taxes in principle. It was rather that the imperial setting meant that paying taxes in India was different from paying taxes in Britain. Indian taxes were sent to Britain, meaning they were not spent on the required education and infrastructure that would spur industrialisation and progress in India. The tax incidence in the Mughal Empire had therefore been better for two reasons. One, the Mughal taxes were spent in India, and two, they had not been too high.[38] Again, the Indian economists judged a policy according to its relevance to India at a particular time.

The rioting peasants, along with the complaints from Dutt and other Indian civil servants, resulted in the Marquess of Ripon, the viceroy of India (1880–4), implementing a compromise: the government could only increase land taxes if prices increased. Yet, once the marquess left his post in 1884, the arrangement was vetoed in Whitehall, 'and a nation of agriculturalists was once more subjected to that *uncertainty* in the state demand which is fatal for successful agriculture'.[39] Dutt complained that after this the taxes started to fluctuate again.

There were internal conflicts among the Indian economists, nevertheless, on the need to expose extortionate land taxes. Naoroji disagreed with Dutt and Wacha that lowering taxes would be the major solution to India's economic problems. In two letter exchanges, Naoroji argued, contrary to Dutt and Wacha, that emphasising high taxes would effectively draw attention away from 'the *real evil* at bottom' and 'the bleeding', referring to the resource drain (see Chapter 4).[40] In an exchange between Wacha and Naoroji in August

---

[37] Chaudhary et al., *A New Economic History of Colonial India*, 102, 108; Washbrook, 'The Indian Economy and the British Empire', 55; Roy, *Economic History of India*, 105.

[38] Dutt, *Indian Famines*, 3, 100; Dutt, *The Economic History of India in the Victorian Age*, 2: xii, 68; Naoroji, *Essays, Speeches, Addresses and Writings*; Naoroji, *Dadabhai Naoroji Correspondence: Correspondence with D.E. Wacha, 30-3-1895 to 5-4-1917*; Naoroji, *Dadabhai Naoroji: Selected Private Papers*.

[39] Gupta, *Life and Work of Romesh Chunder Dutt*, 332 (emphasis in original).

[40] Naoroji, *Dadabhai Naoroji: Selected Private Papers*, 164–5 (emphasis in original).

1900, Wacha drew Naoroji's attention to several articles on the drain published in the *Amrita Bazar Patrika* that year and Dutt's work on excessive land taxes and expressed the hope that these would raise awareness among the publication's numerous readers of the excessive and destructive nature of India's resource drain. Naoroji wrote back that they should refrain from highlighting such a minor issue as land taxes.[41]

In July 1903, Naoroji wrote to Dutt, urging him to realise that self-rule was the more effective and vital solution to India's economic problems. While Dutt insisted that taxes were a large part of the resource drain, Naoroji considered the war repayments forced upon the imperial administration in India to pay for the border disputes (see Chapter 1), and loss of profits from railways and exports much more damaging, and thus held that these should be the only issues discussed with the imperial administration. Dutt reminded Naoroji that in the Parliamentary Committee on Indian Finance (or Fawcett Committee) in 1873, Naoroji had argued for lower taxes. Yet Naoroji wrote to Dutt that he had since changed his mind.[42] 'The drain', declared Naoroji, 'is the *Cause* and *only* cause – all others are consequences, direct and indirect'.[43] Lowering taxes would only tackle the symptoms of India's economic problems. Stopping the drain, which would only happen if and when they gained self-government, was the only appropriate remedy.[44]

A supporter of the Indian economists, A. O. Hume, the founder of the Indian National Congress, had a different opinion about the land taxes. Hume published a pamphlet in 1879 in which he argued that land taxes had remained stable for the last seventy years under the Permanent Settlement in Bengal, despite the period seeing increased productivity, domestic trade and so on. In contrast to Dutt's argument, Hume contended that the constant land taxes had resulted in a loss of 4 or 5 million to Bengali state revenue. If the Permanent Settlement in Bengal had fixed the land tax for twenty to thirty years, instead of indefinitely, which was customary in other areas of India, Bengal would

---

[41] Naoroji, *Dadabhai Naoroji Correspondence: Correspondence with D. E. Wacha, 30-3-1895 to 5-4-1917*, 2:649, 756–7, 766–7.

[42] Naoroji, *Dadabhai Naoroji: Selected Private Papers*, 157, 164–7.

[43] Ibid., 168 (emphasis in original).

[44] Naoroji, *Dadabhai Naoroji Correspondence: Correspondence with D. E. Wacha, 30-3-1895 to 5-4-1917*, 2: 836.

have been in a better position to afford, among other things, famine relief. Taxes, according to Hume, could have enriched Indians rather than impoverishing them.[45]

Improve Irrigation

Ranade, Iyer and Joshi all wrote of how some areas suffered from poor quality of land due to inadequate irrigation.[46] Dutt advocated for more public investment in irrigation and a return to the Mughal policy of building canals and reservoirs, because India was particularly vulnerable to droughts.[47] Joshi proposed that Indians should be trained and subsidised to build irrigation infrastructure.[48] Irrigation needed to be funded by the state.

Irrigation systems had started to collapse by the 1830s and 1840s because the imperial administration failed to invest in the restoration and maintenance of irrigation works damaged during the period of British conquests. Most rural inhabitants had access only to wells, which proved insufficient. The imperial budget prioritised railway construction over effective irrigation systems.[49] Meanwhile, deindustrialisation had increased land use, which meant average land quality had decreased. Only some regions could effectively gain from the growth in exports, resulting in low efficiency gains. While cash crop regions experienced high growth and showed signs of increased standards of living, other regions with poor irrigation were hindered from

---

[45] Hume, *Agricultural Reform in India*, 3–5.
    Similarly, Maddison has more recently argued that higher land revenue would have actually been beneficial to India, enabling the government to spend more on development, as was done in Japan. Maddison, *Class Structure and Economic Growth*, 49.

[46] Joshi, *Writings and Speeches of G. V. Joshi*; Gokhale, *Speeches and Writings of Gopal Krishna Gokhale*, 19; Iyer, *Some Economic Aspects of British Rule in India*, 218; Ranade, *Essays on Indian Economics*, 66.

[47] Dutt, *Speeches and Papers on Indian Questions*, 21, 49, 77–8, 98; Dutt, *Indian Famines*, 86.
    For instance, Dutt wrote about the success of the Kaveri-Pak, an old Hindu reservoir. Dutt, *The Economic History of India under Early British Rule*, 1:199.

[48] Joshi, *Writings and Speeches of G. V. Joshi*, 821.

[49] Some scholars suggest that railways were favoured over irrigation because railways had higher profits, but not enough research has been done. Chaudhary et al., *A New Economic History of Colonial India*, 109–10.

producing higher yields and from expanding their industrial or commercial agriculture (see Chapters 1 and 4).

Some improvement was seen in the 1850s and 1860s when the British set up a centralised system to construct irrigation works. For instance, inundation and perennial canals were built between 1870 and 1920, meaning more land had access to water. Nine canals were built, collectively irrigating over 10 million more acres. Yet the projects were confined to Punjab, Sind, coastal Andhra and western Uttar Pradesh, and the centralisation of irrigation construction destroyed existing systems of water harvesting.[50] Considering the severe famines that came in the late nineteenth century, Ranade, Iyer and Joshi worried that irrigation infrastructure was not sufficient and the state needed to invest and maintain irrigation to avoid poverty and suffering from future droughts.

Industrial Policies

India had been experiencing a gradual decline in its previously large and successful textile industry. Most of the Indian economists spent the majority of their time worrying about deindustrialisation. A dwindling industrial sector meant that the economy became ever more reliant on its agricultural sector to produce sufficient wealth for its population (see Chapter 4). Well-targeted policies were needed to reignite industrialisation.

Mobilise Capital

The major hindrance to industrialisation was the lack of capital mobilised for industry. Ranade proposed a more efficient credit system that would assemble the reservoirs of 'unused Capital' and channel it into industrial enterprises.[51] From his survey of Hungarian, Austrian, French, Italian, Belgian and Swiss credit facilities, Ranade found that ease of access to loans was critical for progress, as it enabled capital-scarce classes to invest. Like the Saint-Simonians of the early nineteenth century, he theorised the need for a central authority to control the

---

[50] Whitcombe, *Agrarian Conditions in Northern India*, 1:64–97; Hardiman, 'The Politics of Water in Colonial India', 113, 115; D'Souza, 'Water in British India'; Mosse, 'Rule and Representation'; Agarwal and Narain, *Dying Wisdom*.
[51] Ranade, *Essays on Indian Economics*, 43.

banks, which he claimed would decrease interest rates in the same way they had in the Austro-Hungarian Boden Credit Institute (1863), France's Credit Foncier (1852) and Italy's Central Credit Foncier (1862).[52] Ranade spoke of how France's and Switzerland's improved credit organisation led to an increase in mortgage advances.[53] He wrote:

> An immense waste of power, time, and money is thus saved to him [the saver, capitalist or depositor] and to the debtor. The business becomes specialised, like any other business, all risks are avoided, and all the benefits of a secure investment and cheap loan are secured to the monied and needy classes.[54]

In other words, assigning certain people and institutions as intermediaries between capitalists and workers would lead to more efficiency.

However, Naoroji, Telang, Joshi, Prithwis Chandra Ray and Iyer all disagreed with Ranade because India had insufficient levels of domestic capital.[55] Naoroji rejected the idea that Indians were hoarders of silver – an argument used by the British to claim that the Indians were at fault for their own aggregate poverty.[56] Naoroji agreed that hoarding was regressive because spending could spur industrial progress, but he challenged the existence of idle capital, as described by the British and Ranade. A better credit system was clearly progressive and necessary for both Ranade and Naoroji, but Naoroji saw this as an end goal and not applicable to a capital-scarce India.

[52] Ibid., 42; Boianovsky, 'Bombay Provincial Banking Enquiry Committee 1929–1930'; Saint-Simon, *The Doctrine of Saint-Simon*, 201–3.
  According to the Saint-Simonian doctrine, the banking sector would be controlled by a central bank and the country's wealth should be held by the banks and not by capitalists. Such a banking system would be more progressive for four reasons. Firstly, the banks' higher sense of morality, which made them realise that lending money is necessary for national well-being, meant more loans would be offered. Secondly, bankers would be more aware of the credit risks, leading to higher returns, more equity (because idle funds would be redistributed from the capitalists to the entrepreneurs) and ultimately greater societal wealth overall. Thirdly, bankers could charge lower interest rates than capitalists because they had lower default rates and thus higher returns overall. Finally, there would be an overall increase in investments made, facilitating industrial growth and making instruments of production more available to workers. General wealth and competition would increase, leading to better conditions for workers.
[53] Ranade, *Essays on Indian Economics*, 49–59, 61, 63.   [54] Ibid., 63.
[55] Telang, 'Free Trade and Protection from an Indian Point of View', 68–9; Joshi, *Writings and Speeches of G. V. Joshi*, 684; Ray, *The Poverty Problem in India*, 39; Iyer, *Some Economic Aspects of British Rule in India*, 104, 329.
[56] Naoroji, *Poverty and Un-British Rule in India*, 92; Naoroji, 'Bimentallism'.

The Indian economists also disagreed on whether to mobilise foreign or Indian capital. In the second half of the nineteenth century, the amount of foreign and British capital flowing into India increased rapidly; British investments rose by £110 million between 1870 and 1885, equal to the total increase between 1885 and 1913.[57] At first, it was invested in railways, canals, mines, plantations and modern industries that seemed to be promoting the desired industrialisation. Some argued that India was capital-scarce and needed the foreign capital. A small group of Indian economists, including Ranade and Banerjea, were pro-foreign capital, claiming that India lacked so much capital that they could not afford to turn any down.[58] Many British economists, statesmen and officials agreed that foreign capital was a major lever for progress; J. S. Mill and Alfred Marshall (1842–1924) both made the case in their economic treatises,[59] and in 1899 the then viceroy, Lord Curzon, declared that foreign capital was 'a *sine qua non* to the national advancement of India'.[60]

Yet foreign capital seemed to dominate India's industrial scene, which dissuaded such optimism. Naoroji used an analogy to explain why having so much foreign capital was bad for India. In a section entitled 'Drain through Investment of English Capital', he wrote that India's condition was

like that of a child to which a fond parent gives a sweet, but to which, in its exhausted condition, the very sweet acts like poison, and as a *foreign substance* by irritating the weak stomach makes it throw out more, and causes greater exhaustion. In India's present condition, the very sweets of every other nation appear to act on it as poison.[61]

According to Naoroji, foreign investments facilitated the penetration of international goods into the Indian market, especially from Britain, rather than developing domestic industry – creating unwanted competition for Indian industrial sectors. Iyer argued that India should borrow capital at home to increase productive investments.[62] Some imperial officials, like George Birdwood (1832–1917), supported the

---

[57] Bloomfield, 'Patterns of Fluctuation in International Investment before 1914', 10.
[58] Cited in Chandra, *The Rise and Growth of Economic Nationalism in India*, 71, 93–4; Mukherjee et al., *India's Struggle for Independence*, 70.
[59] Mill, *Principles of Political Economy*; Marshall, *Principles of Economics*.
[60] Quoted in Mukherjee et al., *India's Struggle for Independence*, 70.
[61] Naoroji, *Poverty and Un-British Rule in India*, 54 (emphasis in original).
[62] Iyer, *Some Economic Aspects of British Rule in India*, 291–5.

anti-foreign capital sentiment.[63] Birdwood urged India to develop its own industries by revitalising its handicrafts sector, limiting exploitative foreign investment and foreign control of existing industries.

Naoroji and Joshi argued that the profits earned from foreign capital investments were then repatriated abroad and consequently could not be reinvested or spent in India.[64] And if capital did not remain in India, there would be less progress, if any at all. British capital was particularly damaging because it perpetuated imperial control, hindering India's ability to achieve eventual independence. For instance, an article in *The Hindu* reported that 'where foreign capital has been sunk in a country, the administration of that country becomes at once the concern of the bondholders'.[65] It continued:

[When] the influence of foreign capitalists in the land is allowed to increase, then adieu to all chances of success of the Indian National Congress whose voice will be drowned in the tremendous uproar of 'the empire in danger' that will surely be raised by the foreign capitalists.[66]

Foreign capital had regressive characteristics in an imperial territory like India. Balanced growth required reinvestment back into the industrial sectors. And British profits in India returned to Britain.

The disagreement among the Indian economists could stem from regional differences. Western textile, primarily cotton, industries were financed by Indian capital, while the eastern, primarily jute, production was predominantly British-owned.[67] The relative success of Indian-owned manufacturers in the west can explain Ranade's optimism, as in evidence in a speech he gave at the 1893 Industrial Conference in Poona, in his home state of Maharashtra. There, Ranade used official statistics from the imperial administration to show that India's manufacturing sector had been showing signs of 'revival' since 1875.[68] However, the

---

[63] Birdwood contributed articles to newspapers like the *Dawn* and published several books.

[64] Naoroji, *Essays, Speeches, Addresses and Writings*, 39–41, 102, 104, 106, 124–7, 130–1, 135; Joshi, *Writings and Speeches of G. V. Joshi*, 652, 757.

[65] *The Hindu*, 23 September 1889.   [66] Ibid.

[67] Kumar and Desai, *The Cambridge Economic History of India*, 2:568; Gupta, 'The Rise of Modern Industry in Colonial India', 67–79; Davis and Huttenback, *Mammon and the Pursuit of Empire*; Roy, *Economic History of India, 1857–1947*; Bagchi, *Private Investment in India*; Dutt, *Conflicting Tendencies in Indian Economic Thought*; Ray, *Entrepreneurship and Industry in India*.

[68] Ranade, *Essays on Indian Economics*, 110.

Indian-owned industry in the east was not doing as well as Ranade's home region in the west.[69]

India could refuse foreign capital, argued Naoroji and Dutt, because India was only capital-scarce due to the British drain of its resources. It was the drain, not India's inherent lack of capital, that created considerable 'disorder'.[70] 'The merit or good of every remedy will depend upon and be tested by its efficacy in stopping this deplorable drain.'[71] Reducing the drain would increase much-needed capital in India. Naoroji and Dutt proposed several ways to reduce the drain, including decreasing public debt and public expenditure. Challenging the extortionate military expenditure in India, Dutt cited a speech given by Henry Campbell-Bannerman (1836–1908), British prime minister from 1905 to 1908, in which he admitted that Britain used Indian troops for its imperial wars in China and South Africa at India's expense. Dutt also held that the imperial administration should follow Queen Victoria's Royal Proclamation of 1858 that guaranteed the employment of natives in the administration, which would allow more salaries and pensions to stay in India. He calculated that almost £14 million was spent on European salaries and pensions for higher positions, compared to only just over £3 million on Indian employees.[72] Employing Indians would thus lower both the drain and public debt.

---

[69] Recent research confirms the barriers to Indian capital and the over-reliance on foreign capital in some sectors. Gopalan Balachandran finds that the Indian credit market developed a dual character: On one side, investments from European traders and London-based banks handled international trade outside of India; on the other, Indian investors were restricted to domestic and regional trade through the closure of the Indian silver mints in 1893, which undermined the power of India's indigenous banking sector and kept India's reserves in London. Indigenous banks remained mere intermediaries for British banks, which were located only in ports and urban areas. Further, Indian banks were often discriminated against with stricter regulation than the European branches, causing inefficiencies. Balachandran, 'Colonial India and the World Economy', 90–1. Moreover, scholars such as Eswar Prasad et al. find that less reliance on foreign capital is associated with higher growth. Prasad, Rajan and Subramanian, 'Foreign Capital and Economic Growth'. Maddison's extensive statistical study finds similar results with regard to the dramatic increase in India's economic growth post-independence. Maddison, 'The Historical Origins of Indian Poverty'.

[70] Dutt, *The Economic History of India under Early British Rule*, 1:49; Naoroji, *Poverty and Un-British Rule in India*, 219.

[71] Naoroji, *Poverty and Un-British Rule in India*, 201.

[72] Dutt included figures on the total money spent on salaries and pensions higher than Rs 1,000 per year (£100, according to Dutt) from 1892, representing the salaries and pensions of higher positions, which, based on the figures were

Impose Tariffs

The next industrial policy concerned trade. The Indian economists debated free trade and protectionism, like many other nineteenth-century economists. The first and probably most representative paper on free trade versus protectionism in India was Telang's 'Free Trade and Protection from an Indian Point of View'. Telang argued that free trade could only exist fairly between equals, as echoed by especially Naoroji, Iyer and Ray.[73] It was protecting the advanced nation's industries – especially Britain's. Similarly, Dutt cited Telang and List to illustrate that

while British Political Economists professed the principles of free trade from the latter end of the eighteenth century, the British Nation declined to adopt them till they had crushed the Manufacturing Power of India, and reared their own Manufacturing Power.[74]

The global trade flows subsequently shifted, making India an exporter of raw materials instead of industrial goods. Iyer included an appendix in his book with protectionist policy examples from Germany and America to show that economic policy was created by national needs and not by economic theories.[75] The lack of duties on imports meant that India had been made into an exporter of raw materials, dependent on European and North American demand. Ranade, Telang and Dutt prescribed temporary protection for infant industries because they could not compete with British industry with free trade policies.

Dutt, Ranade, Joshi and Telang realised that Britain had only implemented free trade once its industries could compete on the international market. Dutt quoted List to make the point that, in reality,

[h]ad [the imperial rulers] sanctioned the free importation into England of Indian cotton and silk goods, the English cotton and silk manufactories must, of necessity, soon come to a stand. India had not only the advantage of

        divided between European and Indian officials, were reserved almost exclusively
        to Europeans. Dutt, *Indian Famines*, 13–14; Dutt, *Papers Regarding the Land
        Revenue System of British India*, 1–23.
[73] Telang, 'Free Trade and Protection from an Indian Point of View', 68–9;
        Naoroji, *Poverty and Un-British Rule in India*, 62; Iyer, *Some Economic
        Aspects of British Rule in India*, 103, 350; Ranade, *Essays on Indian
        Economics*, 748–9; Ray, *The Poverty Problem in India*, 66, 70–3; Dutt,
        Speeches and Papers on Indian Questions, 123–4, 302; List, *National System of
        Political Economy*, 42.
[74] Dutt, *Speeches and Papers on Indian Questions*, 123.
[75] Iyer, *Some Economic Aspects of British Rule in India*, 104–47.

cheaper labour and raw material, but also the experience, the skill, and the practice of centuries. The effect of these advantages could not fail to tell under a system of free competition.[76]

Free trade could be effective in certain circumstances but by no means all. Dutt turned to List, believing a German would be less biased than a Briton. List, argued Dutt, helped explain how free trade was not used to boost Indian industrial growth, like the imperial officials claimed. Free trade was instead used by the British to make India subservient and for the British to gain commercial supremacy. Then once the power loom was adopted in India, the British put excise duties on their goods.[77]

At the same time, Manchester lobbyists imposed restrictions and tariffs on Indian manufacturers (e.g., forcing Indian textile workers to work in the British-owned factories), and the imperial administration forced grain to be exported even during famines.[78] India was both drained of its much-needed raw materials (both food items and raw materials needed for industrial production) and exposed to international competition, leading to the deindustrialisation of its textile industry.[79] 'Our rulers', wrote Banerjea,

profess to be free traders. It is free trade when it suits their interests. It is protection when it benefits them. You know we export large quantities of our gold and silver manufactured articles to England. They levy a heavy duty upon the importation of those articles into England. Is this free trade? I think not.[80]

Not only had Britain practised protection in the past, but their intellectuals advocated for protection in certain situations. As Telang, Ranade, Iyer and Banerjea pointed out, even the dominant discourse from the

---

[76] Dutt, *Speeches and Papers on Indian Questions*, 123.

[77] Ibid., 43–6, 123–4; Dutt, *The Economic History of India under Early British Rule*, 1:viii, 300.

[78] Awasthi, *History and Development of Railways in India*; Bhandari, *Indian Railways*; Ghosh, *Railways in India*; Bogart and Chaudhary, 'Railways in Colonial India', 37–8; Washbrook, 'The Indian Economy and the British Empire', 57; Bagchi, *Private Investment in India*.

[79] Ranade, *Essays on Indian Economics*, 97; Dutt, *Speeches and Papers on Indian Questions*, 49; Stokes, *The English Utilitarians and India*; Sarkar, *Modern India*; Bagchi, 'De-industrialization in India in the Nineteenth Century'; Hurd, 'A Huge Railway System But No Sustained Economic Development'.

[80] Banerjea, *Speeches and Writings*, 43.

likes of J. S. Mill recommended assistance to private enterprise under particular circumstances in colonies that had unequal trade relations with their foreign rulers and for infant industries.[81]

Ranade, Dutt and Telang were especially critical of the theory, often quoted in the imperial discourse from Classical Political Economy, that protection was counterproductive. They rejected the idea that protection would mean less freedom and fewer benefits for Indian consumers and entrepreneurs. Telang showed that it would channel more capital into productive enterprises, rather than that capital being hoarded.[82] Ranade and Dutt argued for subsidies, low-interest government loans for industrial production, and tariffs. According to them, American political economists such as Hamilton and Carey understood the need for protective tariffs to bring about self-sufficient economic development.[83] American Political Economy, asserted Dutt, rightfully assigned appropriate trade policies according to the political context and level of progress and whether the policy was conducive to progress.[84] Much like List and the German Customs Union, Ranade, Dutt and Telang argued that once India's productive powers had increased, its lower classes could consume more.[85] The German example proved it: British exports to Germany increased between 1834 and 1844 despite the tariffs. In fact, they were 50 per cent higher than those to their next six biggest trading partners – Russia, France, Portugal, Spain, Italy and the United States – put together.[86]

In chapter twenty-six of the *National System of Political Economy*, List attacked the 'reigning school', which he regarded as being Smith and French economists like Jean-Baptiste Say (1767–1832). The school, wrote List, argued that import duties on manufactures have an 'unfavourable influence' on agricultural production and thus also on industrial production.[87] 'The school', continued

---

81   Ranade, *Essays on Indian Economics*, 27, 98; Telang, 'Free Trade and
     Protection from an Indian Point of View'; Banerjea, *Speeches and Writings*, 44;
     Iyer, *Some Economic Aspects of British Rule in India*, app. 1.
82   Telang, 'Free Trade and Protection from an Indian Point of View', 14–24.
83   Ranade, *Essays on Indian Economics*, 19–21; Dutt, *The Economic History of
     India under Early British Rule*, 1:300; Dutt, *Speeches and Papers on Indian
     Questions*, 123–4.
84   Dutt, *Speeches and Papers on Indian Questions*, 127.
85   List, *National System of Political Economy*, 458–75.
86   Wendler, *Friedrich List*, 245.
87   List, *National System of Political Economy*, 394.

List, 'does not perceive that, under the operation of unrestricted competition with nations of experience in manufactures, a country not much advanced, however real its vocation for that industry, cannot without protection attain to a complete manufacturing development and to entire independence.'[88] Here was a theory and practice that the Indian economists could agree with. With its shrinking textile industry and the slow mechanisation of its industrial sector, India in the late nineteenth century could not compete with cheap British textile exports.

Furthermore, like List, some of the Indian economists were convinced that the population would be willing to pay the short-term cost of protection in exchange for the long-term gains of lower prices, higher wages and employment, self-sufficiency and more balanced growth. Iyer theorised that a large country like India with rich resources would do well under protection.[89] The benefits, argued Banerjea, Telang and Ray, made the initial cost worthwhile.[90]

Following the same reasoning, Japan also implemented protectionist policies in the last few decades of the nineteenth century. Yukichi Fukuzawa (1835–1901) argued that free trade was used by foreigners to render Japan poor and dependent, as a producer of only primary products. Japanese merchants needed to fight the war of trade against foreign countries and needed help from their government to do so. After the 1868 Meiji Restoration, the government attempted to industrialise Japan through policies such as subsidies, government contracts, the establishment of state-owned companies, acquisition of foreign skills and technology, and development of infrastructure. The policies were successful in rapidly accelerating Japan's industrialisation, and that arguably enabled Japan to defeat China in the First Sino-Japanese War (1894–5) and Russia in the Russo-Japanese War (1904–5).[91]

However, List's prescription of protecting infant industries did not find agreement with all of the Indian economists. Unlike Dutt, Ranade and Iyer, Naoroji never cited List. Naoroji was for free trade, even in his time, if the drain was reduced:

---

[88] Ibid., 394.   [89] Iyer, *Some Economic Aspects of British Rule in India*, 107–8.
[90] Telang, 'Free Trade and Protection from an Indian Point of View', 10–11; Ray, *The Poverty Problem in India*, 136–7; Iyer, *Some Economic Aspects of British Rule in India*, 244–5; Banerjea, *Speeches and Writings*, 44.
[91] Helleiner, 'Globalising the Classical Foundations of IPE Thought', 983–4; Helleiner, *The Neomercantilists*; Sugiyama, *Enlightenment and Beyond*, 49.

Let India have its present drain brought within reasonable limits, and India will be quite prepared for any free trade. With a pressure of taxation nearly double in proportion to that of England, from an income of one-fifteenth, and an exhaustive drain besides, we are asked to compete with England in free trade?[92]

India, argued Naoroji, would not need protection if it were self-governed. He was adamant that if the drain was reduced, India would prosper under free trade.

There were several other proponents of free trade in India and other non-European regions, including merchants from Calcutta, Bengal, who were frustrated at the British East India Company's monopoly in the early nineteenth century. A successful merchant, Dwarkanath Tagore, advocated 'free trade and the abolition of Company monopoly' in the 1830s.[93] Some Bengali liberal reformers argued for the emancipation of the rational self-interested individual following Classical Political Economy's ideal of free exchange, which was denied in the more traditional principles of custom and discrimination found in social conservatism. The Ottoman Empire followed free trade after the implementation of the Anglo-Ottoman Commercial Treaty of 1838, increasing their raw material cotton production, thanks to growing trade with Britain. In Egypt, support for economic liberalism, especially free trade, persisted until well into the 1870s.

Similarly, in early nineteenth-century Latin America there was a liberal critique of the mercantilist trade restrictions under Spanish and Portuguese imperial rule. It is significant that Smith's work was first translated into Portuguese in Brazil in 1811–12 and not in Portugal itself. Likewise it was a Mexican official who financed the first two editions of the most widely circulated Spanish liberal political economy textbook in the nineteenth century. The volume, which denounced mercantilism and argued for Ricardian economics and free trade, was disseminated across Central America by José Cecilio del Valle, a leader of the Central American independence movement.

The disagreements within Indian Economics regarding free trade, along with these global examples, show that free trade was

---

[92] Naoroji, *Poverty and Un-British Rule in India*, 62.
[93] Quoted in Sartori, *Bengal in Global Concept History*, 90.

simultaneously contested and followed across the non-European world in the nineteenth century.[94]

Train the Industrial Workforce

Factory owners needed a technically trained workforce. In Ranade's inaugural address at the first Industrial Conference, held in Poona in 1890, he argued that technical education was part of industrial progress.[95] Ranade observed, through texts from German and American political economists such as List, Hamilton and Carey, that technical education had spurred large-scale industry in Germany, America and Japan. All the Indian economists were pro-European education in India (see Chapter 2) because it provided the most advanced technical training. Ranade wrote:

The superior skill of the Foreigner must be availed of freely by importing it from other Countries, till we train up our own people for the work, first, in Technical Institutes here and in Foreign Countries, and further, in the far more practical disciplines of Factories and Mills at work.[96]

Most Indian newspapers and political leaders prescribed more access to technical education.[97] It was a subject discussed at the Indian National Congress in 1887, 1888, 1891, 1892 and every year from 1894 to 1904. Gokhale spoke of it during the Welby Commission meetings. When Dutt was revenue minister of Baroda in western India, he implemented policies to encourage industry and manufacturing by reducing taxes, removing some taxes and establishing a progressive tax system, as well as getting rid of local custom duties. In his second report, for 1904–5, he noted that the encouragement had helped because 'students were sent to Europe, America, and Japan, to learn mechanical engineering and other useful

[94] Helleiner, 'Globalising the Classical Foundations of IPE Thought', 980; Helleiner, *The Neomercantilists*; Al-Sayyid Marsot, *Egypt in the Reign of Muhammad Ali*, 250–2; Almenar, 'The Reception and Dissemination of Ricardo's Ideas in Spain'; Cardoso, 'The Diffusion of Ricardo and Classical Political Economy in Portugal', 138; Özveren, 'Turkey and the Turkic Linguistic Zone', 348.

[95] Joshi and Iyer made similar arguments. Ranade, *Essays on Indian Economics*, 13–208; Joshi, *Writings and Speeches of G. V. Joshi*, 688–9, 801–2; Iyer, 'Railways in India', 190; Iyer, *Some Economic Aspects of British Rule in India*, 266.

[96] Ranade, *Essays on Indian Economics*, 207.

[97] See, for example, *The Hindu*, 13 June 1904.

professions'.[98] Naoroji, Joshi and Banerjea theorised that technical education was also acquired through experience. The imperial administration therefore needed to employ Indians as engineers and managers so that they could learn the trade.[99] This came only in the twentieth century.

Foster a Middle Class

Industrialisation could only be sustained with a middle class, as they would ensure there was sufficient demand for manufactured goods. The middle class was assumed to grow in urban areas, where it would create the necessary demand for growing industries. Nevertheless, urbanisation and industrialisation could generate either a large upper or middle class. Ranade claimed that if industries primarily catered to the upper classes, their dependents tended to disappear and employment would decrease. The industries that catered to the upper classes included oil-pressing, weavers and spinners of cotton and wool, potters, grocers, peddlers, woodcarvers, embroiderers, dealers in gold and silver, jewellers, priests, musicians, the military and carriers of all kinds.

On the other hand, if policies incentivised the growth of industries catering to the middle classes, more jobs would be created, thanks to the increased demand for goods. The industries that catered to the middle classes included metals, leather, book dealers, paper, stationery, hardware, lamps, matches, timber, stone-workers, watchmakers, railways, cart-makers, butchers, liquor-sellers, jaggery- and sugar-makers, contractors, builders, lawyers, doctors, engineers and factory workers. Ranade was vague as to how India could expand those more progressive industries, only stipulating that

[w]hat we have to do in each case is to learn by organised co-operation to compete with the Foreigner, and take in as much as Raw Produce from

---

[98] Gupta, *Life and Work of Romesh Chunder Dutt*, 415.

[99] Naoroji, *Poverty and Un-British Rule in India*, 54, 194, 228; Naoroji, *Essays, Speeches, Addresses and Writings*, 133, 240, 382, 397–8; Joshi, *Writings and Speeches of G. V. Joshi*, 699–700, 756, 779; Ray, *The Poverty Problem in India*, 322, 324; Banerjea, *Speeches and Writings*, 369–71.

    For secondary literature on the employment of Indian engineers and managers and the general optimism towards European education as a way to industrialise, see, for example, Maddison, *Class Structure and Economic Growth*, chap. 3; Ramnath, *The Birth of an Indian Profession*; Seth, *Subject Lessons*.

Abroad as we need, and work it up here, and to send in place of our Exports of Raw Produce, the same quantities in less bulky, but more valuable, forms, after they have undergone the operation of Art manipulation, and afforded occupation to our Industrial Classes.[100]

Ranade advocated for organised cooperation to divert investments and energy towards those industries catering to middle-class consumption.

Fostering a middle, as opposed to an upper, class would also mean lower levels of inequality. Less inequality was better for progress because, as argued by Ranade and Dutt, only preserving the wealth among a select few was inefficient in that it meant lower capital investment.[101] A large middle class meant that capital was more evenly distributed, offering a greater potential aggregate demand, which would sustain industrial growth. The solution to sustaining such growth was therefore industrialisation that catered to the needs of the middle class.

Construct Efficient Communications

Industrialisation could also only be sustained with efficient communications.[102] Naoroji pointed out that India lacked canals, which could increase communication capabilities.[103] Communication would stimulate production, argued Joshi, and the distribution of goods and wealth across the country.[104] According to Naoroji, the lack of communication channels meant goods produced near the seaports were exported not due to higher prices offered by foreigners but because the produce would perish otherwise.[105]

It is clear from nineteenth-century maps that railways were first built from ports. Until 1870 they primarily catered to the port cities of Calcutta, Bombay, Madras, Beypore and Negapatam. It was only by 1909 that there were several more railways connecting more parts of inland India. Until late into the nineteenth century, the railways thus

[100] Ranade, *Essays on Indian Economics*, 126–7.
       Following this passage, Ranade made a list of the higher-value-added products that could be produced by India.
[101] Ranade, *Essays on Indian Economics*, 24, 98–9, 242; Dutt, *Indian Famines*, 59.
[102] Ranade, *Essays on Indian Economics*, 94–5; Dutt, *Speeches and Papers on Indian Questions*, 76; Naoroji, *Essays, Speeches, Addresses and Writings*, 123.
[103] Naoroji, *Essays, Speeches, Addresses and Writings*, 122.
[104] Joshi, *Writings and Speeches of G. V. Joshi*, 123.
[105] Naoroji, *Poverty and Un-British Rule in India*, 63.

promoted the exporting of raw materials and the importing of foreign goods (primarily British manufactures), rather than the distribution of goods within India. Naoroji may have favoured canals over railways because they would increase ease of communication and transport in inland areas, unlike the railways, which catered almost exclusively to seaports until at least 1870.

As with irrigation infrastructure, the investment in communications needed to be public because existing British private investments in railways were not harnessing progress. Instead of profits being reinvested in the development of further railway infrastructure in India, they were being sent back to Britain.[106] The British capitalists that financed the railways were assured a 5 per cent return on investment – money which, the Indian economists claimed, would leave India.[107] If railways were publicly funded, they would be progressive in India. A natural benefit, according to Naoroji, was that they would ignite growth in the production of higher-value-added goods and more advanced technology, enabling Indian industries to compete with imported goods.[108] Moreover, Ranade believed the state to be more capable of catering to the interests of the nation, meaning that publicly owned railways and canals would further domestic interests and harness progress.[109]

The Indian economists' debates and demands around agricultural, commercial and industrial progress came at a turbulent time. By the early 1890s, the imperial administration had a deficit of Rs 35 million, or £2 million, due partly to investments in large public works but primarily as a result of military spending in Burma and the fall in the value of the rupee. The retiring viceroy, Lord Lansdowne, wrote to the secretary of state, Lord Kimberley, in January 1894, asserting that the only way to reduce the deficit might be to reimpose import duties. India essentially had had no tariffs since 1882. Lord Kimberley refused, knowing that he would lose votes from capitalists and employees in the Lancashire textile industry if he did otherwise.

A month later, the next viceroy, Lord Elgin, quickly realised that the imperial administration had already put together a proposal to impose

[106] Dutt, *Speeches and Papers on Indian Questions*, 76.
[107] Hurd and Kerr, 'Railway Management and Railway Employees in Imperial India', 103.
[108] Naoroji, *Poverty and Un-British Rule in India*, 193.
[109] Ranade, *Religious and Social Reform*, 104.

duties on Indian imports to deal with the deficit. They proposed cutting expenditure on the famine grants and imposing a 5 per cent import duty on all goods. Pressure from Britain pushed Lord Elgin, however, to exempt cotton imports from duties. In particular, pressure came from voters in Lancashire that threatened the sitting government's mandate. Owners of textile companies argued that the tariffs produced an unfair competition in the global market and gave a form of protection to Indian cotton producers. Lancashire capitalists had much to worry about. In the last decade, their exports to big markets in Japan and China had stagnated, while Indian exports to the same had doubled. Britain had also been suffering from the Long Depression since 1873 (see Chapter 1).

Several groups in India burst out in anger against the exemption of cotton goods from the import duty. Six chambers of commerce, three trade associations and eight other public associations registered strong protests. They all asserted that it was unjust on the part of the government to impose tax on kerosene, consumed mostly by the poor, and to completely exempt the cotton goods which could bring substantial revenue. Several newspapers attacked the bill, writing that the government was a puppet of the British and that their attempts to deal with the deficit were inadequate. Military spending was the real issue, not the famine relief grants, which the imperial administration had also proposed reducing. Most importantly, the potential revenue from the cotton import duties was much needed.[110]

In response to the agitation from both Britain and India, an imperial administrator, James Westland (1842–1903), was sent to Bombay in July 1894 to gather data on the large cotton industry there. He wanted to understand what competition the industry posed to Lancashire. His conclusion was that most of the production was in coarser cotton and thus did not compete with the finer cotton produced in England. At the end of 1894, the government of India then proposed that import duties should be imposed on all goods at 5 per cent and, to counteract the protective measures, that there should be an excise duty on all Indian cotton products with a count greater than twenty – the finer cotton that competed with what was produced in Manchester. The final bill, passed in 1896, exempted yarn imports from any tariffs and put a 3.5 per cent duty

---

[110] Malhotra, 'The Internal Administration of Lord Elgin in India', 81–2.

on all woven goods (with some exemptions).[111] In the words of one commentator, it was a 'tax on Indian cloth and free Lancashire yarn'.[112] India's deficit remained.

To make matters worse, India was suffering a country-wide famine (see Chapter 1). Banerjea spoke at the 1896 Indian National Congress of death rates three or four times higher than in 1894.[113] For Indian anti-imperial officers, including the Indian economists, the controversy demonstrated how their politics was governed by British interests, with little or no regard for the financial health of India's government, economy or future prosperity. The unfair tariffs gave the national movement a concrete example of how the imperial government helped British industry to destroy India's prospects for industrialisation.[114]

What followed was a widespread movement to encourage Indian industrialisation. Already in 1894, several newspapers had been urging Indians to boycott foreign products. The boycott quickly expanded to encouraging people to buy local products, a movement later known as Swadeshi. *Swa* means self and *des* nation, together meaning indigenous or home-grown. In particular, the movement encouraged Indians to buy *khaddar* – cloth made of yarn spun by villagers using the *charkha*, a spinning wheel.[115] One of the key moments of Swadeshi was Banerjea's address at the Indian National Congress in 1906. He described how the

infant Hercules was growing in strength and stature, laying for itself a rich reserve fund of energy which was to qualify it for its marvellous achievements in the future. The infant Hercules has now grown into years of adolescence and his labours have just begun.[116]

Swadeshi was not, as its opponents argued, a political movement masked in economic concerns. Banerjea declared it an 'all-comprehensive movement' for their 'growing community'.[117] What is more, it had helped Indians to gather around a goal that was easy to understand:

[W]hen you tell him that the wealth of the country must be kept in the country, that it is to his advantage that it should be so kept and that for this

---

[111] Helm, 'The Indian Duties on Cotton Goods', 110–14.
[112] Malhotra, 'The Internal Administration of Lord Elgin in India', 123.
[113] Banerjea, *Speeches and Writings*, 36.
[114] Klein, 'English Free Traders and Indian Tariffs'.
[115] Goswami, *Producing India*, 197.
[116] Banerjea, 'Speeches by Babu Surendranath Banerjea', 436.   [117] Ibid., 436.

purpose he must purchase country-made articles in preference to foreign articles, he opens wide his eyes and ears and drinks in the lesson.[118]

Swadeshi was based on the foundations of Ranade and Dutt's past stage of civilisation, a golden age before the British invaded and drained all India's wealth (see Chapter 3). Industrialisation would change all that. Some decades later, in the first half of the twentieth century, researchers argued that the efforts of that encouragement to buy local and boycott foreign goods launched the little industrialisation that Bengal experienced.[119] Here was a blueprint for an India-wide industrialisation.

---

[118] Ibid., 437.
[119] Dutt, *Conflicting Tendencies in Indian Economic Thought*, 215.

6 | A Global Win–Win Model for Development[1]

The short-term domestic plan for development in Indian Economics was balanced growth (see Chapter 5); the global development plan in the long run was universal industrialisation and free trade. The widely accepted plan for development in the nineteenth century was broadly based on Ricardo's comparative advantage model, which prescribed industrialisation for western Europe and condemned the rest of the world to producing raw materials. The international division of labour, argued Ranade, would not, like the model theorised, bring Indians the highest level of progress.

Indian Economics envisaged a positive-sum game of global development where an industrialised Asia would not outcompete the already industrialised western Europe. Industrialisation in India would bring higher standards of living and increase global aggregate demand, leading people to buy more goods from Britain and other industrialised countries. Universal industrialisation would, argued the Indian economists, be win–win for the world economy.

While this may seem like an obvious and unsurprising argument today, the common narrative in the late nineteenth century, dominated by imperialism and the firm adoption of the comparative advantage model, did not foresee or prescribe industrialisation outside of western Europe and at best North America. Industrialisation was especially not envisaged for imperial territories like India. India was behind with a history of supposed backwardness (see Chapter 2). List even denied the possibility of Asian progress: 'Hence the entire dissolution of the Asiatic nationalities appears to be inevitable.'[2] The Indian economists, however, produced a rereading of their history that enabled them to envision a different future. India could progress like western Europe (see Chapter 3).

---

[1] This chapter is based on a published article, Bach, 'A Win-Win Model of Development'.
[2] List, *National System of Political Economy*, 126–7, 419.

A Dependent Imperial Economy

Indian Economics' rereading of Indian history enabled theirs to be reconceptualised as a dependent imperial economy. Ranade was the first to put the status of a colonised territory in such terms.[3] Imperialism meant that Britain was extracting Indian resources. The Indian economists understood that the drain caused them to be poorer, spurred deindustrialisation and resigned them to an agricultural economy (see Chapters 3 and 4). A poor India depended on capital, industrial goods and public administration skills from advanced countries. Imperialism, according to the Indian economists, had created a 'dependence' on Britain.[4] The term 'dependence' was not new in this period – 'Dependencies' was commonly used to label territories under the rule of the British Crown[5] – but what the Indian economists added to the idea was consequences. Rather than bringing prosperity, as the civilising mission promised, dependence on the Empire impoverished the Indians.

There were plenty of ways to prove the negative consequences of that dependence. From the very start of the British presence in India, the British East India Company discouraged the manufacturing of silk. As Dutt recorded, '[i]n their general letter to Bengal, dated seventeenth March 1769, the Company desired that the manufacture of raw silk should be encouraged in Bengal, and that of manufactured silk fabrics should be discouraged'.[6] They also forced weavers to work in company factories. As the Indian economy deindustrialised, the British imposed free trade, hindering any chance of reindustrialisation, as India's infant textile industry could not compete with cheap, mechanised textile imports from Manchester (see Chapters 1 and 3). Free trade thus served as a barrier to India becoming internationally competitive again (see Chapter 5). Moreover, Britain's investment in port and railway capacity was not, as they argued, bringing progress to India. On the contrary, the railways increased foreign competition for India's manufacturing industry, as British goods became easier to deliver throughout the subcontinent. India's banking sector was also under foreign control, which damaged Indians' ability to borrow to invest.[7] The Empire had pushed Indian society down to a lower stage of civilisation.

---

[3] Goswami, *Producing India*, 211–2.
[4] Ranade, *Essays on Indian Economics*, 24.   [5] Ibid., 14.
[6] Dutt, *The Economic History of India under Early British Rule*, 1:45.
[7] Ranade, *Essays on Indian Economics*, 93, 199.

Rejecting the International Division of Labour

The Indian economists' rereading of their history and the uncovering of dependence enabled Indian Economics to reimagine the global political economy of development. Universal industrialisation would bring greater growth to the world because it would increase capital accumulation and in turn boost global aggregate demand. Previous theories associated with Classical Political Economy, such as Ricardo's, were Eurocentric, argued Ranade, justifying a zero-sum-game world-view that enriched Europe while impoverishing everyone else.

The comparative advantage model, first formulated by Robert Torrens (1780–1864), was further developed by Ricardo and J. S. Mill.[8] According to the model, western Europe had a comparative advantage in manufacturing, given they had industrialised and the rest of the world remained reliant on agricultural production. Ricardo himself wrote that

England may be so circumstanced, that to produce the cloth may require the labour of 100 men for one year; and if she attempted to make the wine, it might require the labour of 120 men for the same time. England would therefore find it in her interest to import wine, and purchase it by the exportation of cloth.[9]

According to the model, each country had its own comparative advantage. Ranade claimed that the model advocated an international division of labour that kept the rich countries rich and the poor countries poor:

[If] economically backward races must submit to such an arrangement, ... it is fairly open to question whether there is any such inevitable necessity which justifies a line of separation, which has a tendency to accentuate natural deficiencies, and make them a source of permanent weakness.[10]

India's comparative advantage in producing raw cotton, for example, would not yield the benefits Ricardo's model predicted because profits from the prescribed industrial production in western Europe were much higher than the profits from the agricultural production prescribed in the rest of the world. Agricultural production had diminishing returns,

---

[8] Mill, *Principles of Political Economy*, 387–90.
[9] Ricardo, *Principles of Political Economy and Taxation*, 135.
[10] Ranade, *Essays on Indian Economics*, 26.

which kept India capital-scarce and hindered industrialisation – at least in the near future. Ranade used a comparative analysis of imperial policies in British North America, Dutch Java and India to prove his point. He observed how British North America and Dutch Java had harnessed progress through industrialisation. In Java, the Dutch had advanced payments for produce to increase wealth in the biggest sector, agriculture. The higher level of wealth had stimulated industry by increasing capital accumulation (see Chapter 4).[11] India, on the other hand, could not industrialise due to regressive imperial policies such as free trade and excessive taxes.[12]

The industrial sector was more vital for progress than the agricultural sector. Balanced growth, or progress in both the agricultural and industrial, was necessary (see Chapter 5), but industrialisation was a priority over agricultural commercialisation. Agricultural production had decreasing returns. Farmers could never accumulate capital to harness nationwide progress. They produced low-value-added goods, and their profits decreased over time. Industrialists, on the other hand, could accumulate enough capital thanks to increasing returns on their investments. They produced higher-value-added goods that tended to increase their profits over time. The higher profits could fuel further investments to push further industrialisation. There were differences in value between industrial goods,[13] but a country with a larger production of manufactured exports had higher standards of living overall. Industrialisation had to be the number one priority of any nation, whatever its comparative advantage at any point in time.

More trade was not necessarily a sign of progress. Only more high-value-added exchange meant progress. A dominance of raw material exports, asserted Ranade and Naoroji, meant that India was both exporting low-value-added goods and losing out on its former skills in, and wealth from, manufacturing.[14] Throughout the nineteenth century, wrote Dutt, the European 'factories demanded raw produce, the people of India provided the raw produce, forgot their ancient manufacturing skill, lost the profits of manufacture'.[15] India, asserted Ranade, was

---

[11] Ibid., 70–104.   [12] Ibid., 27, 338, 388, 411.
[13] Reinert, 'The Role of the State in Economic Growth'; Reinert, Ghosh and Kattel, *Handbook of Alternative Theories of Economic Development*.
[14] Ranade, *Essays on Indian Economics*, 197; Naoroji, *Essays, Speeches, Addresses and Writings*, 113.
[15] Dutt, *The Economic History of India under Early British Rule*, 1:276.

being clothed by 'distant masters' when it had previously clothed itself (see Chapter 3).[16] The Indian economists theorised that growing trade did not necessarily lead to increasing national wealth, and higher national wealth was necessary because it increased domestic demand, which was essential for sustained industrialisation (see Chapter 5).

Industrialisation, according to Ranade, was both 'inevitable' and desirable.[17] Early civilisation, observed Dutt, exploited raw materials to progress. In modern times, civilisation industrialised through innovations like steam, which harnessed progress.[18] Policies not fostering industrialisation could 'only be temporary palliatives'.[19] India needed 'industrial salvation'.[20] Industrialisation was also more vital than agricultural progress because India's industrial sector was much too small.

The arguments here expose the Eurocentrism of models like comparative advantage because, in practice, it only produces progress for those regions that have a comparative advantage in industrial goods. And those regions were in western Europe, according to the nineteenth-century economists of western Europe. The Indian economists, however, did not accept this global division. They could not imagine a world without an industrialised Britain, but they could imagine a global economy where both Britain and India were industrialised. The Indian economists desired an industrialised India, justified through their rereading of global history. India had previously been progressive, with a large manufacturing sector, and therefore had the potential to reach the same level of industrialisation as Britain (see Chapter 3). Indian Economics' idea of development is therefore more universal than those associated with scholars such as Ricardo or List, advocating the same end goal for all.[21]

A Win–Win Model of Development

Indian Economics theorised that India's return to being a global exporter of manufactured goods would lead to perpetual global progress. Dutt and Naoroji claimed that the whole world, including

[16] Ranade, *Essays on Indian Economics*, 198.   [17] Ibid., 126.

[18] Dutt, *The Economic History of India in the Victorian Age*, 2:1; Dutt, *Speeches and Papers on Indian Questions*, 90.

[19] Ranade, *Essays on Indian Economics*, 126–7, 130–1.

[20] Dutt, *Speeches and Papers on Indian Questions*, 90.

[21] Recent studies also find Ricardo's model Eurocentric. Mehmet, *Westernizing the Third World*; Chang, *Kicking Away the Ladder*.

Britain, would be worse off if India were forced to wait to industrialise.[22] Indian aggregate demand would increase if India could restore its industrial powerhouse by lowering the drain on its resources and boosting investment in industry. Naoroji cited J. S. Mill to argue that foreign exchange brought progress: if India demanded more foreign goods, Britain and other nations would have even greater trade potential.[23] As Mill wrote,

It may be said without exaggeration that the great extent and rapid increase of international trade, in being the principal guarantee of the peace of the world, is the great permanent security for the uninterrupted progress of the ideas, the institutions, and the character of the human race.[24]

Naoroji would have read Mill's book because it was one of the set texts when he was studying at Elphinstone College (see Chapter 2). Britain's trade, reasoned Naoroji, would increase by £250 million if each member of the Indian population could buy British goods worth only £1 per year.[25] More trade meant the potential for higher capital accumulation and further investment in industrial growth. Universal industrialisation, unlike the comparative advantage model, was a win–win model of development.

Indian Economics' win–win model hangs on the need for sufficient domestic demand to sustain industrialisation domestically and internationally. The rural state of India's economy in the late nineteenth century meant a low aggregate demand because peasants tended to only produce enough for their subsistence needs. Demand needed to be restructured, but there was little chance of that happening under imperial rule (see Chapter 1). At the end of the nineteenth century, Indian Economics had already realised the need for greater demand in India.[26]

One solution, argued Naoroji, was to employ more natives in the administration to boost domestic income spent and capital accumulation in India.[27] Naoroji theorised that India's lack of production was

[22] Dutt, *The Economic History of India under Early British Rule*, 1:263; Dutt, *Speeches and Papers on Indian Questions*, 82; Naoroji, *Essays, Speeches, Addresses and Writings*, 354, 516; Naoroji, *Poverty and Un-British Rule in India*, 125, 216, 338.

[23] Naoroji, *Essays, Speeches, Addresses and Writings*, 101.

[24] Mill, *Principles of Political Economy*, 390.

[25] Naoroji, *Essays, Speeches, Addresses and Writings*, 329.

[26] Washbrook, 'The Indian Economy and the British Empire', 64.

[27] Naoroji, *Poverty and Un-British Rule in India*, 49.

primarily due to insufficient income – including a lack of capital to invest in new production ventures and a lack of domestic demand that would make the investment viable and profitable.[28] Domestic demand could also be developed through increased employment in the industrial sector, which had the potential to employ a larger proportion of the population and would raise average income, thanks to increasing returns – as opposed to the overcrowded and lower-paying agricultural sector, dictated by decreasing returns.

Others had similar ideas in the nineteenth and twentieth centuries. List argued that it would be mutually beneficial for Britain and Germany if the latter industrialised because it would increase German aggregate demand.[29] In the 1920s, Yat-sen Sun argued that European governments should help harness progressive forces in China by injecting foreign capital, technology and expertise into state-owned enterprises to also harness more progress in European capitalist powers.[30] Like the Indian economists, Sun was making an argument for industrialisation outside of Europe in order to increase the global surplus and aggregate demand. Global industrialisation was mutually beneficial for all involved.

The win–win model in Indian Economics dealt only briefly with international competition. How would different regions be affected by competition once there was universal industrialisation and global free trade? There was a need for balanced growth and a diversified economy in case of fluctuating international demand. International competition necessitated a diversified economy. A country also needed a large middle class to maintain the high aggregate demand necessary to sustain industrialisation. The middle class incentivised production to cater to their wants and needs, not the upper classes; the upper classes could not, theorised Ranade, foster enough aggregate demand to sustain industrialisation. Dutt argued for lower taxes for peasants to incentivise them to invest more in efficient technology. More efficient technology would, in turn, increase capital accumulation and, although Dutt did not make it explicit, aggregate demand (see Chapter 5). The Indian economists may have assumed that India would recapture its former dominant and prosperous position in the global market, and, if successful, then India would be the most competitive country in the world.

[28] Naoroji, *Essays, Speeches, Addresses and Writings*, 42–5.
[29] Wendler, *Friedrich List*, 245.
[30] Sun, *The International Development of China*.

Universal Nationalism

The nineteenth-century Indian win–win model of development required a focus on both the national and international spheres. 'Swadeshism', the movement to push Indians to buy local products, wrote Banerjea,

does not exclude foreign ideals or foreign learning or foreign arts and industries, but insists that they shall be assimilated into the national system, be moulded after the national pattern and be incorporated into the life of the nation.[31]

The win–win model was a strategy that adapted to the national context, while simultaneously incorporating universal forces coming from abroad. And yet historically there is a tendency for economists and political economists to view nationalist and universalist perspectives as opposites.

Economic nationalism was and is generally seen to place the nation as the unit of focus (the nation's needs, interests and identity) and, consequently, sees the possibility of each having a different path for progress and development.[32] Universalism, or the argument for universalist processes of development, places the individual at the centre of society, instead of the nation, and assumes that all countries progress through the same stages (see Chapters 3 and 4). Economic nationalism aims to maximise the nation's well-being through policies that harness progressive forces within its specific domestic economy. Universalism seeks to allow each person to reach their full potential, most efficiently achieved through individual liberty and with the same recipe for development regardless of context. The Indian win–win model cast the dominant distinction between the national and universal aside. Instead, it combined the two.

Indian Economics theorised a continuous flow of positive and negative societal change that spreads unevenly around the world. During some periods, Asia was progressive, and during others, Europe was. As described by Dutt,

The influence of civilisation will spread, and the light of progress which has been lighted in Southern Europe will yet spread to the shores of the Ganges.

---

[31] Banerjea, 'Speeches by Babu Surendranath Banerjea', 441.
[32] List, *National System of Political Economy*; Helleiner, 'Economic Nationalism as a Challenge to Economic Liberalism?'.

And if the science and learning, the sympathy and example of modern Europe helps us to regain in some measure a national consciousness and life, Europe will have rendered back to modern India that kindly help and brotherly service which India rendered to Europe in ancient days – in religion, science, and civilisation.[33]

In late nineteenth-century India, imperialism was not bringing about sufficient progress. Indian Economics therefore conceptualised an idea of development that adopted universal criteria of progress and development within a nationalist perspective that could cater to the local, historical, social, economic and political context (see Chapter 5).

As imperial subjects, the Indian economists were at the margins of international debates attempting to persuade their foreign rulers to implement a development plan that would harness much-needed progress. The Indian economists were known as the Early Nationalists, being the first group to fight openly for the country's independence. Their idea of development was nationalist in that its content was about India, but also universalist in that it identified certain general criteria that brought about societal change in many different places. As Eric Helleiner argues, economic nationalism is an ideology that is defined by its nationalist content, rather than a form of realism or protectionism, and can be related to several different institutional frameworks, including liberal economic policies more commonly associated with universalist economic thinking such as Classical Political Economy.[34]

The Indian economists mixed nationalists and universalist thinkers. To prove the necessity of balanced growth, Ranade cited List and Smith (see Chapter 5).[35] Economists tend to treat these thinkers' perspectives as contradictory. Either the economy is analysed through different phases of historical development such as Smith's stages of civilisation, most often associated with Classical Political Economy, or the system is analysed from a nationalist perspective such as in List's thought, which brings out the specificities of individual economies in each period.[36] Ranade merged nationalist and universalist views on development by using theories from both approaches.

---

[33] Dutt, *A History of Civilization in Ancient India*, 500.
[34] Helleiner, 'Economic Nationalism as a Challenge to Economic Liberalism?', 307–8; Helleiner, *The Contested World Economy*.
[35] Ranade, *Essays on Indian Economics*, 14–17, 20–1.
[36] Reinert, Ghosh and Kattel, *Handbook of Alternative Theories of Economic Development*, 213.

The nationalist approach was not constructed in a vacuum. Both List and Indian Economics were addressing followers of Classical Political Economy and universalism. They needed to use the same discursive practices to increase their chances of being listened to and understood, and persuading others to change their minds. New discourses are created through dialogue, whether verbally or between texts, by referring to past discourses – usually those dominant. While the distinction between nationalist and universal may be the accepted thinking today, its origins seem to be more nuanced.

There is a canonisation of ideas and discursive practices. This 'is the mechanism through which classic status is ascribed to a text, but then the meaning of the text is increasingly simplified in the interests of producing an easy-to-grasp reading of its allegedly core claims'.[37] Simplification often entails distortion. List, according to Matthew Watson, is found to be more in line with classical liberal ideas associated with Classical Political Economy and particularly Smith.[38] Helleiner has often found that List was misread.[39] In List, nationalism is not only about policies. Economic nationalism is a nationalist ontology, rather than prescriptive policies like tariffs. Yet much of the twentieth-century literature missed the nationalist ontology that the nation is at the centre of any economy, only seeing economic nationalism in terms of non-liberal policies like tariff barriers.[40]

By the late nineteenth century, economic nationalism had become tied to the mercantilist doctrines of the seventeenth and eighteenth centuries unlike List's or Indian Economics' definition of economic nationalism.[41] Economic nationalism is not like mercantilism: mercantilism is statist, centred on the ruling body; economic nationalism focuses on the role of national identities and nationalism in shaping

---

[37] Brown, 'Metanarratives and Economic Discourse', 84.

[38] Watson, 'Friedrich List's Adam Smith Historiography and the Contested Origins of Development Theory', 463–4; Harlen, 'A Reappraisal of Classical Economic Nationalism and Economic Liberalism'.

[39] Helleiner, 'Economic Nationalism as a Challenge to Economic Liberalism?'.
Matthew Watson argues that the misreading of Smith in List's work can be traced back to the interpretations of John Ramsay McCulloch, Dugald Stewart, Georg Sartorius and the Earl of Lauderdale. Ranade cited McCulloch. Watson, 'Friedrich List's Adam Smith Historiography and the Contested Origins of Development Theory', 463–4.

[40] Helleiner, 'Economic Nationalism as a Challenge to Economic Liberalism?', 235.

[41] Gilpin, *Global Political Economy*, 14.

economic policy. Thinkers can be identified as nationalist, therefore, without having to impose certain economic policies. Policies need to be examined separately.[42] The Neomercantilists, such as Ranade, as Helleiner shows, were all nationalists, but, more precisely, they believed in strategic trade protectionism and other types of government economic activism to boost state wealth and power, unlike, for example, Naoroji.[43] Both Ranade and Naoroji were nationalists; while Ranade pushed for protection, Naoroji pushed for free trade.

Context dictates policy prescriptions. A government's goal, argued Naoroji, was to improve the 'material and moral condition of India' by implementing measures that increased the well-being of its people.[44] Dutt's emphasis on self-sufficiency, national insurance and rural development reflected how he prioritised the Indian people. In case of disaster, whether a famine or invasion, India needed the capacity to meet its immediate needs, such as by having a sufficient food supply. 'The function of the State', declared Ranade, was

to help those influences which tend to secure National Progress through the several stages of growth, and adopt Free Trade or Protection as circumstances may require. In this view Free Trade may be good for a Country like England, but not for America and Germany.[45]

The Indian economists' fight for protection for their nation's infant industries reflects a focus on local needs (see Chapter 5).

The attention to regional context is found in List, whose epistemology Ranade and Dutt adopted. List thought you could gain understanding through observation and experience. In translator G. A. Matile's preface to List's *National System of Political Economy*, he cites List as saying, 'My destiny having afterwards again conducted me to the United States, I left behind all my books; they would but lead me astray there.'[46] List held that the world was best understood by the farmers and people, not by some learned cosmopolitans. Similarly, G. A. Matile, the first to translate *National System of Political Economy* into English, asserted

---

[42] Shulman, 'Nationalist Sources of International Economic Integration'; Abdelal, *National Purpose in the World Economy*; Crane, 'Economic Nationalism: Bringing the Nation Back In'; Pickel, 'Explaining, and Explaining with, Economic Nationalism'.

[43] Helleiner, *The Neomercantilists*, 4.

[44] Naoroji, *Essays, Speeches, Addresses and Writings*, 502.

[45] Ranade, *Essays on Indian Economics*, 20.

[46] List, *National System of Political Economy*, xi.

that List's theory was 'at least not founded upon a vague cosmopolitism, but on the nature of things, upon the lessons of history and the wants of nations'.[47] Matile claimed that List's 'system offers a mode of reconciling theory with practices'.[48] Like List, the Indian economists attempted to explain societal change and find an appropriate development plan by reconciling the European theories taught to them with the local and specific practices present in their own country. Most notably, Dutt travelled to the rural areas to observe and interview the peasants, which proved crucial to how he learned about India's most pressing problems (see Chapter 4).

The configuration of economic nationalism in Indian Economics included two elements: the idea that development should be collective and equal, and the long-term goal of a universal society of free trade. It was important for the nation to be prioritised, rather than the individual. Nevertheless, the Indian economists argued that they could not ignore the international context and universal forces that affected every nation. Here is how Indian Economics combined universalism with nationalism, forging their universal nationalism.

Collective and Equal Development

A development plan had to cater to the well-being of the collective and minimise inequality. Collective development was essential because the collective capacity of the state was more effective than the capacity of individuals.[49] Collective development, argued Ranade, 'checked the tendency of individuals to seek immediate gain at the sacrifice of permanent National interests'.[50] 'The State', theorised Ranade, 'was not merely an agency for keeping peace, but ... it was an organisation for securing the progress of the people as widely as possible, and for extending the benefits of the Social Union to all.'[51] The state could and should therefore set up institutions like a judicial system, a schooling system to provide universal education and a postal service. For instance, as the revenue minister of Baroda in the early twentieth century Dutt implemented universal primary education.[52] The state should also pass factory

---

[47] Ibid., xii.   [48] Ibid., xii.   [49] Ranade, *Religious and Social Reform*, 103–4.
[50] Ranade, *Essays on Indian Economics*, 19.   [51] Ibid., 18.
[52] Gupta, *Life and Work of Romesh Chunder Dutt*, 416.

legislation, offer subsidies for railways, and enact policies that would foster commercial development.

As Ranade explained his vision for collective and equal development, he cited Sismondi (see Chapter 2). In the first sentences of Sismondi's pivotal work, published in 1819, he wrote, 'La science du gouvernement se propose, ou doit se proposer pour le but le bonheur des hommes réunis en société.'[53] The state should strive to make the people within its society happy. The legislator, he continued, should help individuals to become as happy as it was possible for them to be, through social organisation and equal participation of all. If a state only made some people happy, then it was at the suffering of others. Sismondi theorised that the state needed to implement unemployment insurance, sickness benefits, a pension scheme, regulated working hours and progressive taxes.[54] The Swiss economist offered Ranade and his peers an argument for what they saw as necessary for dealing with the extreme poverty in India.

There were two central doctrines to Indian Economics' theory of state intervention: first, the state had a right to interfere; and second, communal welfare was more important than industrial interest. Ranade attempted to represent all classes of Indian society, arguing for an 'equitable system of taxation' that would charge those who could afford the tax burden.[55] As revenue minister of Baroda, Dutt implemented a progressive tax system (see Chapter 5). Ranade advocated for a decrease in land and salt taxes, which disproportionately impacted the poorer classes. Moreover, Ranade and Dutt promoted rapid industrialisation through protection (see Chapter 5) because industrial growth would bring about higher wages due to increased demand for manufactured goods, leading to a more equitable distribution of income. Economists, Ranade argued, should not focus on the agent's interests but the collective defence, well-being, social education and discipline – and the agent's duties. Iyer criticised Smith for ignoring the fact that one cultivates sympathy with his or her neighbours, nation and humanity. As a result, he thought it better to follow the economists in the German Historical School and List, who prioritised humanitarian and national interests (see Chapter 2).[56]

---

[53] Sismondi, *Nouveaux principes d'économie politique*, 1:1.   [54] Ibid.
[55] Ranade, *Religious and Social Reform*, 749.
[56] Iyer, *Some Economic Aspects of British Rule in India*, 130–1.

Collective and equal development required India to reunite. The country had been successfully imperialised, according to the Indian economists, due to its inherent disunity. Ranade described how in the seventeenth century the Marathi Confederacy fell apart after its ruler, Shivaji, was replaced and the policies that had united the Maharashtrian state were removed. Without disunity in check, foreigners had been able to conquer India and push it to a lower stage of civilisation (see Chapters 3 and 4). India suffered from internal discords, disorganisation and 'centrifugal' forces that resented discipline and subordination, leaving it 'prey to disorder' and vulnerable to foreign invasion.[57] Naoroji was adamant that the imperial powers were attempting to divide India.[58]

India's many religious and political groups, as well as castes, created a divided nation.[59] Cooperation had been lost,[60] and 'no progress is possible without such co-operation'.[61] In a letter exchange between Wacha and Naoroji, the former worried about the conflicts between Hindus and Muslims, which were 'sure to have an adverse influence on progress'.[62] Dutt said that there were more castes in the late nineteenth century than in ancient times,[63] and Telang argued that caste weakened the chances of uniting India, which was paramount for progress. If the whole society 'levels up' with modern, broader ideas and education,

---

[57] Ranade, *Rise of the Maratha Power*, 24; Ranade, *Select Writings*, 23.

[58] Naoroji, *Dadabhai Naoroji Correspondence: Correspondence with D.E. Wacha, 4-11-1884 to 23-3-1895*, 1:109.

[59] Ranade, *Rise of the Maratha Power*, 24, 29, 58, 92; Ranade, *Religious and Social Reform*, 99–100; Ranade, 'Introduction to the Peishwa's Diaries'; Naoroji, *Essays, Speeches, Addresses and Writings*, 6; Naoroji, *Dadabhai Naoroji Correspondence: Correspondence with D.E. Wacha, 4-11-1884 to 23-3-1895*, 1:336; Naoroji, *Dadabhai Naoroji Correspondence: Correspondence with D.E. Wacha, 30-3-1895 to 5-4-1917*, 2:477; Dutt, *The Peasantry of Bengal*, 8; Dutt, *The Economic History of India in the Victorian Age*, 2:58.

[60] Naoroji, *Dadabhai Naoroji: Selected Private Papers*, 17; Dutt, *England and India*, 14, 40, 118, 154; Dutt, *Indian Famines*, 320; Dutt, *The Economic History of India Under Early British Rule*, 1:324; Dutt, *Speeches and Papers on Indian Questions*, 162.

[61] Ranade, *Religious and Social Reform*, 294.

[62] Naoroji, *Dadabhai Naoroji Correspondence: Correspondence with D.E. Wacha, 4-11-1884 to 23-3-1895*, 1:477; Naoroji, *Dadabhai Naoroji: Selected Private Papers*, 441.

[63] Dutt, *England and India*, 29; Dutt, *The Economic History of India in the Victorian Age*, 2:58, 92.

'caste barriers will break down and vanish away'.[64] But India's rigid societal structure remained.

European nations, wrote Dutt, had had rigid societal structures, but modern civilisation had broken them down and united different classes. Germany had actively dealt with unification, of which Dutt may have been aware, thanks to his travels there (see Chapter 4). List had worried about German disunity, calling for measures that would unite it and produce cooperation. List therefore argued that Germany needed to be a united nation because he saw economic, along with political, unification as vital to the success of a country.[65] Naoroji theorised that one reason for the disunity in India came from the slow diffusion of knowledge due to the multiple languages spoken. While in England, he wrote, 'an idea in the *Times* is known over the whole length and breadth of the land within twenty-four hours, and the whole nation can act as a man'.[66] India needed to unite by making castes less rigid and establishing a common language to build and unite the nation.

A nation could unite and produce collective and equal development through progress. Progressing societies moved from chaos to order (see Chapter 3), and to foster greater order a society should assign a select few the responsibility for establishing it. Each society, prescribed Ranade, needed 'Gurus of the future'. He based his argument on a historical analysis of the Rishi, the pioneers of Indian civilisation in the south that produced a large body of knowledge. These gurus had a 'larger vision' of teaching society to distinguish between progressive and regressive societal forces.[67] At the beginning of the nineteenth century, the Saint-Simonians had theorised something similar. For a society to create order, it needed to assign people who had the capacity to effectively use available resources – land, labour and capital – to do so for the greater good of all. Property was to be placed in the hands of trustees, chosen on their ability to decide where and how society's resources should be invested. The trustees would be bankers who had the most knowledge and connections to choose what was efficient to produce. Bankers possessed greater knowledge because they lived in the

---

[64] Naik, *Kashinath Trimbak Telang*, 51.

[65] List, *National System of Political Economy*, 389, 404–5, 425.

[66] Naoroji, *Essays, Speeches, Addresses and Writings*, 21.

[67] Ranade, *Religious and Social Reform*, 89.

local areas, meaning they tended to be more aware of what a particular place needed.[68]

Collective and equal development required a balance of power between local and central ruling bodies. Ranade narrated the gradual transition from small local units of organisation to a larger democratic political structure. Countries in Europe, America and Asia had all experienced a 'symmetrical development of the little Parish unit into the great Confederacy of States, which appears to be evidently the destined form of the future Political Organisation of the Human Family'.[69] Ranade paraphrased J. S. Mill to explain how the Indian government should be structured:

[P]ower must be localised, while knowledge, especially technical, is most useful when subordinated to a central control. The principal business of the Central Authority should be to give instructions, and to lay down fixed principles, and it should leave the local bodies to apply them in practice.[70]

The central and local public institutions should have different roles and powers. Ranade noted J. S. Mill's argument that the central government should decide on a set of instructions and principles that the local governments would then apply. An imperial official, Charles Lewis Tupper (1848–1910), in the late nineteenth century agreed with Ranade that India needed balanced power between the central and local bodies.[71]

In examining the effective combination of central and local authority, Naoroji drew upon the example of the princely state of Mysore in southern India. The princely states were semi-autonomous regions, each of which had a subsidiary alliance with the British imperial administration. The ruler of Mysore from 1881 to 1894, Maharaja Chamarajendra Wadiyar X, established local and central powers that were progressive for the period. Theirs were the first modern legislatures in princely India.[72] As a result, argued Naoroji, he dramatically improved the state's political and economic condition. Naoroji explained how Mysore managed to accrue more and more wealth, which paid for education programmes and

---

[68] Enfantin, *Économie politique et politique*, 202; Saint-Simon, *The Doctrine of Saint-Simon*, 103–10; Cowen and Shenton, *Doctrines of Development*, 25–6.

[69] Ranade, *Essays on Indian Economics*, 234. [70] Ibid., 260.

[71] Tupper, *Our Indian Protectorate*, 346–7, 407–10.

[72] Chetty, *A Brief Sketch of the Life of Raja Dharma Pravina*.

irrigation projects.[73] Unfortunately, however, this could never be achieved in the Indian states where the British ruled. As Naoroji noted, Mysore was successful because

[s]uch is the result of good administration in a Native State at the very beginning. What splendid prospect is in store for the future if, as heretofore, it is allowed to develop itself to the level of the British system with its own Native Services, and not bled as poor British India is by the infliction of European Services, which are bleeding India to death.[74]

The British drain of Indian resources meant that such progress as Mysore experienced was not possible for those regions directly under the Crown's rule (see Chapter 4).

Moreover, India needed representation to foster collective and equal development. 'It is a truism', stated Dutt, 'that there can be no government for the good of a people without some sort of representation.'[75] The imperial administration would fail to secure balanced growth for the populace until Indians were represented in the executive councils of the Empire. Naoroji was among the major proponents of allowing Indians to take examinations for the Civil Service, and Dutt was ultimately one of the first beneficiaries, going on to serve as a civil servant in the British administration from 1869 to 1882.[76]

Native representation was also important because the imperial administration's European employees did not spend enough of their earnings and pensions in India, exacerbating the drain. European salaries and pensions were much higher than those paid out to Indians. If there were more Indian, and less European, government employees, there would be more capital left over for other things. Moreover, if the administration were to employ more Indians, then the salaries and pensions paid to them would become useful sources of capital. Furthermore, if the 'civilising mission' were to lead to eventual self-government and later independence, then Indians had to train themselves in governing the nation. As things stood, educated Indians were

[73] Naoroji, *Poverty and Un-British Rule in India*, 623.   [74] Ibid., 623.
[75] Dutt, *Speeches and Papers on Indian Questions*, 105.
[76] Gopalakrishnan, *Development of Economic Ideas in India*, 87.
     Other Indian economists, such as Banerjea, argued similarly. Banerjea, *Speeches and Writings*, 45, 190, 219.

being denied an opportunity to utilise and develop the skills they had learned at university.[77] As Naoroji wrote:

The full development of force of character and other qualities depends upon their future exercise and opportunities. When any limb of the body or faculty of mind is not used or exercised, it gradually decays.[78]

Just as a muscle must be exercised in order to function effectively, Indians had to be able to practise the skills they had been taught so that they could govern themselves (see Chapter 5).

Dutt was also in favour, but his reasoning was slightly different. Contrary to the idea of employment in the imperial administration being an educational opportunity, Dutt noted that local representatives spoke the local languages, unlike the imperial officials, and that they also possessed greater knowledge of local customs and land systems than the Europeans.[79] He had had some success in implementing local self-government as revenue minister of Baroda from 1904 to 1907 and later Diwan, 1907–9. There he set up 'Village Boards' under 'Taluka Boards', which sent representatives to the 'District Boards', who in turn sent up 'Councillors to the State Legislative Council'.[80] The village boards oversaw public works, such as wells, which they built with money allocated to them by the district boards. Dutt wrote how the village boards 'executed the works with a degree of efficiency and economy which surpassed all expectations'.[81]

Some imperial officials agreed that Indians should be more involved in the administration. In two speeches in the House of Commons, Henry Fawcett (1833–84), professor of political economy at the University of Cambridge and a Liberal MP, spoke in favour of holding Civil Service examinations in Calcutta, Madras and Bombay to give natives the chance of gaining employment in government. Fawcett had considerable success in influencing public opinion on Indian questions.[82] Additionally, Lord Mayo's resolution of 1870 and Lord Ripon's of 1882 attempted to implement local self-government through financial decentralisation.[83]

---

[77] Naoroji, *Poverty and Un-British Rule in India*, 57–8, 119, 204, 225.
[78] Naoroji, *Essays, Speeches, Addresses and Writings*, 542.
[79] Dutt, *The Economic History of India under Early British Rule*, 1:144, 148–9.
[80] Gupta, *Life and Work of Romesh Chunder Dutt*, 409–10.   [81] Ibid., 410.
[82] Stephen, *Life of Henry Fawcett*, 341–5.
[83] Mathur, *Lord Ripon's Administration in India*; Denholm, *Lord Ripon*; Tinker, *The Foundations of the Local Self-Government in India, Pakistan and Burma*;

Local self-government was important because it would train Indians to manage their own affairs. (Yet Ripon's goal was also to amass more revenue.)[84] Ripon set up local urban and rural boards of natives as an instrument of political education for Indians.

Universal Free Trade in the Long Run

The second element of Indian Economics' economic nationalism was the long-term liberal perspective. While there were disagreements among the Indian economists as to when free trade was beneficial (see Chapter 5), most of them advocated it in the long run. Once universal industrialisation had been attained on a global level, free trade should be universal. Free trade was the end goal of any economy. Like List, Indian Economics saw protective measures such as tariff barriers as temporary until their industry could compete on the international market.[85] 'I am', wrote Banerjea, 'a free trader.'[86] Free trade should be implemented once Indian industry had equal levels of productivity and thus low enough prices to be able to compete with British manufacturers.

Both List and Ranade explained how a tariff was like a 'crutch'.[87] List used the term to explain how early in 1800s Britain's prime minister, William Pitt (1759–1806), should have 'thrown away the protective system as a crutch no longer needed'.[88] The result, argued List, would have meant 'still greater wealth and eminence', and Britain would have come closer to attaining 'the monopoly of manufacturing industry'.[89] Without tariffs, raw materials and agricultural products would have flowed into Britain, and sales of British mechanised textile

Mallik, 'Local Self-Government in India'; de Bercegol, *Small Towns and Decentralisation in India*.

[84] Government revenue was split into imperial, provincial and divided. Imperial revenue included railways, customs, posts and telegraphs, opium, salt, mint, military receipts, land revenue, and so on. Provincial revenue consisted of jails, medical services, printing, roads, general administration, and so on, while the divided revenue included the excise, stamps, forests, registration, and so on, to be split equally between the central and provincial governments. Lord Ripon's Resolution on Local Government, 20 May 1882.

[85] Ranade, *Religious and Social Reform*, 177; Szporluk, *Communism and Nationalism*, 102.

[86] Banerjea, 'Speeches by Babu Surendranath Banerjea', 43.

[87] List, *National System of Political Economy*, 441; Ranade, *Religious and Social Reform*, 177; Ranade, *Essays on Indian Economics*, 15.

[88] List, *National System of Political Economy*, 441.   [89] Ibid.

goods would have increased dramatically. As for Ranade, he praised the French statesman from 1661 to 1683 who served under King Louis XIV, Jean-Baptiste Colbert, for making 'France in his day the most prosperous State on the Continent'.[90] 'He', continued Ranade, 'had a keen perception that State protection and control were but crutches to teach the Nation to walk, and that they should be thrown away when the necessary advance had been made.'[91]

It was in the next century, observed Ranade, that there were 'enormous abuses of State control and direction, of monopolies and restrictions'.[92] The several European East Indian companies had triggered scholars such as Hobbes and Locke to conceptualise an idea of natural liberty. Natural liberty theorised that people were only guided by private interest, and individuals always knew better what they wanted and needed. 'The removal', wrote Ranade, 'of all restrictions and prohibitions became the watchword of this School.'[93] Natural liberty, theorised by Hobbes and Locke, was destructive for nations still developing such as India because, according to Ranade, natural liberty assumed that any state intervention in the market was bad. Ranade realised abuses of state intervention had detrimental effects. Protection, and any state intervention, should thus be treated as a crutch; protective tariffs should be removed when a nascent industry had become competitive enough to compete on the international market.

In the long run, then, when all nations had industrialised, there should be universal free trade. A nation, wrote List, should industrialise to 'prepare it for admission into the universal society of the future'.[94] The universal society of the future meant free trade among all industrialised European nations. Where List differed from the British economists like Ricardo and J. Mill who came before him was on the subject of when free trade should be implemented.[95] List saw free trade for all European nations once they had industrialised. Indian Economics opened this up further to include India as well. The difference, in

---

[90] Ranade, *Essays on Indian Economics*, 15. [91] Ibid. [92] Ibid.
[93] Ibid., 16. [94] List, *National System of Political Economy*, 142.
[95] Ricardo's trade theory also aimed to maximise the world's economic efficiency for the betterment of humankind through free trade. J. Mill saw free trade as a way to keep peace and spread civilisation, ensuring a peaceful, cosmopolitan global society. Helleiner, 'Economic Nationalism as a Challenge to Economic Liberalism?', 313.

other words, between economists like Ricardo, J. Mill and List and the first generation of modern Indian economists is *when* and *where* the universal society of free trade and industrialisation could and should be realised.

India's history with progress within an international context pushed the Indian economists to see a globalised world where the comparative advantage model made no sense. They understood why India was so poor by rereading Indian history and bringing forward the disastrous results of imperialism. They rejected the idea that progress originated in Europe. India had already experienced progress and should be allowed and helped to skip to a higher level of civilisation (see Chapters 3–5). The country was regressing not due to some inherent weaknesses but due to imperial policies. The comparative advantage model condemned India to a sector with diminishing returns. Indian Economics refracted the unequal comparative advantage model with a win–win global framework in which all countries could and should industrialise.

Epilogue: Multiple Definitions of Progress and Development[1]

In the late afternoon of 17 August 1904, Naoroji got up in front of a packed crowd of the world's leading socialist voices. As he slowly approached the podium, 'draped in gorgeous red', the audience stood up and observed a moment of silence for the millions of Indians who had died in the latest famine.[2] Naoroji had been invited as a representative of British India by his socialist friend Henry Hyndman to speak on the question of imperialism at the International Socialist Congress. The congress had rented Amsterdam's Concertgebouw, the concert hall, located in a luxurious part of town. Almost five hundred delegates sat along thirty long tables stretching from the platform where Naoroji stood to the far end of the hall, each next to a sign bearing their country's name. The spacious galleries above, capable of seating some six hundred spectators, were filled with socialists from many parts of the world. The result resembled a stock exchange with speeches held in a variety of languages. The inevitable group of 'non-listeners' who did not understand the language spoken created a 'buzz' during each intervention, walking in and out, and slamming doors.[3] Naoroji, a rare non-European delegate, managed to silence an audience of a thousand people – Rosa Luxembourg, Karl Kautsky and Jean Jaurès among them – as he pleaded for Indian self-government thousands of kilometres from home. A photo of several of the participants was captured where Naoroji stands alongside these leading European socialists of his time (Figure E.1).

Naoroji spoke quietly and clearly with an argumentative manner, 'though at first his voice trembled a little when he attempted to express his gratitude for the great outburst of sympathy for the people of India'.[4] He was thankful for the opportunity to explain what was

---

[1] This chapter is based on a published chapter, Bach, 'Marginalized Knowledge Actors'.

[2] de Leon, *Flashlights of the Amsterdam International Socialist Congress, 1904*, 64.

[3] Ibid., 63.   [4] 'India at the International Socialist Congress'.

Figure E.1 Dadabhai Naoroji at the Amsterdam Socialist Congress, 1904.

happening in India, appealing to the workers of the world to help stop his country from falling into deeper abject poverty. His demand for Indians 'to share in the general progress made by the nations of the world' would have been shared by the owners of the concert hall who had the progressive aim of making musical arts accessible to the poorer classes.[5] From the day it opened, the hall offered cheap concerts regularly. Still today you can enjoy a free lunch concert every Thursday. The owners of the concert hall believed in progress for all, realising that it would benefit even their own privileged class. As this book has shown, Naoroji spread similar notions of progress.

Although the Indian economists followed little of what you could call socialism – indeed, Joshi and Ranade were adamant that their policy plans were not socialistic[6] – Naoroji found in Hyndman and the International Socialist Congress a community that stood by his cries for help to better the conditions of the average poor Indian and to free his people from further political and economic ruin. Naoroji's audience listened to his appeal that day, bursting into another great ovation once Naoroji left the podium. His resolution to allow Indians to rule

---

[5] Ibid.
[6] Joshi, *Writings and Speeches of G. V. Joshi*, 819; Ranade, *Essays on Indian Economics*.

themselves, an 'India for the Indians', passed unanimously.[7] Here was the culmination of a lifetime of fighting, with words and political activism, to gain recognition of India's worsening economic state.

By relocating development economics, I have shown what the first generation of modern Indian economists produced. This first generation mixed various thinkers from across Europe and North America and pushed at the boundaries of existing theories to produce reformulations of economic development that better fit their subcontinent. As Ranade said in his inaugural speech of Indian Economics: '[I]t must be strange indeed that in the Economical aspect of our life one set of general principles should hold good everywhere for all time and place, and for all stages of Civilisation.'[8] Countries under imperial rule, like India, experienced more volatile, at times violent, change than Europe. That experience produced a universal idea of development that accommodated the specificities of such turbulent encounters with societal forces within and outside of India. There was a need, understood the Indian economists, for multiple definitions and trajectories of progress and regress, and subsequently distinct development plans. *Relocating Development Economics* has opened up discursive space to find new ways of thinking about regress, progress and development.

Redefining Progress and Development from and at the Margins

Some ideas get less attention than others. And as much as intellectuals may want to believe that an idea spreads, and only spreads, if it gets us closer to the truth, that is not the only reason an idea may be taken up and circulated. An intellectual's class, caste, gender, nationality, physical location, time period and so forth radically affect whether the knowledge they produce will be read, accepted and passed on. A person's unique localisation in societal and historical space will impact whether they will be considered an actor of knowledge. Knowledge creation, in modern science and especially economics, is notoriously focused on western European and North American intellectuals. There seem, in other words, to be boundaries that define who can produce knowledge. I have questioned those boundaries

[7] 'India at the International Socialist Congress'.
[8] Ranade, *Essays on Indian Economics*, 5.

throughout this book to uncover marginalised economists that are seldom analysed.

Marginalised thinkers are individuals that have been part of dialogues and produced speeches or texts that are largely ignored during, and often after, their time. They are ignored because they are considered inferior, effectively marginalised from societal debates. Sometimes they are ignored on the regional, national or international level, sometimes on all levels. Examples include natives of an imperialised land, women, and working-class men before they gained the right to vote. These economists were or are considered to be incapable of, or at least not good at, producing new ideas or adding anything noteworthy to societal debates. They are considered copiers of existing knowledge. The result is often that they do not get published and their contributions to knowledge are forgotten about all together. Others manage to voice their ideas in lesser-known channels. Still others generate their own channels of communication within which they can publish.

The first generation of modern Indian economists is a good example of marginalised thinkers. They worked within an imperial setting and were treated as inferior, while their addressees, mainly British, were considered superior. The Indian economists were thus producing economic knowledge from the margins. As such, in the ongoing debates around Indian progress and development, the Indian economists often got – and still get – labelled as copiers of existing knowledge from Europe and North America. British officials and some British thinkers interested in Indian history and society, as well as Indian intellectuals, complained that Indian students were only copying the ideas they were taught and failing to contribute to knowledge. Such defeatist thinking foisted upon a whole population must have, at least to some extent, created a blindness to original Indian thought. Like Bayly writes, global historical narratives of European superiority often omit the fact that India had created theories to understand political and socio-economic changes throughout the eighteenth and nineteenth centuries.[9] In the history of economics, even today, these economists are often overlooked.

The question that dominates the history of science is why modern science originated in western Europe and not elsewhere. In an epoch-making paper in the 1960s, George Basalla laid out a three-stage model

---

[9] Bayly, *The Birth of the Modern World*, 79.

that explained the diffusion of European science to the rest of the world.[10] Basalla described how modern science from Europe spread to non-scientific societies in the first stage. These non-European spaces were passive containers of data, providing a 'source for European science'.[11] In the second stage, when European scientific institutions emerged, encouraging further research in their nations, the non-scientific societies became dependent on European empires. In the final stage, imperial territories gained autonomy through independence movements and European-like scientific institutions. The model is full of assumptions that are, at the least, debatable. First, that modern science originated in Europe and is thus European. Second, that modern science is a unified entity. Third, that it spreads everywhere. And fourth, that it spreads the same way in every space and is thus universal.

Basalla's thinking mirrored other well-known and widely diffused arguments of the time, such as Walt Rostow's five-stage model for economic development, where non-European regions would develop like Europe did.[12] Development included economic, political and social phenomena – for example, industrialisation, intellectual progress and democracy. In Rostow's thought, the idea of development is confined to European industrial advancement and that region's specific experience with progress. The idea of development itself is said to have originated in Europe and then been disseminated across the world like the material processes of progress.

And yet many scholars have found that the conventional narrative remains the same in the twenty-first century. Frédérique Apffel-Marglin and Stephen A. Marglin address the role of knowledge in economic development in *Dominating Knowledge*, published in 1990. They argue that 'modern' knowledge, assumed to be Western, wins over 'traditional' knowledge, assumed to be non-Western, not because modern knowledge has a superior cognitive power but because of prestige gained by association with the increasing economic and political power of the West over the past five hundred years, and the perceived richness of its cultural history.[13] In 2000, Dipesh Chakrabarty published his study of the mythical figure of Europe, taken to be the original site of modernity and progress in many histories

---

[10] Basalla, 'The Spread of Western Science'.   [11] Ibid., 611.
[12] Rostow, *The Stages of Economic Growth.*
[13] Apffel-Marglin and Marglin, *Dominating Knowledge*, chap. 2.

of capitalism in non-Western regions. He finds that this illusory idea is built into the social sciences. Non-Western countries are thus perceived as lacking or incomplete, always judged against their Western counterparts.[14] John M. Hobson made a similar argument in 2012, claiming that most international theory has been embedded within various forms of Eurocentrism and that universalist theories defend Western civilisation as the subject in world politics and the ideal from 1760 to 2010.[15]

We have often, consequently, forgotten to look at how other meanings of development came about and what their specific contributions are. Dominant narratives, like the European idea of progress and development, minimise other ways of describing and theorising the world. Within the history of ideas, and more specifically here the history of economics, studies are predominately about well-known figures such as Smith and Ricardo, while lesser-known figures are rarely cited or analysed. There are, of course, some scholars, especially within intellectual history, who have dealt with lesser-known interlocutors. A trend for studying these figures has clearly developed in the last decade or so. However, there is still much to be done in the history of economics. A wider history, as Eric Helleiner labels it, debunks the well-accepted Western diffusion narrative of how knowledge on things like economic development comes from Europe and North America and then diffuses across the world.[16] Expanding the history of economics, which this book is only one example of, provincialises well-known economic theories like economic development and provides perspectives often either ignored or critiqued and quickly forgotten. *Relocating Development Economics* has exposed new ideas not previously taken 'seriously'.[17]

How have I reconstructed narratives from the margins? The British officials in India imposed constraints and limits on these thinkers. The Indian economists' imperial context and the dominant ideas of the age cannot be ignored (see Chapters 1 and 2). Nevertheless, the Indian economists fought to change things over time. What I asked, then, was

---

[14] Chakrabarty, *Provincializing Europe*.
[15] Hobson, *The Eurocentric Conception of World Politics*.
[16] Helleiner, *The Contested World Economy*, 259–70. See also Subrahmanyam, 'Beyond the Usual Suspects'.
[17] This is Zachariah's word choice; for further discussion, see Zachariah, 'Moving Ideas and How to Catch Them', 133.

how this first generation of modern Indian economists functioned in a Eurocentric world on their own terms and in what ways they challenged the status quo.[18]

My relocating approach uncovers how constraints and an inferior position affect the knowledge produced. Dominant narratives overpower thinking in a way that makes it hard for new knowledge to be generated. New discursive practices often appear at the margins as re-articulations of dominant discourse,[19] and on the periphery the knowledge produced by marginalised thinkers is often refracted. The Indian economists were from the margins, but their ideas also changed thought that existed there.

Towards a New Definition of Universal Progress and Development

The win–win model of development produced a universal plan of industrialisation but also insisted on the need for local iterations and paths to that industrialisation (see Chapter 5). Indian Economics combined nationalism with universalism (see Chapter 6). And as historians started to realise in the 1960s, half a century after the Indian economists, western European and North American progress, modernity and development became universal, to an extent, because they were imposed on the rest of the world. Uncovering the Eurocentric assumptions in these well-known, uncontested global concepts and theories yields several results.[20]

The Indian economists realised these assumptions meant that India's history had been misread and delegitimised. Exposed to universal narratives on progress and development, non-European regions such as India were conceptually disconnected from their internal processes of progress and development. India, as well as other imperialised regions, experienced the rise of commerce and a money economy even before Europe modernised. Indian Economics' idea of development rightly assigned

[18] For further discussion and references on how to assign agency of this nature, see Peabody, 'Knowledge Formation in Imperial India'.

[19] See, for example, Muzaka, 'A Dialogic Approach to Understanding Regime Conflicts'; Tilly, *Big Structures, Large Processes, Huge Comparisons*. Bhabha describes this process as a mutation of dominant discourses and genres (Bhabha, 'Unpacking My Library Again').

[20] Washbrook, 'From Comparative Sociology to Global History'; Taylor, 'Two Theories of Modernity'; Habib, *Essays in Indian History*.

agency to India in how it had helped Britain, and other European and North American countries, to rapidly industrialise and develop during the eighteenth and nineteenth centuries. Uncovering the assumptions of progress, modernity and development recovers the many similarities, as well as the interdependence, between western Europe and the rest of the world.

Indian Economics moved away from the dominant idea that progress and development were simply imposed on India exogenously. Ideas of universal progress and development travelled to India. Those who had access to education, including the Indian economists, learned ideas of modernity through the imperial system (see Chapter 2). Nevertheless, the Indian graduates constructed a critique of progress and development. Indians needed, like all other societies, to elaborate an idea of progress and development unique to their space.

Furthermore, stretching the prevailing ideas of progress and development, like the Indian economists did, can resolve the perceived contradictions between nationalist and universalist perspectives. Contrary to dominant thinking, a country can be in favour of universal industrialisation and extensive global trade networks while simultaneously being in favour of acknowledging local or national characteristics. The local national context could, for instance, require protection for infant industries or greater public investment in irrigation due to recurring droughts. At the same time, once a country could compete internationally it could remove its tariff barriers. Indian Economics' economic nationalism included a plan for collective equality, through measures such as income redistribution and a long-term goal of a universal society with global industrialisation and free trade. Its development discourse seems to lie between nationalism and universalism (see Chapters 5 and 6).

The idea of development in Indian Economics proves that progress and development are not inherently European. The processes of positive societal change that occurred in Europe did not only originate there and will not, as a result, manifest in the exact same way across the world. There are universalising forces that make the world ever more connected through, for example, trade networks and migration. Simultaneously, there are local practices and distinct societal processes that have political, economic and social effects long after so-called progressive or homogenising forces have materialised.[21] One consequence, then, of relocating development

[21] Washbrook, 'The Global History of "Modernity"', 297.

economics has been to uncover the complex reactions to such forces. Progress and development need to be understood and defined differently, depending on the specific space and time period. As Jon Wilson put it, 'The history of modernity's emergence is only ever a history of the partial dominance of modern institutions in particular places at particular moments of time.'[22]

The position of these economists at the margins of discursive space offered them a unique perspective. Their distinct positioning pushed them to critique dominant discourse that contradicted their lived experiences and to rework those shared dominant meanings. In the late nineteenth century, India experienced, for instance, famines more severe than it had ever suffered before, and so it seemed to be regressing rather than progressing, despite the dominant idea of progress which saw positive change as a given.

Like the Latin American economists who championed the Dependency School in the 1950s, Indian Economics saw another side to imperialism and the international division of labour. Raúl Prebisch, Hans Singer and Paul Baran explained how integrating peripheral countries like former colonies into the world market made them poorer due to the dependent nature of these weaker economies in the current global, political and economic framework. They saw, just as the Indian economists had at the end of the nineteenth century, imperial rulers force free trade on their countries.[23] The nations of Latin America, like India a half century before, were becoming poorer, while the core of the Empire, Spain and Portugal, became richer. Prebisch, Singer and Baran were responding to modernisation theory, which stipulated that societies progress through similar stages. The Singer–Prebisch thesis, one of the main models in dependency theory, rejected that view and instead argued that peripheral countries were not just primitive versions of the core (more advanced) countries – they had their own unique structures and history. Ranade and Dutt made this clear, too. India had its own history, and the stadial theory had to be reformulated accordingly (as discussed in Chapters 3 and 4).

---

[22] Wilson, 'How Modernity Arrived to Godavari', 407.
[23] Prebisch, *The Economic Development of Latin America*; Singer, 'The Distribution of Gains between Investing and Borrowing Countries'; Baran, *The Political Economy of Growth*.

We need to acknowledge that the dominant idea of development informs the imagination of many scholars and actions across the world. Still, there are often overlooked and forgotten marginal development discourses that can inform our past, present and future. Indian Economics is but one example. Recovering thought from the margins has exposed useful new ways of viewing development. The first generation of modern Indian economists revived the idea that a society can both progress and regress. They exposed the exploitative nature of imperialist regimes that created dependent nations condemned to poverty and regress. And they envisaged an industrialised world that would bring greater progress to all, rather than an international division of labour that condemned the producers of raw materials to poverty.

References

Abdelal, Rawi. *National Purpose in the World Economy: Post-Soviet States in Comparative Perspective.* Ithaca: Cornell University Press, 2001.

Adas, Michael. 'Twentieth Century Approaches to the Indian Mutiny of 1857–58'. *Journal of Asian History* 5, no. 1 (1971): 1–19. www.jstor.org/stable/41929779.

Agarwal, Anil, and Sunita Narain. *Dying Wisdom: Rise, Fall and Potential of India's Traditional Water Harvesting Systems.* New Delhi: Centre for Science and Environment, 1997.

Almenar, Salvador. 'The Reception and Dissemination of Ricardo's Ideas in Spain'. In *The Reception of David Ricardo in Continental Europe and Japan,* edited by Gilbert Faccarello and Masashi Izumo, 152–77. Abingdon: Routledge, 2014.

Al-Sayyid Marsot, Afaf Lutfi. *Egypt in the Reign of Muhammad Ali.* Cambridge: Cambridge University Press, 1984.

Ambirajan, Srinivasa. 'Malthusian Population Theory and Indian Famine Policy in the Nineteenth Century'. *Population Studies* 30, no. 1 (1976): 5–14.

Apffel-Marglin, Frédérique, and Stephen A. Marglin, eds. *Decolonizing Knowledge: From Development to Dialogue.* Oxford: Oxford University Press, 1996.

Apffel-Marglin, Frédérique, and Stephen A. Marglin, eds. *Dominating Knowledge: Development, Culture and Resistance.* Oxford: Clarendon Press, 1990.

Argov, Daniel. *Moderates and Extremists in the Indian National Movement, 1883–1920: With Special Reference to Surendranath Banerjea and Lajpat Rai.* Bombay: Asia Publishing House, 1967.

Arndt, Heinz Wolfgang. *Economic Development: The History of an Idea.* Chicago: University of Chicago Press, 1987.

Arrighi, Giovanni. *The Long Twentieth Century: Money, Power, and the Origins of Our Times.* London: Verso, 1994.

Atkinson, Edward. 'The Railway, the Farmer and the Public'. *Manufacturers' Gazette,* 9 August 1884.

Awasthi, Aruna. *History and Development of Railways in India*. New Delhi: Deep and Deep, 1994.

Bach, Maria. 'A Win-Win Model of Development: How Indian Economics Redefined Universal Development from and at the Margins'. *Journal of the History of Economic Thought* 43, no. 4 (2021): 483–505.

'Marginalized Knowledge Actors'. In *Forms of Knowledge: Developing the History of Knowledge*, edited by Johan Östling, Anna Nilsson Hammer and David Larsson Heidenblad, 121–38. Lund: Nordic Academic Press, 2023.

'Positive Discourse Analysis: A Method for the History of Knowledge?' In *Participatory Knowledge*, edited by Charlotte A. Lerg, Johan Östling and Jana Weiß, Vol. I, 203–24. Berlin: De Gruyter Oldenbourg, 2022. https://doi.org/10.1515/9783110748819-010.

'Poverty Theory in Action: How Romesh Chunder Dutt's European Travels Affected His Poverty Theory, 1868–1893'. *History of Political Economy* 54, no. 3 (2022): 529–46.

'What Laws Determine Progress? An Indian Contribution to the Idea of Progress Based on Mahadev Govind Ranade's Works, 1870–1901'. *The European Journal of the History of Economic Thought* 25, no. 2 (2018): 327–56.

Backhouse, Roger E. 'Marginal Revolution'. In *The New Palgrave Dictionary of Economics*, edited by Steven N. Durlauf and Lawrence Blume, Vol. V, 292–4. London: Palgrave Macmillan UK, 2016.

Bagchi, Amiya Kumar. 'Deindustrialization in Gangetic Bihar 1809–1901'. In *Essays in Honour of Prof. Susobhan Chandra Sarkar*, edited by Arun Das Gupta and Barun De, 499–522. New Delhi: People's Publishing House, 1976.

'De-industrialization in India in the Nineteenth Century: Some Theoretical Implications'. *The Journal of Development Studies* 12, no. 2 (1976): 135–64.

Private Investment in India, 1900–1939. Cambridge: Cambridge University Press, 1972.

Bairoch, Paul. 'International Industrialization Levels from 1750 to 1980'. *Journal of European Economic History* 11, no. 2 (1982): 269–333.

Bakhtin, Mikhail Mikhaĭlovich. *The Dialogic Imagination: Four Essays*. Edited by Michael Holquist. Translated by Ceryl Emerson and Michael Holquist. Austin: University of Texas Press, 1981.

Balachandran, Gopalan. 'Colonial India and the World Economy, c. 1850–1940'. In *A New Economic History of Colonial India*, edited by Latika Chaudhary, Bishnupriya Gupta, Tirthankar Roy and Anand V. Swamy, 84–99. New York: Routledge, 2016.

Banerjea, Surendranath. *Speeches and Writings of Hon. Surendranath Banerjea: Selected by Himself.* Madras: G.A. Natesan, 1917.
Speeches by Babu Surendranath Banerjea, 6th Volume. Calcutta: S.K. Lahiri, 1908.
Banerjee, Sarmila. *Studies in Administrative History of Bengal, 1880–1898.* New Delhi: Rajesh Publications, 1978.
Baran, Paul A. *The Political Economy of Growth.* New York: Monthly Review Press, 1957.
Basalla, George. 'The Spread of Western Science'. *Science* 156, no. 3775 (1967): 611–22.
Bayly, Christopher Alan. *Indian Society and the Making of the British Empire.* Cambridge: Cambridge University Press, 1988.
Recovering Liberties: Indian Thought in the Age of Liberalism and Empire. Cambridge: Cambridge University Press, 2011.
The Birth of the Modern World: 1780–1914. Oxford: Wiley-Blackwell, 2003.
Beckert, Sven. *Empire of Cotton: A Global History.* New York: Alfred A. Knopf, 2014.
Beckwith, Christopher I. *Empires of the Silk Road: A History of Central Eurasia from the Bronze Age to the Present.* Princeton: Princeton University Press, 2009.
Bhabha, Homi K., ed. *Nation and Narration.* Abingdon: Routledge, 2013.
Bhabha, Homi. 'Unpacking My Library Again'. *Midwest Modern Language Association* 28, no. 1 (1995): 5–18.
Bhandari, Ratan Raj. *Indian Railways: Glorious 150 Years.* New Delhi: Publications Division, Ministry of Information & Broadcasting, Govt. of India, 2006.
Bloomfield, Arthur I. 'Patterns of Fluctuation in International Investment before 1914'. Princeton Studies in International Finance no. 21, Department of Economics, Princeton University, Princeton. (1968). http://ies.princeton .edu/pdf/S21.pdf.
Bogart, Dan, and Latika Chaudhary. 'Railways in Colonial India: An Economic Achievement?' In *A New Economic History of Colonial India*, edited by Latika Chaudhary, Bishnupriya Gupta, Tirthankar Roy and Anand V. Swamy, 140–60. Abingdon: Routledge, 2016. https://doi.org/10.2139/ ssrn.2073256.
Boianovsky, Mauro. 'Beyond Capital Fundamentalism: Harrod, Domar and the History of Development Economics'. *Cambridge Journal of Economics* 42, no. 2 (2018): 477–504.
'Friedrich List and the Economic Fate of Tropical Countries'. *History of Political Economy* 45, no. 4 (2013): 647–91.

Bombay Provincial Banking Enquiry Committee 1929–1930, Vols 1–4, Evidence. Bombay: Government Central Press, 1930.

Booth, Charles. *Life and Labour of the People in London.* Vol. II. London: Macmillan, 1897. https://wellcomecollection.org/works/e67mj94f.

Boyer, George R., and Timothy J. Hatton. 'New Estimates of British Unemployment, 1870–1913'. *Journal of Economic History* 62, no. 3 (2002): 643–75.

British Rule in India: Condemned by the British Themselves. London: The Indian National Party, 1915.

Brown, Donald Mackenzie. *The Nationalist Movement: Indian Political Thought from Ranade to Bhave.* Berkeley: University of California Press, 1970.

Brown, Vivienne. 'Metanarratives and Economic Discourse'. *The Scandinavian Journal of Economics* 96, no. 1 (1994): 83–93.

Burrow, John Wyon. *Evolution and Society: A Study in Victorian Social Theory.* Cambridge: Cambridge University Press, 1966.

Burton, Antoinette. 'Making a Spectacle of Empire: Indian Travellers in Fin-de-Siècle London'. *History Workshop Journal*, 42, no. 1 (1996): 126–46.

Bury, John Bagnell. *The Idea of Progress: An Inquiry into Its Origins and Growth.* London: Macmillan, 1920.

Cain, Peter J. 'Character, "Ordered Liberty", and the Mission to Civilise: British Moral Justification of Empire, 1870–1914'. *The Journal of Imperial and Commonwealth History* 40, no. 4 (2012): 557–78.

Cardoso, José Luis. 'The Diffusion of Ricardo and Classical Political Economy in Portugal'. In *The Reception of David Ricardo in Continental Europe and Japan*, edited by Gilbert Faccarello and Masashi Izumo, 137–51. Abingdon: Routledge, 2014.

Caruana-Galizia, Paul. 'Indian Regional Income Inequality: Estimates of Provincial GDP, 1875–1911'. *Economic History of Developing Regions* 28, no. 1 (2013): 1–27. https://doi.org/10.1080/20780389.2013.805510.

Chakrabarty, Dipesh. *Provincializing Europe: Postcolonial Thought and Historical Difference.* Princeton: Princeton University Press, 2000.

Chandra, Bipan. 'Reinterpretation of Nineteenth Century Indian Economic History'. *Indian Economic & Social History Review* 5, no. 1 (1968): 35–75.

The Rise and Growth of Economic Nationalism in India. New Delhi: People's Publishing House, 1966.

Chang, Ha-Joon. *Kicking Away the Ladder: Development Strategy in Historical Perspective.* London: Anthem Press, 2002.

Chatterjee, Kumkum, and Clement Hawes, eds. *Europe Observed: Multiple Gazes in Early Modern Encounters.* Lewisburg: Bucknell University Press, 2008.

Chatterjee, Partha. 'The Social Sciences in India'. In *The Cambridge History of Science*, edited by Theodore M. Porter and Dorothy Ross, Vol. VII, 482–97. Cambridge: Cambridge University Press, 2003.

Nationalist Thought and the Colonial World: A Derivative Discourse. Minneapolis: University of Minnesota Press, 1986.

The Nation and Its Fragments: Colonial and Postcolonial Histories. Vol. XI. Princeton: Princeton University Press, 1993.

Chaudhary, Latika, Bishnupriya Gupta, Tirthankar Roy and Anand V. Swamy, eds. *A New Economic History of Colonial India.* Abingdon: Routledge, 2016.

Chetty, T. Royaloo. *A Brief Sketch of the Life of Raja Dharma Pravina.* Bangalore: T.R.A. Thumboo Chetty, 1909.

Clark, Colin. *The Conditions of Economic Progress.* London: Macmillan, 1951.

Codell, Julie F. 'Reversing the Grand Tour: Guest Discourse in Indian Travel Narratives'. *Quarterly* 70, no. 1 (2007): 173–89. https://doi.org/10.15 25/hlq.2007.70.1.173.

Cohn, Bernard S. *Colonialism and Its Forms of Knowledge: The British in India.* Princeton: Princeton University Press, 1996.

Commander, Simon. 'Malthus and the Theory of "Unequal Powers": Population and Food Production in India, 1800–1947'. *Modern Asian Studies* 20, no. 4 (1986): 661–701.

Cooper, Frederic. 'Writing the History of Development'. *Journal of Modern European History* 8, no. 1 (2010): 5–23. https://doi.org/10.17104/161 1-8944_2010_1_5.

Coquery-Vidrovitch, Catherine. 'La mise en dépendance de l'Afrique noire: essai de périodisation, 1800–1970'. *Cahiers d'Études africaines* 16, no. 61 (1976): 7–58. https://doi.org/10.3406/cea.1976.2888.

Cowen, Michael, and Robert Shenton. *Doctrines of Development.* London: Routledge, 1996.

Crane, George T. 'Economic Nationalism: Bringing the Nation Back In'. *Millennium* 27, no. 1 (1998): 55–75.

Curzon, Lord George. *Speeches by Lord Curzon of Kedleston, Viceroy and Governor-General of India.* Vol. IV. Calcutta: Office of the Superintendent of Government Printing, 1906.

D'Souza, Rohan. 'Water in British India: The Making of a "Colonial Hydrology"'. *History Compass* 4, no. 4 (2006): 621–8.

Dadabhai Naoroji: A Sketch of His Life and Life-Work. Madras: G.A. Natesan, 1908. Pamphlet. London School of Economics Library Archives on Britain and South Asia. Independent Labour Party Papers: ILP/8/1908/7–19.

Dasgupta, Ajit. *A History of Indian Economic Thought.* New York: Routledge, 1993.

Daston, Lorraine. 'Whither Critical Inquiry?' *Critical Inquiry* 30, no. 2 (2004): 361–4. https://doi.org/10.1086/421133.

Davis, Lance E., and Robert A. Huttenback. *Mammon and the Pursuit of Empire: The Political Economy of British Imperialism, 1860–1912.* Cambridge: Cambridge University Press, 1986.

Davis, Mike. *Late Victorian Holocausts: El Niño Famines and the Making of the Third World.* New York: Verso, 2002.

de Bercegol, Rémi. *Small Towns and Decentralisation in India: Urban Local Bodies in the Making.* New Delhi: Springer, 2016.

de Leon, Daniel. *Flashlights of the Amsterdam International Socialist Congress, 1904.* New York: New York Labor News, 1904.

Decker, Corrie, and Elisabeth McMahon. *The Idea of Development in Africa: A History.* Cambridge: Cambridge University Press, 2020. https://doi.org/ 10.1017/9781316217344.

Denholm, Anthony. *Lord Ripon, 1827–1909: A Political Biography.* Canberra: Croom Helm, 1982.

Dinshaw Edulji Wacha: His Life and Labors. Madras: G.A. Natesan, 1909.

Dutt, Romesh Chunder. *A History of Civilization in Ancient India Based on Sanskrit Literature.* Calcutta: Thacker, Spink, 1890.

———. *England and India: A Record of Progress during a Hundred Years, 1785–1885.* London: Chatto & Windus, 1897.

———. *Epochs of Indian History: Ancient India 2000 B.C.–800 A.D.* Edited by John Adams. Bombay: Longmans, Green, 1904.

———. *Indian Famines, Their Causes and Prevention.* London: P.S. King, 1901.

———. *Papers Regarding the Land Revenue System of British India.* London: Darling, 1902.

———. *Speeches and Papers on Indian Questions, 1897 to 1900.* Calcutta: Elm Press, 1902.

———. *The Economic History of India in the Victorian Age: From the Accession of Queen Victoria in 1837 to the Commencement of the Twentieth Century.* Vol. II. London: Kegan Paul, Trench, Trübner, 1904.

———. *The Economic History of India under Early British Rule: From the Rise of the British Power in 1757 to the Accession of Queen Victoria in 1837.* Vol. I. London: Kegan Paul, Trench, Trübner, 1902.

———. *The Peasantry of Bengal.* Calcutta: Thacker, Spink, and Trübner, 1874.

———. *Three Years in Europe, 1868 to 1871: With an Account of Subsequent Visits to Europe in 1886 and 1893.* Calcutta: S.K. Lahiri, 1896.

Dutt, Shib Chandra. *Conflicting Tendencies in Indian Economic Thought.* Calcutta: N.M. Ray-Chowdhury, 1934.

Dyson, Tim. 'The Historical Demography of Berar, 1881–1980'. In *India's Historical Demography: Studies in Famines, Disease and Society*, edited by Tim Dyson, 150–96. London: Curzon Press, 1989.

Enfantin, Barthélemy Prosper. *Économie politique et politique: Articles extraits du Globe*. Paris: Bureau du Globe, 1831.

Escobar, Arturo. *Encountering Development: The Making and Unmaking of the Third World*. Princeton: Princeton University Press, 1995. https://doi.org/10.2307/2076961.

Ferguson, Adam. *Ferguson: An Essay on the History of Civil Society*. Edited by Fania Oz-Salzberger. Cambridge: Cambridge University Press, 1995.

Principles of Moral Political Science: Being Chiefly Retrospective of Lectures Delivered in the College of Edinburgh. Vol. II. Edinburgh: A. Strahan and T. Cadell, 1792.

Fukuyama, Francis. *The End of History and the Last Man*. New York: Free Press, 1992.

Gallagher, John, Gordon Johnson, and Anil Seal. *Locality, Province, and Nation: Essays on Indian Politics 1870 to 1940*. Cambridge: Cambridge University Press, 1973.

Ganguli, Birendranath. *Indian Economic Thought: Nineteenth Century Perspectives*. New Delhi: Tata McGraw-Hill, 1977.

Ghosh, Sitansu Sekhar. *Railways in India – A Legend: Origin & Development (1830–1980)*. Calcutta: Jogemaya Prokashani, 2002.

Gilpin, Robert. *Global Political Economy: Understanding the International Economic Order*. Princeton: Princeton University Press, 2001.

Gokhale, Gopal Krishna. *21st Indian National Congress, Presidential Address*. Calcutta: The Cherry Press, 1905.

Speeches and Writings of Gopal Krishna Gokhale. Madras: G.A. Natesan, 1920.

Gopalakrishnan, Panikkanparambil Kesavan. *Development of Economic Ideas in India, 1880–1914*. New Delhi: People's Publishing House, 1954.

Goswami, Manu. *Producing India: From Colonial Economy to National Space*. Chicago: University of Chicago Press, 2004.

Govindarajan, Swaminath Aduthurai. *G. Subramania Iyer*. New Delhi: Publications Division, Ministry of Information and Broadcasting, Government of India, 1969.

Guha, Amalendu. 'Raw Cotton of Western India: 1750–1850'. *The Indian Economic & Social History Review* 9, no. 1 (1972): 1–41. https://doi.org/10.1177/001946467200900101.

Guha, Ranajit. *Dominance without Hegemony History and Power in Colonial India*. Cambridge, MA: Harvard University Press, 1998.

Gupta, Bishnupriya. 'The Rise of Modern Industry in Colonial India'. In *A New Economic History of Colonial India*, edited by Latika Chaudhary, Bishnupriya Gupta, Tirthankar Roy and Anand V. Swamy, 67–83. Abingdon: Routledge, 2016.

Gupta, Jnanendra Nath. *Life and Work of Romesh Chunder Dutt*. London: J. M. Dent, 1911.

Habib, Ifran. *Essays in Indian History: Towards a Marxist Perception*. New Delhi: Tulika, 1996.

Hadjigeorgiou, Andreas. 'The Legacy of Sir Henry Maine in the 21st Century'. *Noesis*, no. 34 (2020): 159–92.

Harder, Hans. 'Female Mobility and Bengali Women's Travelogues in the Nineteenth and Early Twentieth Centuries'. *South Asia: Journal of South Asian Studies* 43, no. 5 (2020): 817–35. https://doi.org/10.1080/00856401.2020.1791500.

Hardiman, David. *Peasant Resistance in India, 1858–1914*. Edited by David Hardiman. New Delhi: Oxford University Press, 1992.

'The Politics of Water in Colonial India'. *South Asia: Journal of South Asia Studies* 25, no. 2 (2002): 111–20. https://doi.org/10.1080/00856400208723477.

Hardin, Garrett. 'The Tragedy of the Commons'. *Science* 162, no. 3859 (1968): 1243–8.

Harlen, Christine Margerum. 'A Reappraisal of Classical Economic Nationalism and Economic Liberalism'. *International Issues Quarterly* 43, no. 4 (1999): 733–44. https://doi.org/10.1111/0020-8833.00143.

Healy, Kieran. *Social Change: Mechanisms and Metaphors*. Princeton: Princeton University Press, 1998.

Heilbroner, Robert L. 'The Paradox of Progress: Decline and Decay in the Wealth of Nations'. *Journal of the History of Ideas* 34, no. 2 (1973): 243–62. https://doi.org/10.2307/2708728.

Helleiner, Eric. 'Economic Nationalism as a Challenge to Economic Liberalism? Lessons from the 19th Century'. *International Studies Quarterly* 46, no. 3 (2002): 307–29. https://doi.org/10.1111/1468-2478.00235.

'Globalising the Classical Foundations of IPE Thought'. *Contexto Internacional* 37, no. 3 (2015): 975–1010. https://doi.org/10.1590/S0102-85292015000300007.

The Contested World Economy: The Deep and Global Roots of International Political Economy. Cambridge: Cambridge University Press, 2023.

The Neomercantilists: A Global Intellectual History. Ithaca: Cornell University Press. 2021.

Helm, Elijah. 'The Indian Duties on Cotton Goods'. *The Economic Journal* 6, no. 21 (1896): 110–14. https://doi.org/10.2307/2956784.

Hill, Lisa. 'Adam Ferguson and the Paradox of Progress and Decline'. *History of Political Thought* 18, no. 4 (1997): 677–706.

Hobson, John M. *The Eastern Origins of Western Civilisation*. Cambridge: Cambridge University Press, 2004.

  The Eurocentric Conception of World Politics: Western International Theory, 1760–2010. Cambridge: Cambridge University Press, 2012.

Hodge, Joseph M., Gerald Hödl and Martina Kopf, eds. *Developing Africa: Concepts and Practices in Twentieth-Century Colonialism*. Manchester: Manchester University Press, 2014.

Howell, Thomas Bayly. *A Complete Collection of State Trials and Proceedings for High Treason and Other Crimes and Misdemeanors from the Earliest Period to the Year 1783*. Vol. X. London: Longman, Hurst, Rees, Orme, and Browne; J. M. Richardson; Black, Parbury, and Allen; Baldwin, Cradock, and Joy; E. Jeffrey; J. Hatchard; R. H. Evans; J. Booker; E. Lloyd; J. Booth; Budd and Calkin; and T. C. Hansard, 1816.

Hume, Allan Octavian. *Agricultural Reform in India*. London: W.H. Allen, 1879.

Hunter, William Wilson. *England's Work in India*. London: Smith, Elder, 1881.

Hurd, John. 'A Huge Railway System But No Sustained Economic Development: The Company Perspective, 1884–1939: Some Hypotheses'. In *27 Down: New Departures in Indian Railway Studies*, edited by Ian J. Kerr, Vol. XXVII, 314–46. New Delhi: Orient Longman, 2007.

Hurd, John, and Ian J. Kerr. 'Railway Management and Railway Employees in Imperial India'. In *Railway Management and Its Organisational Structure: Its Impact on and Diffusion into the General Economy, Proceedings Twelfth International Economic History Congress*, edited by Clara Eugenia Nunez 103–17. Sevilla: Fundcion Fomento De La Historia Economica, 1998.

Hyndman, Henry Mayers. *England for All*. London: E. W. Allen, 1881.

'Indian Expenditure Report of the Royal Commission'. *Hansard* 86 (1900): 595–618.

'India at the International Socialist Congress. [Text of the] Speech by Mr. Dadabhai Naoroji'. (Reprint from 'India', 2 September 1904). S.l. Second International Archives (ARCH 01299.399), International Institute of Social History (Amsterdam).

Iyer, Ganapathy Subramania. 'Railways in India'. In *Indian Politics*, edited by Iyer, Ganapathy Subramania, 181–94. Madras: Swadesamitran Press, 1898.

  Some Economic Aspects of British Rule in India. Madras: Swadesamitran Press, 1903.

Joshi, Ganesh Vyankatesh. *Writings and Speeches of G. V. Joshi*. Pune: Arya Bhushan Press, 1912.

Kamal, Kajari. *Kautilya's Arthashastra: Strategic Cultural Roots of India's Contemporary Statecraft*. Oxon: Routledge, 2023.

Kamerkar, Mani P. 'Impact of British Colonial Policy on Society Relating to Education in Western India during the 19th Century'. *Bulletin of the Deccan College Research Institute* 60–1, no. 1 (2000): 373–82. www.jstor.org/stable/42936626.

Kapila, Shruti, ed. *An Intellectual History for India*. New Delhi: Cambridge University Press, 2010. https://doi.org/10.1017/UPO9788175968721.

Khan, Gulfishan. *Indian Muslim Perceptions of the West during the Eighteenth Century*. Karachi: Oxford University Press, 1998.

Khodaiji, Sharmin. 'A Nationalistic Framework for Political Economy: Textbooks on Indian Economics during the Early-Twentieth Century'. *Œconomia: History, Methodology, Philosophy* 9, nos. 9–3 (2019): 459–80.

Klein, Ira. 'English Free Traders and Indian Tariffs, 1874–96'. *Modern Asian Studies* 5, no. 3 (1971): 251–71.

Knight, Charles. *The English Cyclopædia: A New Dictionary of Universal Knowledge*. London: Bradbury and Evans, 1854.

Krishnamurty, Jayasankar. *Towards Development Economics: Indian Contributions 1900–1945*. New Delhi: Oxford University Press, 2011.

Krishnamurthy, Jiddu. 'De-industrialisation Revisited'. *Economic and Political Weekly* 11, no. 26 (1976): 964–7.

Kumar, Ashutosh. 'Marx and Engels on India'. *The Indian Journal of Political Science* 53, no. 4 (1992): 493–504.

Kumar, Dharma, and Meghnad Desai, eds. *The Cambridge Economic History of India*. Vol. II. Cambridge: Cambridge University Press, 1983. https://doi.org/10.1017/CHOL9780521228022.

Latham, Anthony. *The International Economy and the Undeveloped World, 1865–1914*. London: Croom Helm, 1978.

List, Friedrich. *National System of Political Economy*. Translated by G. A. Matile. Philadelphia: J.B. Lippincott, 1856.

Lloyd, William Forster. *Two Lectures on the Checks to Population, Delivered before the University of Oxford, in Michaelmas Term 1832*. Oxford: S. Collingwood, 1833.

Luke, Allan. 'Text and Discourse in Education: An Introduction to Critical Discourse Analysis'. *Review of Research in Education* 21, no. 1 (1995): 3–48.

MacDonald, James Ramsay. *Awakening of India*. London: Hodder & Stoughton, 1910.

Macekura, Stephen J., and Erez Manela, eds. *The Development Century: A Global History*. Global and International History. Cambridge: Cambridge University Press, 2018. https://doi.org/10.1017/97811 08678940.

Maclean, James Mackenzie. *A Guide to Bombay: Historical, Statistical and Descriptive. Bombay Gazette Steam Press*. Bombay: Bombay Gazette Steam Press, 1875.

Maddison, Angus. *Class Structure and Economic Growth: India and Pakistan since the Moghuls*. London: Allen and Unwin, 1971.

'The Historical Origins of Indian Poverty'. *Quarterly Review/Banca Nazionale Del Lavoro, Roma* 92, no. 1 (1970): 31–81.

Mahadev Govind Ranade: His Life and Career. Madras: G.A. Natesan, Esplanade, 1901. Pamphlet. London School of Economics Library Archives on Britain and South Asia. (16-Non-ILP Print: Miscellaneous). Independent Labour Party Papers: ILP/16/1901.

Mahmood, Syed. *A History of English Education in India (1781 to 1893)*. Aligarh: M. A. O. College, 1895.

Maine, Henry. *Ancient Law*. London: John Murray, 1861.

Village-Communities in the East and West: Six Lectures Delivered at Oxford. London: John Murray, 1871.

Malhotra, Piarea Lal. 'The Internal Administration of Lord Elgin in India, 1894–1898'. PhD thesis, SOAS University of London, 1966. https://ep rints.soas.ac.uk/33561/.

Mallik, S. N. 'Local Self-Government in India'. *The Annals of the American Academy of Political and Social Science* 145, no. 2 (1929): 36–44.

Malthus, Thomas Robert. *An Essay on the Principle of Population, as It Affects the Future Improvement of Society, with Remarks on the Speculations of Mr. Godwin, M. Condorcet, and Other Writers*. London: J. Johnson, 1798.

Mantena, Karuna. *Alibis of Empire: Henry Maine and the Ends of Liberal Imperialism*. Princeton: Princeton University Press, 2010.

Marshall, Alfred. *Principles of Economics*. London: Macmillan, 1890.

Marx, Karl. *Capital*. Translated by Samuel Moore and Edward Aveling. Vols. 1–3. London: Swan Sonnenschein, 1887.

Mathur, Laxman Prasad. *Lord Ripon's Administration in India (1880–84 AD)*. New Delhi: S. Chand, 1972.

Matin, Kamran. 'Redeeming the Universal: Postcolonialism and the Inner Life of Eurocentrism'. *European Journal of International Relations* 19, no. 2 (2013): 353–77. https://doi.org/10.1177/1354066111425263.

Mayhew, Henry. *London Labour and the London Poor; a Cyclopædia of the Condition and Earnings of Those That Will Work, Those That Cannot*

Work, and Those That Will Not Work. Vol. I. London: George Woodfall, 1851.

McClish, Mark. *The History of the Arthasastra: Sovereignty and Sacred Law in Ancient India.* Ideas in Context. Cambridge: Cambridge University Press, 2019. https://doi.org/10.1017/9781108641586.

Meek, Ronald L. 'Smith, Turgot, and the "Four Stages" Theory'. *History of Political Economy* 3, no. 1 (1971): 9–27.

Mehmet, Ozay. *Westernizing the Third World: The Eurocentricity of Economic Development Theories.* London: Routledge, 1995.

Mill, James. *The History of British India.* London: Baldwin, Cradock, and Joy, 1817.

Mill, John Stuart. *Memorandum of the Improvements in the Administration of India during the Last Thirty Years, and the Petition of the East-India Company to Parliament.* London: W. H. Allen, 1858.

Principles of Political Economy with Some of Their Applications to Social Philosophy. Manchester: George Routledge, 1848.

Mitra, Iman. 'Exchanging Words and Things: Vernacularisation of Political Economy in Nineteenth-Century Bengal'. *Indian Economic and Social History Review* 53, no. 4 (2016): 501–31. https://doi.org/10.1177/0019464616662143.

Mosse, David. 'Rule and Representation: Transformations in the Governance of the Water Commons in British South India'. *The Journal of Asian Studies* 65, no. 1 (2006): 61–90.

Mukherjee, Aditya. 'Empire: How Colonial India Made Modern Britain'. *Economic and Political Weekly* 45, no. 50 (2010): 73–82.

Mukherjee, Aditya, Bipan Chandra, K. N. Panikkar, Mridula Mukherjee and Sucheta Mahajan. *India's Struggle for Independence 1857–1947.* New Delhi: Viking, 1988.

Mukherjee, Haridas. *Benoy Kumar Sarkar: A Study.* Calcutta: Das Gupta, 1953.

Mukhopadhyay, Aparajita. 'Colonised Gaze? Guidebooks and Journeying in Colonial India'. *South Asia: Journal of South Asian Studies* 37, no. 4 (2014): 656–69. https://doi.org/10.1080/00856401.2014.952972.

Mulhall, Michael George. *The Progress of the World.* London: Edward Stanford, 1880.

Muthiah, Subbiah. 'Willing to Strike and Not Reluctant to Wound'. *The Hindu*, 13 September 2003. https://web.archive.org/web/20121107181430/http://www.hindu.com/th125/stories/2003091300770200.htm.

Muzaka, Valbona. 'A Dialogic Approach to Understanding Regime Conflicts: The Case of the Development Agenda'. *Third World Quarterly* 38, no. 1 (2017): 61–83.

Naik, Vasant N. *Kashinath Trimbak Telang: The Man and His Times*. Madras: G.A. Natesan, 1915.

Naoroji, Dadabhai. 'Bimentallism'. *The Times*, 23 December 1886.

Dadabhai Naoroji Correspondence: Correspondence with D.E. Wacha, 4–11-1884 to 23-3-1895. Edited by R. P. Patwardhan. Vol. I. Bombay: Allied, 1977.

Dadabhai Naoroji Correspondence: Correspondence with D.E. Wacha, 30–3-1895 to 5–4-1917. Edited by R. P. Patwardhan. Vol. II. Bombay: Allied, 1977.

Dadabhai Naoroji: Selected Private Papers. Edited by Sri Ram Mehrotra and Dinyar Patel. New Delhi: Oxford University Press, 2016.

Essays, Speeches, Addresses and Writings (on Indian Politics,) of Hon'ble Dadabhai Naoroji. Edited by Chunilal Lallubhai Parekh. Bombay: Caxton Printing Works, 1887.

Poverty and Un-British Rule in India. London: Swan Sonnen Schein, 1901.

Nayar, Pramod K. *Colonial Voices: The Discourses of Empire*. Chichester: John Wiley, 2012.

Nisbet, Robert A. *Social Change and History: Aspects of the Western Theory of Development*. Vol. 313. New York: Oxford University Press, 1969.

Nurullah, Syed, and Pangal Jayendra Naik. *History of Education in India during the British Period*. Bombay: Macmillan, 1943.

Omkarnath, Goddanti. 'Indian Development Thinking'. In *Handbook of Development Economics*, edited by S. Reinert Erik, Jayati Ghosh and Rainer Kattel, 212–27. Cheltenham: Edward Elgar, 2016.

Özveren, Eyüp. 'Turkey and the Turkic Linguistic Zone: The Case That Doesn't Quite Fit'. In *Routledge Handbook of the History of Global Economic Thought*, edited by Vincent Barnett, 179–88. New York: Routledge, 2015.

Park, Y. Goo. 'Depression and Capital Formation: The United Kingdom and Germany, 1873–1896'. *Journal of European Economic History* 26, no. 3 (1997): 511–30.

Parliament of Great Britain. *Hansard's Parliamentary Debates*. Vol. XIX. London: T.C. Hansard, 1833.

Patel, Dinyar. *Naoroji: Pioneer of Indian Nationalism*. Boston: Harvard University Press, 2020.

Patel, Sujata. 'Towards Internationalism: Beyond Colonial and Nationalist Sociologies'. In *Theories about and Strategies against Hegemonic Social Sciences*, edited by Michael Kuhn and Shujiro Yazawa, 119–32. Tokyo: Centre for Global Studies, Seijo University, 2013.

Peabody, Norbert. 'Knowledge Formation in Imperial India'. In *India and the British Empire*, edited by Douglas Peers and Nandini Gooptu, 75–99. Oxford: Oxford University Press, 2012.

Pick, Daniel. *Faces of Degeneration*. Cambridge: Cambridge University Press, 1989. https://doi.org/10.1017/cbo9780511558573.

Pickel, Andreas. 'Explaining, and Explaining with, Economic Nationalism'. *Nations and Nationalism* 9, no. 1 (2003): 105–27.

Poovey, Mary. 'The Limits of the Universal Knowledge Project: British India and the East Indiamen'. *Critical Inquiry* 31, no. 1 (2004): 183–202. https://doi.org/10.1086/427307.

Porter, Roy, and Mikuláš Teich, eds. *The Scientific Revolution in National Context*. Cambridge: Cambridge University Press, 1992.

Prakash, Gyan. *Another Reason: Science and the Imagination of Modern India*. Princeton: Princeton University Press, 1999.

Prasad, Eswar, Raghuram Rajan and Arvind Subramanian. 'Foreign Capital and Economic Growth'. *NBER Working Papers*, 2007.

Prebisch, Raúl. *The Economic Development of Latin America and Its Principal Problems*. New York: United Nations, 1950.

Quesnay, François. 'Analyse de la formule arithmétique du tableau économique de la distribution des dépenses annuelles d'une Nation agricole'. *Journal de l'Agriculture, du Commerce et des Finances* 2, no. 3 (1766): 11–41.

Raj, Kapil. *Relocating Modern Science: Circulation and the Construction of Knowledge in South Asia and Europe, 1650–1900*. Delhi: Permanent Black, 2007.

Ramnath, Aparajith. *The Birth of an Indian Profession: Engineers, Industry, and the State, 1900–47*. Oxford: Oxford University Press, 2017.

Ramos, Imma. 'Contesting the Imperial Gaze: Image Worship Debates in Nineteenth-Century Bengal'. *South Asian Studies* 31, no. 2 (2015): 237–46.

Ranade, Mahadev Govind. *Essays on Indian Economics: A Collection of Essays and Speeches*. Madras: G.A. Natesan, 1906.

'Introduction to the Peishwa's Diaries: a paper read before the Bombay branch of the Royal Asiatic Society'. Poona: Printed at the Civil Military Orphanage Press, 1900.

Religious and Social Reform: A Collection of Essays and Speeches. Edited by Mangesh Bal. Kolasker. Bombay: G. Claridge, 1902.

Rise of the Maratha Power Girgaum. Bombay: Punalekar, 1900.

Select Writings of the Late Hon'ble Mr. Justice M.G. Ranade on Indian States. Edited by Vasudeo Waman Thakur. Indore: Datta Printing Works, 1942.

The Miscellaneous Writings of the Late Hon'ble Mr. Justice M.G. Ranade. Edited by Ramabai Ranade and Dinshaw E. Wacha. Bombay: The Manoranjan Press, 1915.

Ray, Prithwis Chandra. *The Poverty Problem in India: Being a Dissertation on the Causes and Remedies of Indian Poverty*. Calcutta: Thacker, Spink, 1895.

Ray, Rajat Kanta. *Entrepreneurship and Industry in India, 1800–1947*. New Delhi: Cambridge University Press, 1994.

Reinert, Erik S. 'The Role of the State in Economic Growth'. *Journal of Economic Studies* 26, nos. 4–5 (1999): 268–326.

Reinert, Erik S., Jayati Ghosh and Rainer Kattel, eds. *Handbook of Alternative Theories of Economic Development*. Cheltenham: Edward Elgar, 2016.

Reinert, Sophus A. 'Darwin and the Body Politic: Schäffle, Veblen, and the Shift of Biological Metaphor in Economics'. Tallinn University of Technology Working Papers in Technology Governance and Economic Dynamics (2006).

'Report of the Indian Famine Commission'. Simla: Government Central Printing Office, 1898.

Ricardo, David. *Principles of Political Economy and Taxation*. London: John Murray, 1817.

Rostow, Walt Whitman. *The Stages of Economic Growth: A Non-Communist Manifesto*. New York: Cambridge University Press, 1960.

Roy, Tirthankar. *Economic History of India, 1857–1947*. Oxford: Oxford University Press, 2011.

Said, Edward W. *Orientalism*. London: Routledge and Kegan Paul, 1978.

Saint-Simon, Claude-Henri Comte de. *The Doctrine of Saint-Simon: An Exposition; First Year, 1828–1829*. Edited and translated by Georg G. Iggers. Boston: Beacon Press, 1958.

Sarkar, Sumit. *Modern India 1886–1947*. New Delhi: Macmillan, 1983.

Sartori, Andrew. *Bengal in Global Concept History: Culturalism in the Age of Capital*. Chicago: University of Chicago Press, 2008.

Satya, Laxman. *Cotton and Famine in Berar, 1850–1900*. New Delhi: Manohar, 1997.

Saul, Berrick. *Studies in British Overseas Trade, 1870–1914*. Liverpool: Liverpool University Press, 1960.

Sen, Amartya. *Poverty and Famines: An Essay on Entitlement and Deprivation*. Oxford: Oxford University Press, 1981.

Seth, Sanjay. *Subject Lessons: The Western Education of Imperial India*. Durham: Duke University Press, 2007.

Sharma, Ram Sharan. *Early Medieval Indian Society*. Hyderabad: Orient Longman, 2001.

Shulman, Stephen. 'Nationalist Sources of International Economic Integration'. *International Studies Quarterly* 44, no. 3 (2000): 365–90.

Sims, George. *How the Poor Live*. London: Chatto & Windus, 1883.

Singer, Hans Wolf. 'The Distribution of Gains between Investing and Borrowing Countries'. *The Journal of Development Studies* 11, no. 4 (1975): 376–82.

Singh, Vir Bahadur. *From Naoroji to Nehru: Six Essays in Indian Economic Thought*. New Delhi: Macmillan and Company of India, 1975.

Sismondi, Jean-Charles-Léonard Simonde. *Nouveaux principes d'économie politique, ou de la richesse dans ses rapports avec la population*. Vol. I. Paris: Delaunay, Treuttel and Wurtz, 1819.

Smith, Craig. *Adam Smith's Political Philosophy: The Invisible Hand and Spontaneous Order*. New York: Routledge, 2006.

Spencer, Herbert. *The Principles of Biology*. London: Williams and Norgate, 1864.

Stein, Burton. *A History of India*. Oxford: John Wiley, 1983.

Stephen, Leslie. *Life of Henry Fawcett*. Cambridge: Cambridge University Press, 1885.

Stokes, Erik. *The English Utilitarians and India*. Oxford: Oxford University Press, 1959.

Subrahmanyam, Sanjay. 'Beyond the Usual Suspects: On Intellectual Networks in the Early Modern World', *Global Intellectual History* 2, no. 1, (2017): 30–48. https://doi.org/10.1080/23801883.2017.1332884.

Sugiyama, Chūhei, and Hiroshi Mizuta, eds. *Enlightenment and Beyond: Political Economy Comes to Japan*. Tokyo: University of Tokyo Press, 1988.

Sullivan, John. *Are We Bound by Our Treaties? A Plea for the Princes of India*. London: Effingham Wilson, Cornhill, 1853.

Sun, Yat-sen. *The International Development of China*. Shanghai: Commercial Press, 1920.

Szporluk, Roman. *Communism and Nationalism: Karl Marx versus Friedrich List*. Oxford: Oxford University Press, 1993.

Taylor, Charles. 'Two Theories of Modernity'. *Public Culture* 11, no. 1 (1999): 153–74.

Telang, Kashinath Trimbak. 'Free Trade and Protection from an Indian Point of View'. In *Selected Writings and Speeches*, edited by V. N. Naik, Vol. I, 97–181. Bombay: Manoranjan Press, 1916.

Selected Writings and Speeches. Edited by Dhananjayrao Gadgil. Bombay: Manoranjan Press, 1916.

Temple, Sir Richard. *India in 1880*. London: John Murray, 1880.

'The Indian Nation Builders, Part I'. 6th ed. Madras: Ganesh, 1920.

Thorner, Daniel, and Alice Thorner, eds. *Land and Labour in India*. Bombay: Asia Publishing House, 1962.

Tilly, Charles. *Big Structures, Large Processes, Huge Comparisons*. New York: Russell Sage Foundation, 1984.

Tinker, Hugh. *The Foundations of the Local Self-Government in India, Pakistan and Burma*. Vol. I. London: University of London, Athlone Press, 1954.

Trincado, Estrella, Andrés Lazzarini and Denis Melnik, eds. *Ideas in the History of Economic Development: The Case of Peripheral Countries.* New York: Routledge, 2020.

Tupper, Charles Lewis. *Our Indian Protectorate: An Introduction to the Study of the Relations between the British Government and Its Indian Feudatories.* London: Longmans Green, 1893.

Unger, Corinna R. *International Development: A Postwar History.* London: Bloomsbury Academic, 2018. https://cadmus.eui.eu/handle/1814/58724.

Washbrook, David. 'From Comparative Sociology to Global History: Britain and India in the Pre-history of Modernity'. *Journal of the Economic and Social History of the Orient* 40, no. 4 (1997): 410–43. https://doi.org/10.1163/1568520972601495.

'Intimations of Modernity in South India'. *South Asian History and Culture* 1, no. 1 (2009): 125–48. https://doi.org/10.1080/19472490903387274.

'The Global History of "Modernity"—A Response to a Reply'. *Journal of the Economic and Social History of the Orient* 41, no. 3 (1998): 295–311.

Washbrook, David A. 'Progress and Problems: South Asian Economic and Social History c. 1720–1860'. *Modern Asian Studies* 22, no. 1 (1988): 57–96.

'The Indian Economy and the British Empire'. In *India and the British Empire*, edited by Douglas M. Peers and Nandini Gooptu, 44–74. Oxford: Oxford University Press, 2012.

Watson, Matthew. 'Friedrich List's Adam Smith Historiography and the Contested Origins of Development Theory'. *Third World Quarterly* 33, no. 3 (2012): 459–74.

Wendler, Eugen. *Friedrich List (1789–1846): A Visionary Economist with Social Responsibility.* Translated by Donna Blagg. Berlin: Springer, 2014.

Whitcombe, Elizabeth. *Agrarian Conditions in Northern India: The United Provinces under British Rule, 1860–1900.* Vol. I. Berkeley: University of California Press, 1971.

Wilson, Jon. 'How Modernity Arrived to Godavari'. *Modern Asian Studies* 51, no. 2 (2017): 399–431.

India Conquered: Britain's Raj and the Chaos of Empire. London: Simon and Schuster, 2016.

Young, Robert J. C. *White Mythologies: Writing History and the West.* London: Routledge, 1990.

Zachariah, Benjamin. *Developing India: An Intellectual and Social History c. 1930–50.* Oxford: Oxford University Press, 2005.

'Moving Ideas and How to Catch Them'. In *After the Last Post: The Lives of Indian Historiography*, 129–48. Berlin: De Gruyter Oldenbourg, 2019.

Annex I Archival Sources – Major Works of the First Generation of Modern Indian Economists, 1870–1905

Dadabhai Naoroji (1825–1917)

1887 *Essays, Speeches, Addresses and Writings (on Indian Politics)*
1887 *Indian Exchanges and Bimetallism*
1889 *The Parsi Religion*
1901 *Poverty and Un-British Rule in India*

Mahadev Govind Ranade (1842–1901)

1877 *Revenue Manual of the British Empire in India*
1881 *Land Law Reform and Agricultural Banks*
1894 *A Note on the Decentralization of Provincial Finance*
1900 *Rise of the Maratha Power*
1900 'Introduction to the Peshwa's Diaries' in the *Journal of the Bombay Branch of the Royal Asiatic Society*
1902 *Religion and Social Reform: A Collection of Essays and Speeches*
1906 *Essays on Indian Economics: A Collection of Essays and Speeches*
1915 *The Miscellaneous Writings of the Late Hon'ble Mr. Justice M. G. Ranade*
1942 *Select Writings of the Late Hon'ble Mr. Justice M.G. Ranade on Indian States*

Dinshaw Edulji Wacha (1844–1936)

1910 *Recent Indian Finance*
1913 *Rise and Growth of Bombay Municipal Government*
1920 *Speeches and Writings of Sir Dinshaw Edulji Wacha*

Romesh Chunder Dutt (1848–1909)

1874 *The Peasantry of Bengal*
1891 *A History of Civilization in Ancient India Based on Sanskrit Literature*
1896 *Three Years in Europe, 1868 to 1871*
1895 *The Literature of Bengal*
1897 *England and India: A Record of Progress during a Hundred Years, 1785–1885*
1900 *Open Letters to Lord Curzon on Famines and Land Assessments in India*
1901 *Indian Famines, Their Causes and Prevention*
1902 *The Economic History of British India: From the Rise of the British Power in 1757 to the Accession of Queen Victoria in 1837*
1902 *Speeches and Papers on Indian Questions*
1902 *Papers Regarding the Land Revenue System of British India*
1903 *The Economic History of India in the Victorian Age: From the Accession of Queen Victoria in 1837 to the Commencement of the Twentieth Century, Vol. I*
1904 *Epochs of Indian History: Ancient India 2000 B.C.–800 A.D.*

Ganesh Vyankatesh Joshi (1851–1911)

1912 *Writings and Speeches*

Ganapathy Dikshitar Subramania Iyer (1855–1916)

1898 'Railways in India' in *Indian Politics*
1903 *Some Economic Aspects of British Rule in India*

Gopal Krishna Gokhale (1866–1915)

1908 *Speeches of the Honourable Mr. G.K. Gokhale*
1920 *Speeches and Writings of Gopal Krishna Gokhale*

Kashinath Trimbak Telang (1850–93)

1877 *Free Trade and Protection from an Indian Point of View*
1885 *Selected Writings and Speeches*

Surendranath Banerjea (1848–1925)

1908 *Speeches by Babu Surendranath Banerjea, 6th Volume*

1909 *The Trumpet Voice of India: Speeches of Babu Surendranath Banerjea*

1917 *Speeches and Writings of Hon. Surendranath Banerjea: Selected by Himself*

1925 *A Nation in the Making: Being the Reminiscences of Fifty Years of Public Life*

Index

181

Other Books in the Series (*continued from page ii*)

Printed in the United States
by Baker & Taylor Publisher Services